Cuisine at home.

VOLUME 7

AUGUST HOME
SPECIAL PUBLICATIONS

2200 Grand Avenue
Des Moines, IA 50312
www.augusthome.com

HEART AND SOUL

That's what we put into every issue of *Cuisine at home*: Heart and Soul. Our staff works very hard to create recipes sure to become family favorites. That's not always an easy task! There are always a few ideas that don't make it to photography... Articles can take a totally different direction late in the day... And there are some recipes we'd "sampled" a little too often for our own good. Yes, there can be *too* much of a good thing (thank goodness for a gym membership)!

How do we go about developing a recipe? Well, it always starts with a lot of discussion and attention to our magazine mission. What's our mission? Here's a scaled-down version:

1) First and foremost, *always* be a teacher
2) Offer creative solutions to cooking problems
3) Provide question-free instruction
4) Make it flavorful, colorful, and interesting
5) Above all else, will you, our reader, enjoy it?

Tall order, isn't it? But we always have a great time developing something new and working out recipe "bumps."

This year seemed to fly by, but we were able to stay true to our mission—you! Enjoy another complete year of all that *Cuisine at home* brings to you and your family.

Cuisine at home

THE YEAR AT A GLANCE

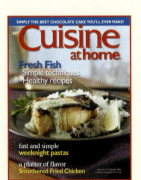

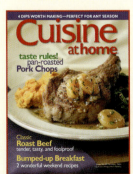
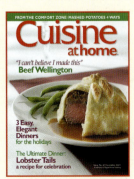

Cuisine at home.

Please contact us to find out about other *Cuisine at home* products and services:

By Phone: 1-800-311-3995
By Mail: 2200 Grand Avenue, Des Moines IA 50312
By Email: CuisineAtHome@CuisineAtHome.com
Or Visit Our Web-Site: www.CuisineAtHome.com

Cuisine at home.

Fresh Fish
Simple techniques
Healthy recipes

fast and simple
weeknight pastas

a platter of flavor
Smothered Fried Chicken

Issue No. 37   February 2003
A publication of August Home Publishing

Cuisine at home

Publisher
Donald B. Peschke

Editor
John F. Meyer

Art Director
Cinda Shambaugh

Senior Editor
Susan Hoss

Assistant Art Director
Holly Wiederin

Assistant Editor
Sara Ostransky

Graphic Designer
April Walker Janning

Test Kitchen Director
Kim Samuelson

Image Specialist
Troy Clark

Photographer
Dean Tanner

Contributing Food Stylist
Jennifer Peterson

AUGUST HOME
PUBLISHING COMPANY

Corporate:

Corporate Vice Presidents: Mary R. Scheve, Douglas L. Hicks • *Creative Director:* Ted Kralicek • *Professional Development Director:* Michal Sigel *New Media Manager:* Gordon C. Gaippe • *Senior Photographer:* Crayola England *Multi Media Art Director:* Eugene Pedersen • *Web Server Administrator:* Carol Schoeppler • *Web Content Manager:* David Briggs • *Web Designer:* Kara Blessing *Web Developer/Content Manager:* Sue M. Moe • *Controller:* Robin Hutchinson *Senior Accountant:* Laura Thomas • *Accounts Payable:* Mary Schultz • *Accounts Receivable:* Margo Petrus • *Research Coordinator:* Nick Jaeger • *Production Director:* George Chmielarz • *Pre-Press Image Specialist:* Minniette Johnson • *Electronic Publishing Director:* Douglas M. Lidster • *Systems Administrator:* Cris Schwanebeck *PC Maintenance Technician:* Robert D. Cook • *H.R. Assistant:* Kirsten Koele *Receptionist/ Administrative Assistant:* Jeanne Johnson • *Mail Room Clerk:* Lou Webber • *Office Manager:* Natalie Lonsdale • *Facilities Manager:* Kurt Johnson

Customer Service & Fulfillment:

Operations Director: Bob Baker • *Customer Service Manager:* Jennie Enos *Customer Service Representatives:* Anna Cox, Kim Harlan, April Revell, Deborah Rich, Valerie Jo Riley, Tammy Truckenbrod • *Buyer:* Linda Jones • *Administrative Assistant:* Nancy Downey • *Warehouse Supervisor:* Nancy Johnson • *Fulfillment:* Sylvia Carey

Circulation:

Subscriber Services Director: Sandy Baum • *New Business Circulation Manager:* Wayde J. Klingbeil • *Multi Media Promotion Manager:* Rick Junkins • *Promotions Analyst:* Patrick A. Walsh • *Billing and Collections Manager:* Rebecca Cunningham *Renewal Manager:* Paige Rogers • *Circulation Marketing Analyst:* Kris Schlemmer *Circulation Marketing Analyst:* Paula M. DeMatteis • *Art Director:* Doug Flint *Senior Graphic Designers:* Mark Hayes, Robin Friend

www.CuisineAtHome.com

talk to *Cuisine at home*

Questions about Subscriptions and Address Changes? Write or call:

Customer Service

2200 Grand Avenue,
Des Moines, IA 50312
800-311-3995,
8 a.m. to 5 p.m., CST.

Online Subscriber Services:
www.CuisineAtHome.com

Access your account • Check a subscription payment • Tell us if you've missed an issue • Change your mailing or email address • Renew your subscription • Pay your bill

Cuisine at home® (ISSN 1537-8225) is published bi-monthly (Jan., Mar., May, July, Sept., Nov.) by August Home Publishing Co., 2200 Grand Ave., Des Moines, IA 50312. *Cuisine at home*® is a trademark of August Home Publishing Co. ©Copyright 2003 August Home Publishing. All rights reserved. Subscriptions: Single copy: $4.99. One year subscription (6 issues), $24.00. (Canada/Foreign add $10 per year, U.S. funds.)

Periodicals postage paid at Des Moines, IA and at additional mailing offices. "USPS/Perry-Judd's Heartland Division automatable poly". Postmaster: Send change of address to *Cuisine at home*®, P.O. Box 37100 Boone, IA 50037-2100. *Cuisine at home*® does not accept and is not responsible for unsolicited manuscripts. **PRINTED IN CHINA**

editor's letter

The holidays may be over but the joy of cooking continues! Oh sure, the once-a-year recipes are fun, but there is still plenty of enjoyment left in the kitchen. We have some exciting dinners in this issue of *Cuisine* that are guaranteed to start the year off right.

If one of your New Year's resolutions is to watch what you're eating, the *Cuisine Class* about cooking fish is a good start. Find out how to buy a fresh piece of fish and then three different ways to prepare it. Even if you're not concerned about a waistline, try one of these terrific recipes—there's something for everyone. The Mahimahi in "Crazy Water" is perfect for dinner parties while Fish Tacos are a great way to introduce the kids to healthy eating.

If you're searching for a little more comfort, don't look much further than our *Chef at home* article. Usually, we invite a well-known chef or cookbook author to share one of their favorite recipes. This time, we invited the King Arthur Flour Company to show us how to bake bread; after all, they've been doing this for two hundred years. Never mind what the aroma can do to a home—the anticipation of just-out-of-the-oven bread mingling with sweet cream butter can create quite a stir around the house.

But don't eat too much freshly baked bread because you have to leave room for the Beef Bourguignonne. This recipe is more than satisfying with all the fresh mushrooms, pearl onions, and rich red wine sauce. But when it's served over butter-drizzled potatoes, it hits the decadent mark. Put this on your "must try" list.

For most of us, winter brings plenty of cold Sundays. Our two chicken dinners are made for these days, especially the Smothered Chicken with big-time flavor and plenty of gravy. Surprisingly, it's skinless and cooked with little oil—just a bit healthier for you.

And finally, I haven't forgotten all the deserving Valentines—an unbelievably moist (and simple) chocolate cake. You may never try another chocolate cake recipe again. Happy cooking.

table of contents

Issue No. 37 February 2003

departments

features

from **our** readers

tips *and techniques*

Food on the go

When I transport prepared foods in the car to a picnic or other social gatherings, I place a piece of non-skid liner in and under the box. That way the food doesn't slide around and spill in the car (or even inside the box). I also put a non-skid mat in my pie carrier so the pie doesn't slide around and break off my decorative crust edges.

Sue Martinez
Burlington, NC

Liners
Non-skid liners are sold by the roll and come in a variety of colors. Rolls are inexpensive and can be cut to size. You can find them in most grocery and department stores in the housewares aisle.

Softened Butter

When you forget to soften butter for cookies or other baking recipes, use this simple technique to soften it quickly. Place the cold butter in a food processor fitted with a steel blade, then pulse until it's soft enough to use.

Glenda Goldwater
Portland, OR

Easy Cake Slicing

I've found an easy and clean way to slice sheet cakes—I use a large pizza cutter! It wheels right through the cake and the frosting doesn't build-up like it does when using a knife.

Kelly Zdrojewski
Fishers, IN

Pitting 101

To pit olives easily, place a few in between double layers of paper towels. With your hand, roll the olives back and forth to loosen the flesh from the pits—use a little bit of pressure as you do this. Then peel back the paper towels and remove the olive flesh. This works best with slightly soft olives, such as kalamatas.

Kit Cassidy
Stuart, FL

Heated Through?

Here's an easy way to tell if the casserole you're heating is hot throughout. Insert the blade of a paring knife into the center for a few seconds, then draw it out. Touch it with the tip of your finger—it should be hot.

Michael Wall
Churton, MD

Spinning Spinach

To eliminate some of the mess created when squeezing water out of thawed frozen spinach, line a salad spinner with paper towels. Then scatter the spinach on the paper towels and spin it just as you would salad greens.

Jan Laus
Tuscaloosa, AL

Stuck-up Recipes

When I have a recipe card that I want to keep handy, I put a bit of "Fun Tak" on the back. That way, I can stick it up on a kitchen cabinet door at eye level. It's a great trick because it keeps me from spilling on the recipe!

Linda Jawitz
New York, NY

Editor's note: Fun Tak is a brand name for a removable tacky-like material. There are other manufacturers of similar products.

Pith-free Citrus

No matter how carefully I peel citrus, there's still the tedious job of removing the unattractive, bitter-tasting pith (the white fiber under the peel). But I finally found a solution.

Place the whole fruit, peel and all, in a 350° oven for 15–20 minutes. Peel while it's still warm and the skin will pull away with the pith. The flesh stays relatively cool and can be used immediately. This works with all types of citrus.

A word of caution: The peel does get pretty hot, so use an oven mitt or towel to protect your hand from burns.

Tricia Littleton
Harlan, IA

The pith is the white layer that lies between the skin and the fruit. It's bitter, so you want to remove it. ►

Test Kitchen Tip
Always cook beans halfway through before adding salt, acidic ingredients, or sugar. These harden the skins and prevent beans from cooking.

Portioning Sausage

When I buy a roll of breakfast sausage, I portion it into patties before freezing. It's convenient because then I don't have to thaw a whole roll if I only need a few servings.

To do this, partially freeze the sausage first (about 30 minutes) so it's easier to slice. Then slice the roll into patties about $1/2$"-thick, arrange them on a parchment-lined baking sheet, and place them in the freezer. When the patties are completely frozen, transfer them to a plastic freezer bag for storage.

Dorothy Chilson
Elmira, OR

Easy Meatball Rolling

When making meatballs I find that if you dampen your hands first with cool water, the meat mixture will not stick to them. Makes rolling easier too!

Ann Castelli
Chicago Heights, IL

Cork Protector

After uncorking wine with a screw type opener, ensure the cork covers the tip and leave it on the opener. It will keep the worm sharp and prevent it from puncturing you or other items while being stored in the utensil drawer.

Gerry Phillips
San Francisco, CA

share your **tips** with *Cuisine at home*
and techniques

If you have a unique way of solving a cooking problem, we'd like to hear from you, and we'll consider publishing your tip in one or more of our works.

Just write down your cooking tip and mail it to *Cuisine at home*, Tips Editor, 2200 Grand Ave., Des Moines, IA 50312, or contact us through our email address shown below. Please include your name, address, and daytime phone number in case we have questions. We'll pay you $25 if we publish your tip.

Email: CuisineAtHome@CuisineAtHome.**com**
Web address: CuisineAtHome.**com**

cuisineclass

Cooking
fresh fish

Do not fear fish! This article paths the way to three healthy, fish-centered meals.

Chances are, most of us would rather eat fish at a restaurant than cook it ourselves at home. Is it any wonder? The danger of cooking it to death coupled with its lingering smells in the kitchen are enough to keep most self-respecting cooks at bay.

It shouldn't be like that. Delicious *and* healthy fish dishes can be a reality in your kitchen. Just keep these things in mind.

First, shop carefully. A truly great dish is only as good as the quality of the fish you buy, *see below*. Seek out the best—do not settle or you'll be disappointed.

Second, don't hesitate to try these interesting varieties of fish with their unique preparations. Of course, if you can't find a certain kind of fish, other types may be used (each recipe comes with substitution suggestions).

Fish sense

To find the freshest fish it's critical to use a few of your senses.

Smell: Fish should smell like the ocean, *see Figure 1*. If there's any hint of "off" odors, don't buy it. (The same goes for the establishment in which it's sold.)

Touch: If possible, squeeze the fish gently, *see Figure 2*. It should be firm and moist, not slimy or sticky. (The store may not allow this due to health regulations.)

Sight: Fresh fish should be stored on ice and well drained so water doesn't pool around it. The flesh, skin, and eyes should be vibrant—avoid fish that's dull, cloudy, or discolored. If you must buy frozen fish (a distant second to fresh), look for it in Cryovac packaging with few if any ice crystals inside, *see Figure 3*. Crystals indicate freezer burn.

Frozen fish can be good if it's been handled well—in good packaging with few, if any, ice crystals. Thaw frozen fish completely before cooking.

poaching
fresh fish

MAHIMAHI IN "CRAZY WATER"

MAKES 4 SERVINGS
TOTAL TIME: 35–40 MINUTES

FRY IN 1 T. OLIVE OIL; REMOVE:
1   small lemon, thinly sliced, seeded
2   T. capers, drained

SAUTE:
4   cloves garlic, thinly sliced
1/4 t. crushed red pepper flakes

ADD:
1 1/2 cups water
1   cup tomato, chopped (or 1 cup grape tomatoes, halved)
1/2 cup dry white wine
4   sprigs fresh thyme

POACH:
4   4–6 oz. fresh mahimahi fillets

REMOVE FISH, REDUCE BROTH, AND FINISH WITH:
      Fried lemon slices and capers
      Drizzle of extra-virgin olive oil
      Coarse sea salt to taste

Fry lemon slices and capers in olive oil in a large saute pan over medium-high heat. Cook lemons on both sides until they begin to brown around the edges, and the capers start to shrivel slightly, 3–4 minutes. Remove and set aside.

Saute garlic and pepper flakes in the pan, stirring constantly, just until fragrant, about 30 seconds.

Add water, tomato, wine, and thyme and bring to a simmer.

Poach fish fillets in simmering liquid, covered, just until cooked through, 8–10 minutes. Lift the lid occasionally to make sure the poaching liquid isn't boiling hard and adjust heat accordingly.

Remove fish, transfer to shallow serving bowls, divide lemons and capers among fish, and cover to keep warm. Increase heat; boil broth 3–4 minutes to reduce, then taste for seasoning and divide among fish. To finish, drizzle with oil and sea salt to taste.

mahimahi
in "crazy water"

This is a variation of an Italian dish which gets its name from the broth—bland water morphs into a flavorful broth with just a few simple ingredients.

The critical thing to remember when poaching is to keep the liquid at a gentle simmer. You don't want a rolling boil—it's too harsh for delicate fish. A lid on the pan retains heat and creates steam for faster cooking.

Mahimahi [MAH-hee-MAH-hee] is a fairly firm, lean fish. Its rosy flesh turns off-white when cooked, with brownish striping along the backbone area. For freshness, buy a large piece (have the skin removed), then cut into portions yourself. Halibut and red snapper are good substitutes.

▲ *Fried lemons and capers flavor the simple broth and act as a garnish as well.*

▲ *Bring liquid to a simmer before adding the fish. Cover and poach gently until cooked through.*

oven-roasting
fresh fish

Fish tacos sound strange, but try them. It's easy to see why they're so popular on Mexico's beaches.

Most fish for tacos is fried, but oven-roasting is a great way to achieve optimum flavor while limiting the fat. Placing the fillets on a preheated baking sheet helps crisp up the coating. The same goes for the tortillas—a brief toasting boosts their flavor and gives them a little crunch.

Tilapia [tuh-LAH-pee-uh] is a firm, dense white fish that, today, is nearly all farm-raised. Skinless, boneless fillets are typical, but it may also be sold whole. Raw, the fillets are pearl-pink with a dark stripe near the backbone area. Cooked, the fish is white, juicy, and *very* mild. The assertive flavors of fresh salsa and chipotle mayonnaise are perfect with it. Red snapper is a good substitute.

Preparing tilapia
Halve the fish fillets by slicing down the dark pink center. One half will be thicker than the other—it's okay and won't affect the cooking time.

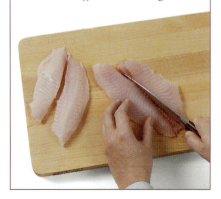

FISH TACOS

MAKES 4 SERVINGS
TOTAL TIME: 30 MINUTES

MARINATE IN LIME JUICE:
4   4 oz. fresh tilapia fillets, halved, see *left*

BLEND; COAT FISH IN:
3   T. all-purpose flour
3   T. yellow cornmeal
1   t. chili powder
1   t. kosher salt
$^{1}/_{4}$ t. cayenne

SPRAY, THEN OVEN-TOAST:
8   7" corn tortillas

SERVE WITH:
3   cups napa cabbage, shredded Mango-Avocado Salsa and Creamy Chipotle Sauce, *Page 9*

Preheat oven to 500° with racks on the top and bottom levels.

Marinate tilapia fillets in lime juice for 10 minutes, turning to coat. Place a baking sheet on each oven rack and preheat 5 minutes. **Blend** flour, cornmeal, and seasonings in a shallow dish. Coat marinated fish on both sides with flour mixture. Remove a hot pan from oven and spray with nonstick spray. Place fillets on hot pan and roast on top rack 5 minutes. **Spray** both sides of tortillas with nonstick spray. (Meanwhile, carefully turn fish over and return to oven 3–4 minutes.) Oven-toast tortillas on the second heated baking sheet after turning the fillets over. Toast tortillas just until they're lightly crisp around the edges, 2–3 minutes. **Serve** fish and tortillas with shredded cabbage, mango salsa, and chipotle sauce.

fish tacos

MANGO-AVOCADO SALSA

MAKES ABOUT 3 CUPS
TOTAL TIME: 15 MINUTES

COMBINE:

- 1   ripe yet firm mango, peeled, diced
- $1/2$ cup grape tomatoes, halved
- $1/2$ cup cucumber, diced
- $1/4$ cup red onion, minced
- 1   T. jalapeño, seeded, minced
- 1   t. sugar
- $1/4$ t. kosher salt
- $1/4$ t. ground cumin
-     Juice of one lime

BEFORE SERVING, STIR IN:

- 1   firm yet ripe avocado, pitted, peeled, thinly sliced
- 2   T. coarsely chopped fresh cilantro

Combine mango, tomatoes, cucumber, onion, jalapeño, seasonings, and lime juice in a large bowl. Let stand 10 minutes to blend flavors.
Before serving, stir in avocado and cilantro.

Halve, pit, and peel avocado, then slice crosswise into half-moons. ▼

CREAMY CHIPOTLE SAUCE

MAKES ABOUT $1/2$ CUP
TOTAL TIME: 5 MINUTES

STIR TOGETHER:

- $1/4$ cup plain lowfat yogurt
- $1/4$ cup reduced-calorie mayonnaise
- 2   t. sugar
- 1–2 chipotle chiles in adobo sauce, minced
-     Juice of $1/2$ lime

Stir all ingredients together in a small bowl and adjust seasonings to taste. Let stand at least 10 minutes to allow flavors to blend. (May be made several days ahead. Keep chilled until ready to serve.)

Dredge both sides of marinated tilapia in flour-cornmeal mixture. ▼

To shred napa cabbage, halve the head lengthwise, then thinly slice. ▼

Place fillets on preheated baking sheet and roast 5 min. Turn with a spatula and roast 3–4 minutes. ▶

Indian-style
sea bass

sauteing
fresh fish

Avid fish eaters appreciate new preparations—grilling gets old after a while! This Indian-inspired dish may be just the ticket for livening up your fish repertoire.

It centers around a yogurt and spice marinade similar to what Indian cooks use in their chicken or lamb Tandoor oven dishes. By sauteing the fish, a slightly smoky flavor is created, mimicking the flavors of the tandoori oven. It's important to use a nonstick skillet, plenty of heat, and a little oil in the pan—don't worry, the dish is still quite healthy. The oil isn't so much a preventative measure to keep the fish from sticking as it is a way to avoid scorching the marinade.

Chilean sea bass is a beautiful white, firm, fatty fish with mild flavor. However, its skyrocketing popularity over the last decade has resulted in overfishing to the point of its endangerment. If Chilean sea bass fillets are unavailable, or you'd rather abstain from using them, halibut fillets make a fine substitute.

INDIAN-STYLE SEA BASS

If you don't have all the spices for the marinade, it's okay to leave one or two out. Finishing the fish with butter at the end adds richness.

MAKES 4 SERVINGS
TOTAL TIME: ABOUT 30 MINUTES + MARINATING

COMBINE:

1/2   cup plain lowfat yogurt

2   T. fresh ginger, minced

2   T. garlic, minced

1   T. fresh lime juice

1   T. jalapeño, seeded, minced

1   t. paprika

1   t. kosher salt

1/2   t. cayenne

1/2   t. ground cumin

1/2   t. ground cinnamon

1/2   t. ground coriander

1/4   t. ground turmeric, *optional*

ADD AND MARINATE:

4   4–6 oz. fresh sea bass fillets

SAUTE FISH IN:

1   T. olive oil

TOP FISH WITH:

4   t. unsalted butter, *optional*

SERVE WITH:

  Apple-Coconut Raita, *right*

  Basmati Rice with Peas,

  see *online extra*

Combine yogurt, ginger, garlic, lime juice, jalapeño, and spices in a shallow, nonreactive dish (such as a glass pie plate).

Add sea bass fillets and coat both sides with yogurt mixture. Cover with plastic and marinate in the refrigerator for at least 1 hour and up to 4. Before sauteing, scrape off most (but not all) of the yogurt marinade. Discard remaining yogurt mixture.

Saute fish in oil in a large non-stick skillet over medium-high heat. It will splatter, so cover the skillet with a screen to prevent burns from popping oil. Cook fish on one side 4–5 minutes, carefully turn with a spatula, and continue to cook another 3–4 minutes. Remove skillet from heat.

Top each fillet with the optional 1 tsp. butter, cover skillet with a lid, and let stand for 1 minute.

Serve fish with raita and rice.

APPLE-COCONUT RAITA

Raita [RI-tah] is a traditional Indian yogurt-based condiment used as a cooling element to a spicy meal.

MAKES ABOUT 1 1/2 CUPS
TOTAL TIME: 10 MINUTES

PROCESS:

1/2   cup sweetened shredded coconut

ADD AND BLEND:

1   Granny Smith apple, diced

1   small jalapeño or serrano, seeded, coarsely chopped

1   bunch cilantro leaves and stems

1/4   t. ground cumin

  Juice of half a lime

  Pinch salt

STIR IN:

3–4 T. plain lowfat yogurt

Process coconut in food processor fitted with a steel blade until finely chopped.

Add apple, chile, cilantro, cumin, lime juice, and salt. Process until finely chopped (but do not over-process to a paste).

Stir in yogurt. Chill until ready to serve. (Raita is best served within an hour of being made.)

Preparing sea bass
Whole fish is fresher than precut fillets. So buy a 1–1 1/2 lb. chunk of fish, then portion it into fillets.

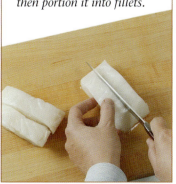

▲ *Coat fish fillets with the marinade and chill 1–4 hours.*

37

online **extra**

Want to make basmati rice with peas? Visit www.CuisineAtHome.com for a recipe.

◄ *Saute fish 4–5 min., then carefully turn and cook 3–4 more minutes. The marinade will darken but watch out that it doesn't scorch.*

5-ingredient pastas

orzo risotto
with mushrooms and chard

Pasta is always warm and inviting. Here are three quick pastas that will fit comfortably into your weeknight schedule.

Dinner doesn't always have to take a long time, nor does it need to take a lot of ingredients. You probably have most of the ingredients in your kitchen for each of these pasta dishes.

Besides the short shopping list and cooking time, these pasta recipes are unique because each uses a different cooking procedure. The first one is cooked like risotto, another uses a reduction, and one recipe is hardly cooked at all!

Sound a little confusing? Don't worry, each dish is really simple to make. Now, while I say these are 5-ingredient dinners, that's actually a bit of a stretch. At the right, you'll notice a brief list of common items that are often used to prepare Italian dishes. You'll only need to use a few of these in each recipe.

As with most recipes, be sure to have all ingredients at hand. Cooked pasta gets gummy if not used right away in the recipe.

Pantry items
Stock these ingredients for the following recipes:

Extra-virgin olive oil
Kosher salt
Freshly ground black pepper
Crushed red pepper flakes
Garlic
Shallots
Parmesan cheese
Fresh lemons
Dry white wine
Unsalted butter
Low-sodium chicken broth

ORZO RISOTTO WITH MUSHROOMS AND SWISS CHARD

The combination of cooking pasta like risotto and then adding sauteed mushrooms make this meatless pasta dish extraordinarily hearty.

MAKES 6 CUPS; TOTAL TIME: 40 MINUTES

FOR THE MUSHROOMS—
SAUTE IN 2 T. OLIVE OIL:
1   lb. white mushrooms, sliced
1   t. garlic, minced

FOR THE SWISS CHARD—
BLANCH:
1   bunch Swiss chard, stemmed, chopped (10–12 cups)

FOR THE RISOTTO—
SAUTE IN 2 T. OLIVE OIL:
1/4   cup shallots, minced
ADD:
2   cups dry orzo pasta
DEGLAZE WITH:
1/2   cup dry white wine
ADD:
3 1/2   cups low-sodium chicken broth, warmed, divided
STIR IN:
     Sauteed mushrooms
     Blanched Swiss chard
FINISH WITH:
1/2   cup Parmesan cheese
2   T. unsalted butter
1   T. minced fresh sage
     Kosher salt and black pepper to taste

Saute mushrooms in olive oil until they soften and most of their liquid is evaporated. Add garlic and saute for 1 minute. Transfer to a bowl and set aside.

Blanch the chard in boiling water for 1 minute. Drain and immediately plunge into ice water to stop the cooking. Squeeze out excess moisture; set aside.

Saute shallots in oil until softened using the same pan that the mushrooms were cooked in.

Add the orzo and continue cooking over medium heat until the pasta browns lightly.

Deglaze pan with wine, scraping up the flavorful bits at the bottom.

Add 1 1/2 cups of warmed chicken broth to the orzo and stir well. Continue cooking for 10 minutes. Add another cup of warmed broth and cook another 5 minutes. Add the last cup of broth and taste orzo for doneness.

Stir in the reserved mushrooms and chard.

Finish with Parmesan, butter, sage, salt, and pepper.

Orzo

[OHR-zoh]
Orzo is a small riced-shaped pasta that is commonly used in soups. Translated, it is Italian for "barley." If you can't find orzo, use any tiny pasta ending in *ine, ini, ette,* or *etti,* which indicates small. Pastas like anellini (little rings), ditalini (thimbles), or stelline (stars) will work fine.

▲ *When pasta is thoroughly cooked and all the liquid is absorbed, add mushrooms, chard, cheese, butter, and sage.*

▲ *Saute mushrooms until most moisture is gone. Add garlic and cook briefly.*

▼ *After removing mushrooms, saute shallots and add orzo. Cook until lightly browned.*

▲ *Deglaze pan with wine, scraping up the flavorful bits. Add warmed chicken broth and stir.*

faster **with** fewer

WARM LILY SALAD

Nothing cooking here except the pasta. The hot pasta and warm garlic oil enhance the delicate flavors of the fresh tomatoes, herbs, and cheese.

MAKES 8–9 CUPS
TOTAL TIME: 30 MINUTES

COMBINE:

1½ cups grape tomatoes, halved
½   cup kalamata olives, pitted,
     halved
4   oz. feta cheese, crumbled
     (about 1 cup)
3   T. torn fresh basil
3   T. chopped fresh parsley
1   t. lemon zest, minced

PREPARE:

1   lb. campanelle pasta

WARM IN ¼ CUP OLIVE OIL:

1   T. garlic, minced

TOSS PASTA WITH:

    Prepared vegetables,
    cheese, and herbs

FINISH WITH:

    Garlic infused olive oil
    Sea salt and freshly ground
    black pepper to taste

Combine tomatoes, olives, cheese, herbs, and lemon zest in a large bowl; set aside.
Prepare pasta according to package directions.
Warm garlic in olive oil. Don't allow it to burn or it'll taste bitter.
Toss hot, drained pasta with vegetables, cheese, and herbs.
Finish with garlic oil, sea salt, and black pepper to taste.

warm lily salad

◄Drain the pasta and immediately toss with the fresh vegetables, cheese, and herbs.

Drizzle salad with the warm garlic oil and toss well. Season and serve immediately. ►

Campanelle

This family of pastas consists of flower shapes. They are particularly good with chunky-type sauces because the folds and cavities can hold large pieces of vegetables. Other names you might see are riccioli or gigli (Italian for lilies). Some good substitutes might be ziti, penne, rigatoni, or conchiglie (shells).

LITTLE EARS WITH SAUSAGE AND BROCCOLI

A bold but simple dish. Reducing the sauce not only intensifies the flavors but also helps it cling to the pasta.

MAKES 8 CUPS
TOTAL TIME: 30 MINUTES

COOK:
¹/₂ lb. sweet Italian link sausage

FOR THE SAUCE—
BOIL AND REDUCE:
2 cups low-sodium chicken broth
¹/₂ cup dry white wine
1 t. garlic, minced
1 t. crushed red pepper flakes

PREPARE:
2 cups orecchiette

ADD:
3 cups broccoli florets

FINISH WITH:
1 T. unsalted butter

Start boiling water for the pasta and broccoli. Preheat the oven to 375° for the sausage.

Cook sausage in a skillet. Add a little water to the pan and cook in the oven for 15–20 minutes. Turn it over halfway through to brown on both sides. Slice sausage into ¹/₄"-thick rounds and set aside.

Boil the broth, wine, garlic, and pepper flakes for the sauce until reduced to ³/₄ cup, 10–15 minutes.

Prepare the pasta according to package directions.

Add the broccoli to the pasta water during the last 4 minutes of cooking. Drain, but do not rinse. Toss the sausage, pasta, and broccoli together. Pour the sauce over all the ingredients and stir to combine.

Finish with butter.

▲ *Cook sausage in the oven with a little water to prevent it from drying out.*

When pasta is nearly cooked, add broccoli to the water. Drain with pasta. ▶

Orecchiette

[oh-rayk-kee-EHT-teh]
In Italy, orecchiette (little ears) is made from small pieces of dough that are pressed and pulled to form hollowed, oval shapes. This shape is popular in both northern and southern regions of Italy because it holds sauces well. If you can't find orecchiette, a medium shell works fine.

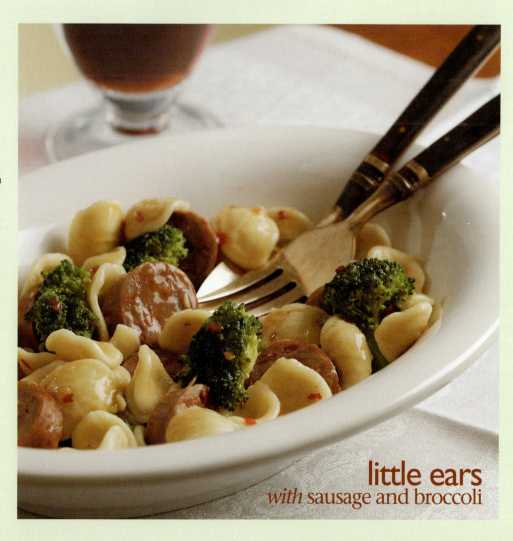

little ears
with sausage and broccoli

oven-fried chicken

All the flavor and texture of fried chicken but with fewer calories. How come? This crunchy treat is skinless and cooked in the oven!

Fried chicken tastes great because it's cooked in *hot* oil. That does several things to make it taste good. First, it creates steam inside the meat which makes for juicy, tender chicken. Second, while that meat is steaming, the crust (made from the flavorful, fatty skin) is turning golden and crunchy. Done right, it's these contrasts that make fried chicken so appealing. But, oh my, the calories! So how can you get fried chicken qualities with a little less fat? Oven-frying. Get the flavor and texture by following a few simple techniques.

Brining: Simply put, frying in oil moisturizes meat while dry-roasting extracts moisture. By using a brine of sugar and salt, you add moisture, flavor, and texture to the meat. Sugar is used for flavor and browning, while salt tends to retain moisture within the meat. I found that a short two-hour brine is sufficient. After that, you experience diminishing results.

Use paper towels to grip the chicken skin and pull it away. Trim any excess fat. ▶

▲ *For even cooking, cut breasts in half at an angle so that they are the same size as the thighs and legs.*

Pierce each piece of chicken several times to make sure the brine penetrates the meat. ▼

OVEN-FRIED CHICKEN
Makes 8–10 Pieces; Total Time: 2–3 Hours

FOR THE BRINE—
DISSOLVE:

¹/₂	cup kosher salt
¹/₂	cup brown sugar
4	cups hot water

ADD:

4	cups ice cubes

PREPARE:

8–10 chicken pieces (thighs, legs, and breasts), skin removed, pierced

FOR THE COATING—
COMBINE:

3	cups all-purpose flour
2–3	T. black pepper
1	T. kosher salt
1	T. paprika

BEAT:

2	egg whites

ADD:

1	cup buttermilk

HEAT:

3	T. vegetable oil

Dissolve salt and sugar for brine in hot water in a large container. **Add** ice and stir to cool mixture. **Prepare** chicken pieces by removing the skin and piercing the meat with a knife. Add to brine and refrigerate for 1¹/₂–2 hours.

Preheat oven to 450°. Coat a 4-quart Pyrex baking dish with nonstick cooking spray. **Combine** flour, pepper, salt, and paprika in a large, heavy bag. Remove chicken pieces from the brine and lightly pat dry. Place a few pieces into the bag of seasoned flour and toss to coat. Shake off excess flour and place on a rack. Let sit 10 minutes. **Beat** egg whites to soft peaks. **Add** buttermilk and stir gently. Dip floured chicken pieces into the egg white-buttermilk mixture. Put the dipped pieces back into the seasoned flour bag. Shake gently and transfer to the rack. Repeat with remaining chicken. **Heat** oil in the prepared Pyrex dish by placing it in the oven for 5 minutes.

  Set the prepared chicken pieces, meaty-side down, into the hot Pyrex dish; roast for 30 minutes. Remove dish from the oven and carefully turn the pieces over. Return to the oven and roast 20 minutes more. Remove chicken from the oven and let rest 15 minutes before serving.

Place a few chicken pieces into the bag of seasoned flour and toss to coat. Shake off excess flour and place on rack. ▼

◄ *Beat egg whites to soft peaks (when they begin to hold their shape). Gently stir in the buttermilk.*

Dip floured pieces into the egg white-buttermilk mixture. ►

Coating: By removing the fatty skin, you eliminate two good crust characteristics—something for the coating to cling to, and the natural crispness that skin provides. This makes using the right ingredients and procedures all the more important.

  Since the skin is gone, double coating is imperative. It helps reestablish some of the needed surface texture. Remove pieces from the brine and pat dry. Lightly coat each piece with seasoned flour. I put all the flour in one large bag and use it for both the first and second coatings.

  After the first coating, let the chicken sit for 10 minutes so flour has time to bond to the meat.

  For the second coating, whip egg whites to soft peaks and then fold in buttermilk. Whipping the whites puts air into the coating so the high temperature can penetrate the coating easily. Now dip each piece into the buttermilk mixture and then the flour.

  Pan: Use a glass baking dish (like Pyrex) for best results. Glass retains the hot temperature without fluctuating.

Place prepared chicken pieces in hot Pyrex dish, meaty-side down. Bake 30 minutes, turn, and roast 20 minutes more. ►

◄ *Place dipped pieces back into seasoned flour bag. Shake gently to coat thoroughly. Return to rack.*

sides for
chicken

You're going to need some mighty good side dishes to pair with oven-fried chicken. Here are two that can cook right along with this crispy treat.

menu

Oven-fried Chicken

Hot Coleslaw

3-Cheese Potato Gratin

HOT COLESLAW

Fried chicken and coleslaw just go together. Here's a warm winter version that's reminiscent of German potato salad. Use red cabbage for color.

MAKES 4 CUPS; TOTAL TIME: 25 MINUTES

FRY:
1/2   lb. thick-sliced bacon, diced
ADD:
1   cup yellow onion, diced
WHISK IN:
1   T. all-purpose flour
STIR IN:
2/3   cup white wine vinegar
1/3   cup sugar
1/4   cup low-sodium chicken broth
    Salt and pepper to taste
ADD; TOSS:
8   cups red cabbage, thinly shredded
STIR IN:
1/4   cup chopped fresh parsley

Fry bacon in skillet. Pour off all but 1/4 cup drippings.

Add onion to bacon and drippings. Cook on medium heat until softened, about 5 minutes.

Whisk in flour. Cook 1–2 minutes to remove the starchy taste of the flour.

Stir in vinegar, sugar, broth, salt, and pepper to taste.

Add the cabbage and toss to wilt, 4–5 minutes.

Stir in parsley before serving.

▲ *Halve cabbage and remove core. Divide into quarters and slice very thinly.*

Add shredded cabbage to pan and toss to wilt and combine flavors. Cook 4–5 minutes. ▶

3-CHEESE POTATO GRATIN

The key to making this gratin is first simmering the potatoes with flavored milk and cream.

MAKES 4–6 SERVINGS
TOTAL TIME: 1 HOUR

COMBINE:
1½ cups whole milk
½ cup heavy cream
1 clove garlic, peeled, smashed
1 t. kosher salt
½ t. white pepper
⅛ t. cayenne
⅛ t. ground nutmeg

ADD; SIMMER:
3 lb. russet potatoes, peeled, thinly sliced

TOSS; LAYER WITH POTATOES:
½ cup sharp Cheddar cheese, grated
½ cup Gruyere or Swiss cheese, grated
¼ cup Parmesan cheese, grated
1 T. all-purpose flour

Preheat oven to 450°. Coat a 2-quart casserole dish with nonstick cooking spray.

Combine milk, cream, garlic, and spices in a large saucepan.

Add potatoes and bring to a boil. Cover, reduce heat to low, and simmer 8 minutes. Discard garlic.

Toss grated cheeses with flour; set aside. Layer half the potatoes in the casserole dish. Sprinkle half the cheese mixture over the potatoes. Add remaining potatoes and pour the milk mixture over the top. Sprinkle with the remaining cheese mixture.

Coat a piece of foil with nonstick spray and tightly cover baking dish; bake for 30 minutes. Remove foil and bake an additional 20 minutes, or until gratin is browned and bubbly. Let gratin rest 10–15 minutes before serving.

▲ *A mandoline works great to slice potatoes about ⅛" thick.*

◄ *Combine milk, cream, and seasonings. Add potatoes, cover, and reduce heat to low. Simmer 8 minutes.*

Layer half the potatoes into the prepared casserole dish. Cover with half the cheese. ►

◄ *Layer with remaining potatoes, cover with milk mixture, and top with cheese.*

smothered
oven-fried chicken

You've made the oven-fried chicken. Now smother it with this easy-to-make gravy. It'll warm up a winter Sunday better than your favorite sweater.

Simple gravy

Smothered chicken isn't exactly calorie-free, but I've reduced them without sacrificing flavor.

This isn't a hard gravy to make—it actually makes itself in the oven. But the rich flavor comes from caramelized onions that are slowly cooked on top of the stove. Here's what to do.

In a saute pan, slowly cook the onions over low heat. Stir often until they turn golden. This means the sugars in the onions are caramelizing and a deep, rich flavor is developing.

Once golden, add the flour and cook 2–3 minutes to eliminate the starchy taste. Then add liquids and stir thoroughly to incorporate the flour.

After chicken is cooked, pour liquid mixture around the chicken and bake another 10 minutes. Remove chicken and place on a platter. Stir parsley into thickened sauce and pour over chicken.

GRAVY FOR SMOTHERED CHICKEN
MAKES 2 CUPS; TOTAL TIME: 35 MINUTES

PREPARE:
Oven-fried Chicken, *Pages 16–17*

MELT:
2   T. unsalted butter

ADD; CARAMELIZE:
2   cups yellow onions, sliced

STIR IN:
3   T. all-purpose flour

STIR IN:
3   cups low-sodium chicken broth
1/3 cup dry white wine

ADD:
2   T. chopped fresh parsley
     Salt to taste

SERVE WITH:
Oven-fried Chicken
Cooked white rice

Prepare oven-fried chicken as on Pages 16–17.

Melt butter in a large saute pan over medium heat while chicken is in the last 20 minutes of cooking.
Add onions and cook on low heat until caramelized, about 15–20 minutes.
Stir in flour and cook 2–3 minutes to cook out starchy taste.
Stir broth and wine into onion mixture. Pour the gravy into the baking dish with the chicken. Try not to pour it on top of the pieces—they will get soggy. Place chicken back into the oven for 15 minutes to thicken gravy. Remove baking dish from oven and transfer chicken pieces to a serving platter.
Add parsley to gravy just before serving and season with salt.
Serve with chicken and cooked white rice.

▼ *Melt butter in saute pan. Add onions and cook slowly 15–20 minutes to caramelize. Stir often.*

▼ *When the onions are nice and brown it's time to stir in the flour.*

▲ *Stir in the broth and the wine. Scrape up the bits off the bottom.*

▼ *Pour gravy over chicken to "smother" it. Serve with rice.*

▲ *Pour gravy mixture into baking dish—avoid pouring on top of the chicken. Return to oven to thicken.*

▲ *Remove chicken pieces to a serving platter. Add parsley to gravy right before serving.*

beef bourguignonne

Don't let the fancy French name scare you—it's simply beef stew. But what a stew it is.

It's winter and it's cold—what could be more satisfying than something steaming and rich?

When the craving hits, try this in lieu of the usual chili. The ingredient list and cooking process are a bit long, but you're not tied to the stove the whole time. It's worth it, I promise.

Beef bourguignonne [boor-gee-NYON] is a French classic, and this recipe doesn't stray too far from the norm—I mean, why change a good thing? In bistros, bourguignonne is often serve by itself, perhaps with a baguette. But I recommend buttered potatoes, *Page 25*. It's a perfect match.

Getting ready—the beef and the wine

Beef bourguignonne revolves around two primary ingredients: meat and wine.

Beef: This stew is braised (simmered in liquid for a long time) so it's important to use the proper cut of beef—one well marbled with connective tissues and fat. During cooking, the fat and tissues melt into the sauce giving it body and richness. Then, at the same time, the meat softens and becomes fork-tender.

I got the best results by cutting a chuck pot roast into pieces. Precut meat ("beef for stew") worked quite well, but by cutting a pot roast yourself, you get more consistent quality. Grocery store stew meat is mostly just trimmings from all types of cuts.

This stew also includes a knuckle bone (often labeled "soup bone"). French chefs sometimes add veal bones to bourguignonne—collagen-rich, they give the sauce incredible smoothness. A knuckle bone does a similar job, but if you can't find one, just omit it.

Wine: Pinot noir, made entirely from pinot noir grapes, is the traditional bourguignonne wine. But I found that blended wines (made with several types of grapes, not just one variety) give the stew a fuller flavor— Coppola Rosso 2001 is very good. No matter what you choose, don't spend more than 10 bucks on it. Pricier bottles are for drinking.

BEEF BOURGUIGNONNE
MAKES 6 CUPS; TOTAL TIME: ABOUT 2 1/2 HOURS + MARINATING

TRIM AND CUBE:
2 lb. chuck pot roast

COMBINE; MARINATE BEEF IN:
1 bottle (750 ml) red wine
1 yellow onion, diced
1 carrot, diced
1 rib celery, diced
3 cloves garlic, crushed
2 bay leaves

REMOVE BEEF; DREDGE IN:
1/2 cup all-purpose flour
1 t. kosher salt
1/2 t. black pepper
1/4 t. cayenne

SAUTE:
4 strips thick-sliced bacon, diced

BROWN BEEF IN BACON FAT; ADD:
2–4 T. olive oil

SWEAT:
Reserved vegetables from marinade
1 beef knuckle soup bone
1 T. tomato paste

ADD:
1/4 cup brandy, *optional*

TIE TOGETHER:
6 sprigs fresh thyme
1 t. whole black peppercorns

ADD AND BRAISE:
Herb bundle
Reserved marinade, bacon, and browned beef

STIR IN; COOK:
8 oz. white mushrooms, halved
8 oz. pearl onions, peeled
1 T. red wine vinegar

FINISH WITH:
1/4 cup chopped fresh parsley
1 T. lemon zest, minced
Salt and pepper to taste

SERVE OVER:
Buttered potatoes, *Page 25*

Trim roast and cut into 2" cubes.
Combine wine, vegetables, garlic, and bay leaves, in a large bowl. Place meat in a strainer and submerge in the marinade. Marinate 4 hours, preferably overnight.
Remove meat from marinade; pat dry. Drain vegetables from marinade, reserving both. Combine flour and seasonings in a large resealable plastic bag. Dredge beef in flour mixture.
Saute bacon in a large Dutch oven over med.-high heat until crisp. Remove with slotted spoon and drain on paper towel-lined plate.
Brown beef in batches in bacon fat left in pan—do not crowd the pan or meat won't brown well. Remove browned beef before adding more. If the pan becomes dry, add a little olive oil. Remove last batch of meat before continuing. Preheat oven to 350°.
Sweat reserved vegetables, soup bone, and tomato paste in pan, stirring to loosen the browned bits from the bottom. Cook until vegetables soften, 5 minutes.
Add brandy; cook until evaporated.
Tie thyme and peppercorns in a paper coffee filter; secure with cotton kitchen string.
Add herb bundle, reserved marinade, bacon, and beef. Cover with a tight-fitting lid, transfer to oven, and braise 1 hour.
Stir in mushrooms, onions, and vinegar. Return to oven and cook, covered, until meat is tender, 30–40 minutes. Remove herb bundle and soup bone.
Finish with parsley, lemon zest, salt, and pepper to taste.
Serve over buttered potatoes.

◄ *Put beef in a strainer, then submerge it into the wine and vegetables (to prevent sorting out the beef later). Stir meat once or twice during marinating.*

Three steps to stew

Browning, deglazing, and braising are the three key steps to great beef bourguignonne.

Step One—Browning

This is the cornerstone for flavor and color. The browner the meat gets, the better the stew will be.

There are four keys to good browning. The first is a large, heavy stock pot or Dutch oven that has a tight fitting lid. Thinner pots create "hot spots" and are more likely to scorch. Second, the meat must be patted dry. Surface moisture causes steam, preventing a good sear. Third, brown the meat over fairly high heat and, to prevent burning, use a good amount of oil in the pot. The bacon contributes some fat, but you'll need to add more oil. Finally, brown the meat in small batches or it will steam, not sear.

Watch the condition of the pot while browning the meat. The dredging flour and natural sugars in the beef create that dark layer on the bottom of the pot—the flavor foundation and thickening agent for the stew's sauce. But be careful that it doesn't scorch. If you see or smell smoke, reduce the heat and add more oil before continuing.

Step Two—Deglazing

To release and incorporate the stuck-on layer from the bottom, you need to "deglaze" the pot.

Normally this is done with a liquid—water, broth, or wine. But here, the vegetables from the marinade are the deglazer. Their natural juices, as well as any wine left on them, loosen the bits.

Reduce the heat to medium and add the vegetables, scraping the pot with a wooden spoon. Then cover and "sweat" them (cook the vegetables without browning) for five minutes. This generates steam, loosening additional stuck spots. Then add the wine marinade to start braising.

▲ *Remove beef cubes from marinade and pat dry. Strain vegetables from wine; reserve both separately.*

▼ *Combine flour mixture in a resealable plastic bag; dredge beef cubes in mixture to coat.*

▲ *Saute bacon and remove. Brown beef in batches in bacon drippings. Remove before adding next batch.*

▲ *Deglaze with vegetables from marinade, soup bone, and paste. Scrape brown bits from the bottom of the pan.*

◄ *Sweat vegetables until softened. Tie thyme and peppercorns in coffee filter; add to pot. Return beef, bacon, and reserved wine to pot.*

Step Three—Braising

Braising is one of the simplest cooking methods around—most of the work is up front in browning and deglazing. Once the stew is in the oven, you can almost turn your back on it.

A braise, by definition, is to slowly cook food, tightly covered, in liquid. The slow cooking causes the connective tissues and muscle fibers in the meat to break down and make it tender. The melted connective tissues also transform the wine into a thick, glossy sauce. It's *the* method to use with tough cuts of meat such as pot roast. Quicker techniques, like sauteing, don't allow the meat to cook long enough to tenderize it.

Now, in today's hurry-up world, it's hard to imagine beef bourguignonne as a weeknight meal, especially with the marinating and lengthy braising times. But this is one of those dishes that tastes *better* the next day. So here's what I recommend you do: Make the stew one weekend, have half for dinner, then chill or freeze the rest. After that, it's feasible to have dinner on the table in the time it takes to boil potatoes. Now *that's* fast food!

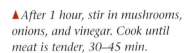

▲ *After 1 hour, stir in mushrooms, onions, and vinegar. Cook until meat is tender, 30–45 min.*

▲ *Remove soup bone and herb bundle. Finish stew with parsley, lemon zest, and salt to taste.*

Serve the stew over Buttered Potatoes, right. Noodles or rice are also a good accompaniment. ▶

BUTTERED POTATOES
Yes, these are simple boiled, buttered potatoes—nothing fancy. But don't eat bourguignonne without them!

MAKES 4–6 SERVINGS
TOTAL TIME: 20–25 MINUTES

COOK; DRAIN AND MASH:
2–3 lb. russet potatoes, peeled, cut into chunks

TOP WITH:
    Butter
    Salt to taste

Cook potatoes in salted water to cover until they can be pierced easily with a skewer. Drain, then mash coarsely on serving plates.
Top with butter and salt before serving, then ladle Beef Bourguignonne on top.

37

online **extra**

How do you peel pearl onions? Visit our web site at **www.CuisineAtHome.com** for a step-by-step guide.

bean Soups

Besides being a wealth of health, the humble bean packs a punch in these soups.

With today's schedules, it's hard to imagine actually *cooking* dried beans. It's just easier to reach for a can instead. But cooked dried beans are so different than those from a can. In terms of flavor, texture, and nutrition, it's worth taking the plunge and cooking them. It isn't much work at all—simply a few extra quick steps.

No matter what type of dried bean you use (black, navy, red, white, speckled), cooking them actually starts with soaking. This reduces cooking time (the longer they soak, the less time they'll take to cook) and helps purge them of the enzymes that can cause digestive mayhem. An important note: Don't use the bean soaking water for cooking, or the beans will reabsorb the enzymes they were purged of.

Cook soaked beans in fresh water to cover by two inches. If the water boils down, add more. Depending on their age and variety, cooking times may vary, so test often for doneness. If the first one you try is done, test a few more to be sure they're consistently cooked throughout.

▲ *Medium-sized thick-skinned beans include black, pinto, red, cannellini, great Northern, navy, black-eyed pea, and many heirloom varieties.*

COOKED DRIED BEANS

MAKES 6 CUPS
SOAK TIME: 4–12 HOURS
COOK TIME: 1–1½ HOURS

SORT AND SOAK:
1   lb. medium-sized thick-skinned dried beans
DRAIN, RINSE, AND COOK:
     Soaked beans

Sort beans to remove pebbles or dirt. Rinse well. Soak in a large pot with cold water to cover by 2". Cover and chill 4–12 hours. **Drain** and rinse soaked beans. Place beans in pot, add 6 cups cold water, and bring to a boil. Reduce heat and simmer 1–1½ hours, partially covered. Add more water during cooking if needed. Test a few beans for tenderness after 1 hour. Drain and chill up to 3 days.

◄ *Sort through and rinse beans before soaking to remove any pebbles or dirt.*

red beans & rice

RED BEANS AND RICE SOUP

MAKES 10 CUPS
TOTAL TIME: 50 MINUTES + SOAKING AND COOKING BEANS

SAUTE IN 1 T. VEGETABLE OIL:
1/2   lb. kielbasa, diced

STIR IN:
1   cup yellow onion, diced
3/4   cup celery, diced
1/2   cup red bell pepper, diced
2   T. garlic, minced
2   t. brown sugar
1 1/2 t. dried thyme
2   bay leaves
       Salt to taste

DEGLAZE WITH:
2   T. apple cider vinegar
1   T. Tabasco, *optional*

ADD:
6   cups low-sodium chicken broth
6   cups cooked red beans, *Page 26*
2/3   cup converted white rice

GARNISH WITH:
       Chopped scallions, green parts only

Saute kielbasa in a large pot over medium-high heat, 4–5 minutes.
Add onion, celery, bell pepper, garlic, and seasonings. Cook, stirring constantly, 3–4 minutes.
Deglaze the pot with vinegar and Tabasco.
Add broth, beans, and rice. Partially cover and simmer 25–30 minutes, or until rice is tender.
Garnish servings of soup with chopped scallions.

◄ *Saute kielbasa; stir in vegetables and seasonings.*

Deglaze with vinegar and Tabasco. Add broth, beans, and rice. Partially cover and simmer 25–30 minutes. ▼

add in

Add to hot soup right before serving:
6   cups mustard greens, stemmed, chopped into bite-size pieces

CUBAN black Bean

CUBAN BLACK BEAN SOUP

MAKES 8 CUPS
TOTAL TIME: 50 MINUTES + SOAKING AND COOKING BEANS

SIMMER:
- 6 cups cooked black beans, *Page 26*
- 6 cups low-sodium chicken broth

PUREE:
- Half the cooked beans and broth

SAUTE:
- 2 slices bacon, diced small

SAUTE IN 1 T. BACON DRIPPINGS:
- 1 cup white onion, diced
- 2 T. garlic, minced
- 2 t. paprika
- 1 t. ground cumin
- 1 t. dried oregano
- ½ t. ground coriander
- ¼ t. cayenne
- Pinch of sugar and salt

DEGLAZE WITH; ADD:
- 1 T. red wine vinegar
- 1 can (14.5 oz.) diced tomatoes
- Reserved bacon

COMBINE FOR GARNISH:
- ½ cup jalapeño jelly
- ¼ cup grape tomatoes, diced

GARNISH WITH:
- Sour cream
- Jelly–tomato mixture

Simmer cooked beans and broth in soup pot over medium heat, 20–30 minutes.

Puree half of the bean-broth mixture in a food processor fitted with a steel blade. Return pureed beans back to pot. Keep warm over low heat.

Saute bacon in skillet until crisp and drain on paper towels. Remove all but 1 T. drippings.
Saute onion, garlic, and seasonings in drippings until softened, about 5 minutes.
Deglaze pan with vinegar. Add tomatoes with juice. Simmer to reduce and then mash tomatoes lightly. Add reserved bacon into black beans.
Combine jelly and tomatoes.
Garnish with sour cream and jelly-tomato mixture.

add on

Serve soup over mashed potatoes:
- 2 lb. russet potatoes, peeled, quartered
- ½ cup whole milk
- ¼ cup unsalted butter
- Salt to taste

Cook, drain, and mash potatoes. Combine with milk, butter, and salt.

Puree half the bean-broth mixture and add back to soup pot. ▼

▲ *Wrap a towel around the food processor to prevent burns and spills.*

▲ *Saute onion, garlic, and seasonings in bacon drippings. Stir into beans.*

PASTA E FAGIOLI SOUP

Makes 8 Cups
Total Time: 50 Minutes + Soaking and Cooking Beans

Cook:
1 cup small shell pasta (reserve 2 cups pasta water)

Saute in $^1/_4$ Cup Olive Oil:
$^1/_2$ cup yellow onion, diced
1 t. black pepper
$^1/_2$ t. crushed red pepper flakes

Stir in:
1 T. garlic, minced
2 t. minced fresh rosemary
1 t. anchovy paste, *optional*

Add and Simmer:
6 cups cooked great Northern beans, *Page 26*
4 cups low-sodium chicken broth
    Reserved pasta water

Stir in:
1 T. fresh lemon juice
    Cooked pasta
    Salt to taste

Combine; Garnish with:
$^3/_4$ cup Parmesan, finely grated
$^1/_4$ cup chopped fresh parsley

Cook pasta according to package directions. Drain pasta reserving 2 cups water for the soup; set aside.

Saute onion, black pepper, and pepper flakes in oil in a large pot over medium-high heat.

Stir in garlic, rosemary, and anchovy paste. Cook for 1 minute.

Add beans, broth, and pasta water. Bring to a boil, reduce heat, and simmer 20–25 minutes.

Stir in lemon juice, pasta, and salt.

Combine Parmesan and parsley. Pass at the table to sprinkle on top of soup.

Pasta e fagioli

Saute onion and seasonings in oil until onion softens. ▼

▲ *Add cooked white beans to the soup mixture.*

Combine Parmesan and parsley to pass at the table. ►

add in

Stir into soup:
2 cups Roma tomatoes, seeded, diced

Stir tomatoes into the soup with the beans, broth, and pasta water.

allabout

Salt *to* taste

Don't think for a moment that salt is salt. If you're into cooking, here's the information you need to know to make all your food taste even better.

Salt just might be one of the most important commodities in our world—thank goodness there is plenty of it.

I'm frequently asked why food in restaurants tastes so much better than food prepared at home. The secret? Besides years of training, chefs use plenty of butter and salt. What's not to love? Real butter makes everything better, but salt is a different story. The proper amount of salt is imperative, but the *kind* of salt is even more important. Top chefs know this and have been using specialty salts for years.

Salt has always played a role in society. The ancient Greeks traded salt for slaves resulting in the phrase "not worth his salt." Roman soldiers were partially paid in salt—the word "salt" comes from the Latin word *salarium,* meaning salary. Today, salt has over 40,000 applications from manufacturing to medicine, but to most of us, its main function is in the kitchen.

Like so many things, salts have become trendy—red salt from Hawaii, Jurassic salt from Utah, and the multitude of sea salts from Europe. Is the salt trend overrated, or are some of those Mediterranean sea salts really worth $30 a pound? Well, maybe, but you need to know the basics before deciding.

Table salt

Table salt (granular salt) is what most of us know. It is mined and processed to form small, uniformly shaped cubes. Additives are added to prevent caking and some medical problems. Most table salt is mined like coal or extracted by forcing water down into subterranean salt deposits. The resulting brine is pumped out and processed to form tiny, dense, cube shapes that don't dissolve very well.

Kosher salt

Kosher salt is made by compacting granular salt between rollers which produces large irregular flakes. This shape allows the salt to easily draw blood when applied to freshly butchered meat (part of the koshering process). Unlike table salt, kosher salt contains no additives.

Sea salt

Sea salt is created when ocean waters flood shallow beds along coastlines. During the summer months, the water evaporates leaving large salt crystals. The different waters and minerals from the surrounding land lend their flavors to these flaky salts.

What to use

At $30 a pound, you need to exercise good judgment when selecting salts for your kitchen—especially exotic salts.

For regular cooking, nothing beats 70¢ a pound kosher salt. It blends well, is clean-tasting, easy to cook with, and additive free. All of the qualities of expensive salts get lost during cooking. Their value is geared towards finished food—that is, sprinkling on top of food just before serving. Texture as well as taste become important for a finishing salt.

My favorites, hands down, are Fleur de Sel and Maldon sea salts. Their flavors are mild and their textures pleasingly crisp.

Maldon Sea Salt

Besides Fleur de Sel, England's Maldon sea salt is worth its $11 a pound price. A good "finishing salt" that gets its delicate flavor from a tradition of boiling the sea water to form hollow pyramid-shaped crystals. You can actually crush the crystals between your fingers. This makes for a light taste on your tongue.

Sel Gris

"Gray salt" is harvested on France's Atlantic coast where shallow basins are flooded with ocean water. Evaporation takes place between May and September when artisan harvesters rake the salt to the edge of each bed. The salt picks up its gray color and distinct flavor from minerals in the bed's clay bottom.

Fleur de Sel

A finishing salt that I think is worth its high price tag. A by-product of Sel Gris, Fleur de Sel is created only when the winds are calm and the days are warm. It is on these rare few days that the gray salt "blooms" lacy, white crystals. This is the "flower of salt" and is carefully skimmed from the surface. Use sparingly on foods just before serving.

Table Salt

Except for baking, I haven't used table salt in years. It always seems to taste really salty and harsh. The reality is that it isn't any saltier than other salts, it's just that the crystals are small and don't dissolve well. Because of this, the crystals tend to linger on the surface of the tongue.

Kosher Salt

Kosher is granular salt that's pressed together. If you look at it microscopically, each grain resembles an ancient Egyptian pyramid—stacked cubes that have weathered. Why am I telling you this? It's the design that makes kosher so good. This structure dissolves easily and imparts plenty of flavor (without over-salting) because of its large surface area. We use it in our test kitchen.

Red Alae Hawaiian Sea Salt

Hawaiian red and black sea salts (black not shown) are specialty finishing salts. While they look cool, their flavor is a bit strange. Red salt has an iron taste from the soil that's used to add color while the black salt tends to have a sulfuric aroma from added purified lava.

basic
white bread

What could be better on a winter day than eating home-made bread? Not a fancy artisanal loaf, but old-fashioned white bread, slathered with loads of real butter.

We've all experienced it at least once—opening a door and being embraced by the aroma of baking bread. It just might be one of the best smells in the whole world.

We wanted to make *that* kind of memory again, so we went to the experts—King Arthur Flour. Their white bread has a thick, tender crust, and a moist, light interior that's full of flavor.

Our instructor is Jeffrey Hamelman, Director of the King Arthur Flour Bakery and Baking Education Center. Translating his knowledge and experience into classes for every level of baker, Jeffrey stresses three principles for producing a flavorful loaf of bread. Begin with a starter, let dough rise at room temperature, and use time to develop flavor.

Dating back to 1790, King Arthur Flour is America's oldest flour company. While chemical-free flour remains their foundation, they are dedicated to being an education resource and inspiration to bakers.

*To fulfill that mission they've expanded into a premier source for professional quality baking equipment and ingredients with their Baker's Catalogue. Their retail store, bakery, and Baking Education Center make Norwich, Vermont a bakers destination. Check out their website, **bakerscatalogue.com**, for recipes and products, and to find when a free King Arthur Flour bread baking class will be in your area.*

Evening start

The best way to build flavor into bread is to begin the night before with a *pre*-ferment. It's a starter that ferments overnight. There are several kinds of pre-ferment—we're using a biga (BEE-gah).

Biga basics: A biga is a combination of flour, water, and a very small amount of yeast. It's really just a portion of the final dough that gets an early start. The little bit of yeast growing for a long period of time produces a lot more flavor than does more yeast rising for less time. It's the long, slow fermentation process that builds flavor. By morning the biga has developed and can be mixed into the final dough.

Ingredients: If available, use King Arthur's unbleached all-purpose flour. Go to their website to find a store in your area that carries King Arthur products, or see Resources, *Page 43*, to order.

Both the biga and the final dough are made with quick-rise, or instant, yeast. Don't confuse it with active dry yeast which has larger particles that must be dissolved in water before mixing. Quick-rise yeast can go directly into the dough.

Yeast of choice
Quick-rise yeast has very fine granules that dissolve directly into the dough, eliminating the need for proofing.

WHITE BREAD

A starter called a biga gets this bread going the night before the dough is mixed and baked. The biga takes less than five minutes to mix.
MAKES 2 LOAVES; TOTAL TIME: 3$\frac{1}{2}$ HOURS + OVERNIGHT FOR BIGA

FOR THE BIGA—
COMBINE AND KNEAD:
1$\frac{3}{4}$ cup unbleached all-purpose flour
$\frac{2}{3}$ cup cool water (65–70°)
$\frac{1}{4}$ t. quick-rise yeast
FOR THE FINAL DOUGH—
MIX:
Developed biga
5 cups unbleached all-purpose flour
$\frac{1}{2}$ cup nonfat dry milk
3 T. unsalted butter, softened
2 T. sugar
1 T. table salt
2 t. quick-rise yeast
1$\frac{3}{4}$ cups cool water (65–70°)
FOR THE EGG WASH—
BRUSH WITH:
1 egg, beaten

FOR THE BIGA—
Combine flour, water, and yeast. Turn biga out onto a lightly floured surface; knead until fully mixed. Place in bowl, cover with plastic, and let sit at room temperature overnight, 10–15 hours.
FOR THE FINAL DOUGH—
Mix biga and dough ingredients in stand mixer on first speed for 3 min. Increase to second speed; mix 5 min., scraping hook occasionally.

Knead dough by hand a few times then shape into ball. Place in oiled bowl; cover with plastic, let rise at room temperature 45 min.

Turn the dough out onto a lightly floured surface and press out the gas. Then fold the dough in thirds (like a letter). Give it a quarter turn and repeat the fold. Turn dough over, return it to the bowl, cover, and let rise another 45 minutes.

After second rise, turn dough out onto lightly floured surface and press out the gas for the second time. Divide dough in half, shape into two loaves, and place in greased 8$\frac{1}{2}$ x 4$\frac{1}{2}$" loaf pans (see photos on Page 34). Cover loosely with plastic, let rise a final 45–60 minutes, or until 1" above rim. With rack in center of oven, preheat to 425°.

Brush top of each loaf with beaten egg, then lightly mist with water. Place loaves in oven and mist again. Bake 5 minutes at 425°, then lower oven to 375° and bake 45–50 minutes, or until tops are russet and there's a hollow sound when tapped. Remove immediately from pans and cool 30 minutes on a rack.

▲ *The initial biga is dry and shaggy. Gather it together and knead briefly, about 20 times.*

After kneading, it forms into a rough, sticky ball. ▼

▲ *The biga is fully developed when it has risen and expanded into a bubbled mass.*

chef at home: *King Arthur Flour*

Morning mix and bake

▼ *After kneading in a mixer the dough is smooth and elastic.*

No Mixer?
Knead by hand—the bread will turn out just as well. Dough will be sticky at first, but don't add extra flour. Knead 8 minutes, cover with plastic, and let rest 10 minutes. Then knead for 5 more minutes.

▲ *Press all the gas bubbles out of the risen dough (there will be more bubbles after second rise).*

▼ *Fold dough into thirds, like a letter. Turn, and repeat fold.*

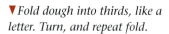

After mixing, the dough rises three times—twice in a bowl, and a final time in the pans.

Rising and shaping: Let the dough rise at room temperature (about 70°). Warmer air would definitely speed up the process, but the dough will develop more flavor and moisture if it rises slowly at room temperature.

Once it has risen, press the gas bubbles out of the dough. Then fold into thirds, turn, and fold again. This redistributes the yeast so it can keep working.

After the second rise and pressing, divide dough in half and shape into two loaves. For nicely shaped bread, fold each half into thirds (like the first time), then turn it and fold in *half*. Now stretch the folded dough to 7 or 8" long (gently squeezing the sides) so it will fit into the loaf pan without folding the ends. But don't worry if it doesn't look absolutely perfect— it'll still taste fantastic.

▲ *After dough is cut, shape each half into a loaf by gently stretching folded dough to 7 or 8" length.*

Put the dough into shiny or light-colored pans for baking. Dark surfaces tend to overbrown before the bread is fully baked.

The dough should rise in the pans until it's about an inch above the rim (not quite fully risen). This gives it room for a final rise in the oven.

Baking: Once risen, mist the loaves with a few sprays of water just before going into the oven. The moist surface allows the bread to stretch and rise better during baking. To create a little steam, spray the loaves a second time just after placing in oven.

The bread is baked at two temperatures—425° for the first 5 minutes, then 375° for the remaining time. The initial high temperature gives the bread a final burst or rise, while the lower temperature allows it to bake through. Cool the loaves at least 30 minutes before cutting them. An electric knife makes clean cuts without squashing the loaf.

◄ *The loaves are misted twice, just before and after going into the hot oven.*

Optional: *To make sure the bread is done, you can check its temperature. It should be 200–210°.* ►

Adding **on**

cinnamon bread

Really good basic white bread easily transforms into *unbelievably* good cinnamon bread. Eat it warm or toast it the next morning.

CINNAMON BREAD

Follow the White Bread recipe until shaping the loaves.
MAKES TWO LOAVES; TOTAL TIME: 3¹/₂ HOURS + OVERNIGHT FOR BIGA

FOR THE CINNAMON FILLING—
COMBINE:
²/₃   cup sugar
4   t. cinnamon
FOR THE EGG WASH—
WHISK:
1   egg

Combine sugar and cinnamon. **Whisk** egg for egg wash. Grease two 8¹/₂ x 4¹/₂" loaf pans. After dough has risen the second time, turn out onto a lightly floured surface, press out the gas, and divide dough in half. Press each half into a 7 or 8 x 12" rectangle. Brush with egg wash and sprinkle with half the sugar-cinnamon mixture. Roll into a log, then carefully transfer to prepared pan, seam

Press and stretch dough into a 7 or 8 x 12" rectangle so it will fit into pan without tucking ends.▼

side down. Cover loosely with plastic; let rise 45–60 minutes, or until 1–2" above rim. Before baking, brush top with egg wash, mist with water, place in oven, and mist again. Bake in preheated 425° oven for 5 minutes; lower to 375° and bake 50–55 minutes, until crust is russet and internal temperature is 200–210° degrees. Remove from pan; cool on rack.

◄*Beginning at narrow end closest to you, roll the dough into a log, ending with seam on the bottom.*

Dough is ready to be baked when it has risen 1–2" above the rim of the pan. ►

37

online extra

Want an alternate recipe with raisins? Visit www.CuisineAtHome.com for a step-by-step guide.

cuisinereview

Wares
toasters

The real requirements of a toaster are simple: to brown evenly and operate easily. Looks and extra features are just a bonus.

Our staff does its best to be unbiased going into testing. But I have to admit, I was pretty sure that a few of the extra high-end toasters would come out on top. Our testing proved otherwise.

Toaster testing: Toasting is a combination of cooking and drying bread. Even browning from side to side and top to bottom is what you should expect from a toaster. Besides the differences in models, there are some bread variables that affect toast outcomes—moisture content, density, and thickness. So to ensure fair testing comparisons, we used soft white bread from the grocery store, and toasted on medium settings.

Feature presentation: The features on a toaster are only meaningful if they offer a real benefit to you, and then deliver.

Defrost features usually just allow extra time for toasting. And *reheat* options are supposed to warm without darkening. In reality they often add a bit of color.

Some toasters have a really cool *bagel* feature. It toasts bagels on the cut side, while merely warming the back side for the perfect crunchy-chewy bite. But watch out for bogus bagel features. On some models it only means it toasts a little longer to heat the bagel through. Worse yet, some "bagel toasters" just have wide slots for bagels—which virtually all toasters now have.

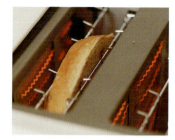

▲ *Bread guides are wire cages that adjust to hold bread evenly between elements. But they also block toasting, often leaving white stripes on toast.*

▲ *Most heating elements are wire (top), but Krups has a quartz heating tube (above).*

Expensive lesson: The pricey, hip toasters from upscale catalogs really appealed to me. But *completely* uneven toasting and tedious mechanics revealed that looks aren't everything. It seems "commercial quality" means it's not at all suited for home use.

The long haul: There's one consideration we couldn't test—longevity. But there *are* built-in safeguards: All toasters are subject to UL requirements to toast at least 6000 cycles (over eight years used twice a day!). And warranties provide security against lemons.

The bottom line: If a toaster doesn't brown evenly, its features or life span don't matter. Our top picks browned consistently and all happened to land in the middle price range. Neither the expensive trophy models or flimsy cheap ones could compete.

These toasters are all recommended after testing in the Cuisine Test Kitchen.

Farberware "Down Right" — $69.95

The "Down Right" toaster has no lever to lower the toast—it goes down automatically when the bread is put in. This slick model manages uniform browning with minimal striping on toast. The bagel button is legitimate—only the inner coils heat to toast cut sides, and defrost extends the toasting cycle.

Hamilton Beach IntelliToast — $24.95

Even browning is the result of a microchip "brain" that reacts to temperature and adjusts toasting time for consistent results. This means it will even compensate for frozen bread. The bagel feature adds extra time to the toasting cycle. Also available in black.

Toastmaster New Classics — $29.99

Simple and straightforward mechanics allow this retro version of the classic Toastmaster to focus on toasting bread evenly from crust to crust. Thin items (like toaster pastries) are held upright by shutters that close over the top. Bread guides can produce striping on toast. Also available in full chrome.

Krups ToastControl — $49.95

A sleek, contemporary design isn't the only thing to set the solid Krups apart. It toasts with a quartz heating element. Coils are placed inside two quartz tubes that act as heat diffusers reflecting onto side panels for an even heat spread. Metal bread guides are especially sturdy on this easy-to-operate toaster.

Hamilton Beach Portfolio — $29.99

The traditionally shaped Portfolio is made exclusively for Target stores by Hamilton Beach. Bagel feature means only the outside elements will toast (an illustration is printed on top to remind to face cut sides out). Defrost button adds time to toasting cycle, and reheat does the job well. Noticeable white stripes from bread guides.

KitchenAid Digital — $59.95

This single-slot digital model delivers consistent results. The heat is even because there are only two sides to heat instead of four. And KitchenAid's exclusive bagel feature was the best tested. It toasts the cut side while warming the back at 50% power. Adds extra time for frozen bread, gently warms, has nine shade settings, comes in four colors.

old-fashioned
chocolate cake
with glossy chocolate icing

This is not a molten-middle, blacker-than-night chocolate cake. It's the kind of cake grandma used to make, with "Betty Crocker" looks and one-of-a-kind flavor.

This cake is special. If you're a believer in (and user of) Duncan Hines, then you need to try this recipe. I'll be willing to bet that you never go back to the box again.

Why? For one thing, this cake is super-moist due to the oil. It also means the cake keeps well (not that there will be many leftovers!). But the big reason this cake is so great

is that it's *easy*—easier than a mix, actually. In fact, you probably have all the ingredients on hand, and making cake from a mix requires a trip to the store!

The cake isn't complete until it's iced, and a thick layer of chocolate really seals this deal. But you won't go wrong with either of the other icings on Pages 40–41.

Besides making two 8" rounds, this recipe also makes one 9 x 13" rectangular cake (bake 35–40 minutes) or 24 cupcakes (bake 20–25 minutes). Cooled cakes may be frozen—thaw slightly before frosting.

The Glossy Chocolate Icing must cool completely to be spreadable. You may cool it at room temperature (it takes about three hours) or chill it, then gently rewarm in the microwave. Before frosting, line the platter with four strips of waxed paper, then place the cake on the plate. Pull out the strips after frosting.

▼ *Combine wet ingredients with dry, whisking just to combine. Do not overmix or cake could be tough.*

◄ *When a toothpick inserted in center of cakes comes out clean, they're done. Cool cakes completely.*

▲ *For the icing, add cream mixture to chocolate mixture. Cook just until smooth.*

CHOCOLATE CAKE

MAKES ONE 8", 2-LAYER CAKE
TOTAL TIME: 45 MINUTES +
COOLING

WHISK TOGETHER:
3 cups all-purpose flour
2 cups sugar
1/2 cup unsweetened cocoa powder
2 t. baking soda
1 t. table salt

COMBINE; ADD:
2 cups hot water
3/4 cup vegetable oil
2 T. white vinegar
1 T. instant coffee granules
1 T. vanilla extract

GLOSSY CHOCOLATE ICING

This icing is quite soft. If it seems too thin to stay put, stir in powdered sugar 1 T. at a time until it's easily spreadable.
MAKES ABOUT 4 CUPS
TOTAL TIME: 10 MINUTES +
COOLING

MELT:
1 stick (8 T.) unsalted butter
STIR IN:
1 1/2 cups sugar
1 1/4 cups unsweetened cocoa powder
   Pinch salt
COMBINE; GRADUALLY ADD:
1 1/4 cups heavy cream
1/4 cup sour cream
1 t. instant coffee granules
OFF HEAT, ADD:
2 t. vanilla extract

▼ *Spread 1 cup icing all the way to the edges of first layer.*

Preheat oven to 350° with rack in the center. Spray two 8" round cake pans with nonstick spray.
Whisk dry ingredients together in a large mixing bowl.
Combine water, oil, vinegar, instant coffee, and vanilla in a large measuring cup. Add to the dry ingredients and whisk just until combined—a few lumps are okay. Divide batter among pans (3 cups in each), then bake until toothpick inserted in center comes out clean, 35–40 min. Cool cakes for 15 minutes on a rack, then invert them onto the rack. Leave cakes upside down to cool completely (this flattens domed cakes), then frost.

Melt butter in a large saucepan over medium heat.
Stir in sugar, cocoa, and salt. Mixture will be thick and grainy.
Combine heavy cream, sour cream, and instant coffee in a large measuring cup, mixing until smooth. Gradually add cream mixture to chocolate until blended and smooth. Cook until sugar has dissolved, and mixture is smooth and hot to the touch. Do not boil.
Off heat, add vanilla. Cool icing at room temperature until spreadable, about 3 hours. (Icing may be chilled until completely cold, then warmed gently in the microwave until spreadable. Heat at high power in 20-second intervals, stirring well after each interval.)

◄ *Top first layer with second cake, and spread with 1 cup of icing. "Blob" more icing on the sides, then spread around.*

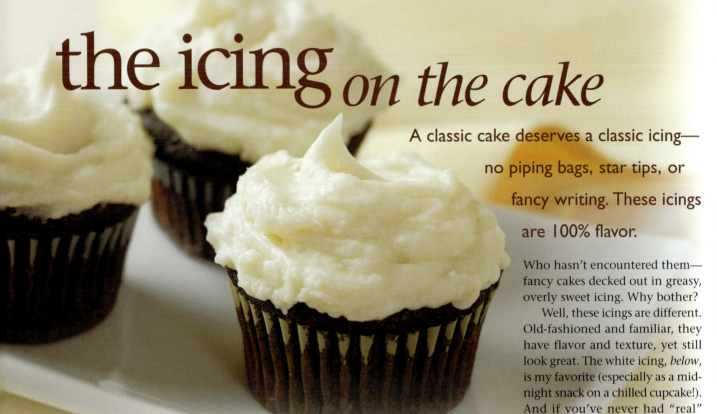

the icing *on the cake*

A classic cake deserves a classic icing—no piping bags, star tips, or fancy writing. These icings are 100% flavor.

Who hasn't encountered them—fancy cakes decked out in greasy, overly sweet icing. Why bother?

Well, these icings are different. Old-fashioned and familiar, they have flavor and texture, yet still look great. The white icing, *below*, is my favorite (especially as a midnight snack on a chilled cupcake!). And if you've never had "real" German chocolate icing before, do yourself a favor and try this recipe—it's awesome.

BUTTERY WHITE ICING

Because of this icing's high proportion of butter, any cake frosted with it is best stored in the refrigerator. Wrap it well to avoid "off" flavors.
MAKES ABOUT 3 1/2 CUPS; TOTAL TIME: 15 MINUTES + COOLING

BRING TO A BOIL; COOL:
1 1/2 cups whole or 2% milk
7 T. all-purpose flour
BEAT:
1 1/2 cups (3 sticks) unsalted butter, softened (*not* melted)
1/2 t. kosher salt
ADD:
1 1/2 cups sugar
BEAT IN:
  Milk-flour mixture
1 T. vanilla extract

Bring milk and flour to a boil in a heavy saucepan over medium heat, whisking constantly to avoid scorching. Cook until mixture thickens into a paste, about 5 minutes. *Cool flour mixture completely before using.*

Beat butter and salt in a large mixing bowl until combined.

Add sugar and beat until fluffy.

Beat in cooled flour mixture and vanilla extract until well blended and smooth, about 4 minutes. Icing will not be glossy smooth, but a bit rough-looking. Frost cake and chill until ready to serve (to firm up icing). Store any leftover cake in the refrigerator to keep the icing firm.

◄ *Cook flour in milk until pasty. Boil briefly to eliminate starchy taste.*

◄ *Beat butter and sugar, then add cooled milk-flour mixture and vanilla. Beat icing until well blended.*

▲ *Icing should resemble loosely mashed potatoes.*

GERMAN CHOCOLATE CAKE ICING

This large batch easily covers four cake layers. If you're frosting a sheet cake or cupcakes, you'll have extra. Warmed, it's good on ice cream.

MAKES ABOUT 5 CUPS
TOTAL TIME: 30 MINUTES + COOLING

COMBINE:

3   cups sweetened shredded coconut
2   cups pecans or walnuts, toasted, coarsely chopped
1   cup brown sugar, lightly packed
1   cup heavy cream
10   T. unsalted butter, cubed
$1/3$ cup sugar
5   egg yolks, lightly beaten
    Large pinch salt

OFF HEAT, STIR IN:

1   T. dark rum, *optional*
2   t. vanilla extract

FROST:

2   8" Chocolate Cake rounds, *Page 39*, halved horizontally (see online extra, right)

Combine coconut, nuts, brown sugar, cream, butter, sugar, yolks, and salt in a large heavy saucepan. Bring mixture to a low boil over medium-high heat, stirring with a wooden spoon. Cook at a low boil 5–8 minutes, or until mixture thickens, stirring constantly. Icing is done when it has thickened, appears shiny, and has turned a deeper shade of brown.

Off heat, stir in rum and vanilla. Transfer icing to a bowl and let cool 20–25 minutes, stirring occasionally. It may be spread when it is warm to the touch.

Frost the four split cake layers but leave the sides unfrosted (it's traditional). Let frosted cake stand at least one hour before slicing and serving. Slice cake using an electric knife—the rapid sawing motion of the blades cleanly cuts through the thick coconut and caramel. A regular slicing knife, no matter how sharp, will drag and tear through the cake. (Do not refrigerate cake or icing will turn grainy and cloudy.)

When the icing reaches a low boil, stir it constantly to avoid scorching and sticking.▼

It's important to cook the icing long enough or it will be too thin, soak into the cake, and make it soggy. ►

▲*Halve cakes horizontally into 4 layers. Spread 1¼ cups icing on each layer.*

▲*Use an electric knife for slicing—a regular knife will stick and tear the cake.*

37

online **extra**

How to halve cake layers? Visit www.CuisineAtHome .com for a step-by-step photo guide.

from **our** readers

Q&A
questions & answers

CREAM OF TARTAR

What is cream of tartar and what is it supposed to do?

Becky Jans
Yorba Linda, CA

A by-product of wine making, cream of tartar comes from a crystalline acid that forms on the inside of wine barrels.

Cream of tartar's acidic quality gives it many uses. It helps stabilize egg whites in souffles and angel food cake, making them less prone to collapse. In candy making it slows the crystallization process. Cream of tartar also helps whiten foods, like angel food cake, boiled potatoes, or cauliflower. And it is also sometimes used in food additives and medicines.

GARLIC STORAGE

How should I store garlic and how long will it last?

Tom Nash
Pine Bluff, AR

The folks at the Gilroy Garlic Festival say that garlic will keep for four to five months stored in a basket or hanging from a braid. The important thing is that it has plenty of ventilation.

They also offer freezing as an alternative for longer-term storage. Garlic frozen in a plastic container will keep for more than a year without deterioration. The skin will pull free easily after defrosting, and the flesh will retain its pungency.

PANKO SOURCE

I don't have access to an Asian market to buy panko. Do you know of a mail order source?

Natalie Ness
Fullerton, NE

We use the coarse Japanese bread crumb, panko, in the Coconut Shrimp and Pork Cutlet recipes. A standard item in Asian markets, panko is also available by mail from **asiamex.com** for $2.49 a bag, Item #1850. Or call to order at **(877) 274-2639**.

BRUSCHETTA OR CROSTINI?

What's the difference between bruschetta and crostini?

David Casperson
Columbus, GA

The main difference between bruschetta (brew-SKET-ta) and crostini (kroh-STEE-nee) is found in their size.

Basic bruschetta are toasted or grilled slices of Italian bread that have been rubbed with garlic and then brushed with olive oil. From there they can be sprinkled with salt and pepper, topped with the classic chopped tomatoes and basil, or layered with about anything you like.

Crostini translated means "little toasts." They're actually just smaller, usually thinner versions of bruschetta.

OIL REUSE

Can I reuse the vegetable oil that I use for deep-fat frying?

Virginia Stanley
Springfield, OH

Oil from deep frying *can* be reused after straining, but for safety and quality reasons we don't recommend it. High frying temperatures cause rapid breakdown of the fat. This lowers the flash point, which means it can catch fire at a lower temperature. And fats can turn rancid when combined with oxygen, moisture, or food particles.

Foods fried in reused oil will be darker and fat will soak into the food faster.

UNSWEETENED COCONUT

Where can I find unsweetened coconut to make the Coconut Shrimp in Issue 35?

Jennifer Allen
North Bend, WA

You can usually find unsweetened coconut at a natural food store. It's also available by mail from King Arthur Flour, Item #1253, at **bakerscatalogue.com** or **(800) 827-6836.**

SUBSTITUTING STARCHES

Why would I use potato starch instead of cornstarch?

Kaye Boyer
Camden, NJ

Probably the most common reason for the substitution would be an allergy to corn. But it could also be an advantage if you need a thickener that gels clear, as potato starch does, rather than cloudy, as cornstarch does.

But don't confuse potato starch with potato *flour*. While potato starch is derived from the starch of potatoes, potato flour is made from 100% dehydrated potatoes. The flour has a pronounced potato flavor and is best used when you want to boost or add potato flavor to soup, potato bread, or rolls.

MEXICAN VANILLA

What is Mexican vanilla?

Allie Catlin
Chicago, IL

Vanilla beans derive their names from where they are grown, so vanilla grown in Mexico is Mexican vanilla. Flavor is also determined by the growing region. Soil, climate, and curing methods all contribute to taste differences. Mexican vanilla has a hint of spice making it especially well suited to savory foods.

In fact, the vanilla bean was first discovered in Mexico, in 1520. It was later carried to other equatorial growing regions. Today Madagascar raises the largest crop, followed by Indonesia, then Mexico.

Look for Mexican vanilla that's processed in the United States. Mexico does not have strict labeling requirements, so tonka beans (not for consumption) are often added to stretch precious vanilla. They contain coumarin, a potentially toxic substance that the FDA has banned. See Resources, *right*, to order extract processed in America.

resources

grand**finale**

cream cheese filled Cupcakes

CREAM CHEESE FILLING FOR CHOCOLATE CUPCAKES

Due to the filling, these cupcakes take longer to bake than unfilled ones. To test for doneness, insert a toothpick in a cupcake's center. It should come out clean. But remember—it may have melted chocolate on it from the chips!

MAKES ENOUGH TO FILL 24 CUPCAKES
TOTAL TIME: 5 MINUTES + BAKING AND FROSTING CUPCAKES

BLEND:
4   oz. cream cheese, softened
1/3 cup sugar
1   egg
1   t. vanilla extract
     Pinch salt

FOLD IN:
2/3 cup semisweet chocolate
     chips

Blend cream cheese, sugar, egg, vanilla, and salt with a hand mixer until smooth.
Fold in chocolate chips.

To make filled cupcakes, line two 12-cup muffin pans with paper liners. Prepare one recipe Chocolate Cake, *Page 39*, and fill each muffin cup 1/2 to 2/3 full of cake batter. Drop a heaping teaspoon of the filling into each cupcake and bake as directed on Page 39 (increase baking time to 30–35 minutes). Cool cupcakes completely, then frost them with one recipe Glossy Chocolate Icing, *Page 39*.

Cuisine at home®

tiramisù
a fancy favorite made simple

Crab Cakes
easy steps with pure crab taste

braised Lamb Shanks
extreme flavor, tender results

Issue No. 38 April 2003
A publication of August Home Publishing

Cuisine at home®

Publisher
Donald B. Peschke

Editor
John F. Meyer

Art Director
Cinda Shambaugh

Senior Editor
Susan Hoss

Assistant Art Director
Holly Wiederin

Assistant Editor
Sara Ostransky

Graphic Designer
April Walker Janning

Test Kitchen Director
Kim Samuelson

Image Specialist
Troy Clark

Photographer
Dean Tanner

Contributing Food Stylist
Jennifer Peterson

AUGUST HOME
PUBLISHING COMPANY

Corporate:

Corporate Vice Presidents: Mary R. Scheve, Douglas L. Hicks • *Creative Director:* Ted Kralicek • *Professional Development Director:* Michal Sigel *New Media Manager:* Gordon C. Gaippe • *Senior Photographer:* Crayola England *Multi Media Art Director:* Eugene Pedersen • *Web Server Administrator:* Carol Schoeppler • *Web Content Manager:* David Briggs • *Web Designer:* Kara Blessing *Web Developer/Content Manager:* Sue M. Moe • *Controller:* Robin Hutchinson *Senior Accountant:* Laura Thomas • *Accounts Payable:* Mary Schultz • *Accounts Receivable:* Margo Petrus • *Research Coordinator:* Nick Jaeger • *Production Director:* George Chmielarz • *Pre-Press Image Specialist:* Minniette Johnson • *Electronic Publishing Director:* Douglas M. Lidster • *Systems Administrator:* Cris Schwanebeck *PC Maintenance Technician:* Robert D. Cook • *H.R. Assistant:* Kirsten Koele *Receptionist/ Administrative Assistant:* Jeanne Johnson • *Mail Room Clerk:* Lou Webber • *Office Manager:* Natalie Lonsdale • *Facilities Manager:* Kurt Johnson

Customer Service & Fulfillment:

Operations Director: Bob Baker • *Customer Service Manager:* Jennie Enos *Customer Service Representatives:* Anna Cox, Kim Harlan, April Revell, Deborah Rich, Valerie Jo Riley, Tammy Truckenbrod • *Buyer:* Linda Jones • *Administrative Assistant:* Nancy Downey • *Warehouse Supervisor:* Nancy Johnson • *Fulfillment:* Sylvia Carey

Circulation:

Subscriber Services Director: Sandy Baum • *New Business Circulation Manager:* Wayde J. Klingbeil • *Promotions Analyst:* Patrick A. Walsh • *Billing and Collections Manager:* Rebecca Cunningham • *Renewal Manager:* Paige Rogers • *Circulation Marketing Analyst:* Kris Schlemmer • *Circulation Marketing Analyst:* Paula M. DeMatteis • *Art Director:* Doug Flint • *Senior Graphic Designers:* Mark Hayes, Robin Friend

www.CuisineAtHome.com

talk to Cuisine at home
Questions about Subscriptions and Address Changes? Write or call:

Customer Service
2200 Grand Avenue,
Des Moines, IA 50312
800-311-3995,
8 a.m. to 5 p.m., CST.

Online Subscriber Services:
www.CuisineAtHome.com
Access your account • Check a subscription payment • Tell us if you've missed an issue • Change your mailing or email address • Renew your subscription • Pay your bill

Cuisine at home® (ISSN 1537-8225) is published bi-monthly (Jan., Mar., May, July, Sept., Nov.) by August Home Publishing Co., 2200 Grand Ave., Des Moines, IA 50312. **Cuisine at home®** is a trademark of August Home Publishing Co. ©Copyright 2003 August Home Publishing. All rights reserved. Subscriptions: Single copy: $4.99. One year subscription (6 issues), $24.00. (Canada/Foreign add $10 per year, U.S. funds.)

Periodicals postage paid at Des Moines, IA and at additional mailing offices. "USPS/Perry-Judd's Heartland Division automatable poly". Postmaster: Send change of address to **Cuisine at home®**, P.O. Box 37100 Boone, IA 50037-2100. **Cuisine at home®** does not accept and is not responsible for unsolicited manuscripts. PRINTED IN CHINA

editor's letter

As a kid, some of my best vacation days were spent crabbing on the coast of South Carolina—there was nothing more exciting than pulling up a cage full of big blue crabs. You'd take your bounty home, boil them up, and then spend hours picking the meat out of every corner and crevice of the crab. Looking back, it seems like a lot of work for the amount of meat that was actually harvested, but it was definitely worth it at the time.

As nice as those memories may be, picking fresh crabs just doesn't fit into my schedule anymore, but crab cakes sure do! That's why the crab cake article beginning on Page 6 hits the mark. Easy-to-find crabmeat and simple ingredients can quickly bring back plenty of good times.

Unfortunately, all memories aren't that good. I can recall some pretty poor tasting mutton and, as a result, lamb has never been on my short list. I rarely order it if there are other choices available. Well, I'm here to tell you that the lamb shanks on Page 28 are some of the best melt-in-your-mouth meat I've ever eaten. And don't overlook the cheese grits side dish either. We made sure to use Quaker Quick Grits (they're available everywhere) so you have no excuse not to try this. The rosemary buttered noodles are really good, too, but the cheese grits drizzled with slow-braised barbecue sauce is just this side of heaven. It's spring and if there were ever a desire to serve lamb this time of the year, this is your recipe and your moment.

There are plenty more outstanding recipes in this issue, from chopped salads to velvet cream soups to quick chicken dishes. But they all have one thing in common—they'll all taste better if finished with the easy-to-make tiramisù. I'm sure you've had the Italian dessert plenty of times, but this one is different. It not only delivers knock-out flavor, it also has a high-priced Fifth Avenue look. This is a perfect end to any one of the special dishes in this issue. Enjoy.

table of contents

Issue No. 38 April 2003

from **our** readers

tips *and techniques*

Frozen Pastry Brush

Instead of trying to clean a pastry brush that's been used in butter or oil, place the brush in a resealable plastic freezer bag and store it in the freezer. Next time you need the brush, either dip it into hot butter or microwave it for a few seconds.

Bill Ray
Hershey, PA

Editor's Note
For even more sauce "protection," fill the cast iron skillet with water.

Peeling Garlic

I have arthritis in my hands and have trouble peeling garlic. But not anymore! Instead of struggling, I just put on a pair of heavy rubber gloves (the type with a good grip). Then I can rub a clove or two of garlic in the palm of my hands using a circular back-and-forth motion. The peel slips right off. This tip is especially helpful when you have a lot of garlic cloves to peel.

Demetra Derro
Northville, MI

Safe Sauce Warmer

I have a hard time turning my burner low enough to keep delicate sauces warm. The answer is to place the saucepan inside a cast-iron skillet set over a low flame. The cast-iron pan helps "buffer" the heat.

Bryan Emery
Houston, TX

Checking the Date

Whenever I open a container of milk or other perishables, I write the expiration date boldly on a piece of freezer tape with a permanent marker. I then tape it to the front of the product. This way I can keep track of the age at a glance and use up the old before starting new.

Linda Jawitz
New York, NY

Easy Seeding

Seeding a tomato by giving it a squeeze can leave it a bit misshapen. Here's a more gentle solution—a chopstick!

First, slice the tomato in half across its middle as shown in the photo above. This opens up all the seed chambers. If you cut it from top to bottom, you'll be fishing around for trapped seeds.

Now simply use either end of the chopstick to push the seeds out and into a bowl.

James Komar
Athens, GA

Caper Removal

Brined capers are a pain to remove and measure—the jar opening is just too narrow for a spoon to fit inside.

In frustration, I came up with a solution—a melon baller! It's small enough for the opening, and the hole in the bottom of the melon baller will allow the brine to drain away.

Rachel Johannes
Steamboat Springs, CO

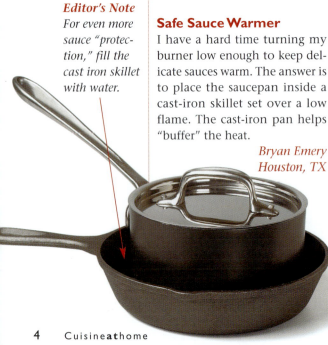

Frozen Assets

I often bake more cookies, cakes, and breads than I need, then place any extras in the freezer. However, the freezer tends to dry out cookies and rolls, even with good plastic freezer wrap.

To keep baked goods as soft and fresh as the day they were made, try this. First, moisten a paper towel and place it in a fold-top sandwich bag—but don't close the top. Then tuck the bag and paper towel in with the baked goods that are being wrapped for the freezer. That extra little bit of moisture keeps cookies soft and bread wonderfully fresh.

Candy Boustead
Sargeant Bluff, IA

Evenly Cooked Asparagus

To cook asparagus evenly, place the trimmed spears in a large, wide skillet with enough water to cover (be sure the tips are all pointing in the same direction). Put the pan on the burner so the stems (thick ends) are over the heat and the tips (tender ends) are well off the heat.

Clair Sumner
Little Rock, AR

Fish Beds

I like to bake fish on a bed of chopped onion, celery, and parsley. Not only does this make the fish more flavorful, it also raises the fish above the baking surface—no more sticking!

Darlene Goble
Des Moines, IA

Card Extender

If a recipe is too long for a single card, hinge two cards together with transparent tape, and fold to file. This is also handy if you need to include a picture of the finished product with the recipe.

Ann Castelli
Chicago Heights, IL

Cabbage Keeper

My family likes fresh coleslaw, but I only use part of a head of cabbage at a time. So I came up with a good storage idea. Take off the larger, normally discarded outer leaves, wash them well, and set aside. Slice the head of cabbage as needed for the recipe.

Then, to the store the unused portion of the cabbage head, wrap the reserved outer leaves around the cabbage (especially the cut side), place it in a resealable plastic bag, and store in the refrigerator. The outer leaves prevent the cut edges of the cabbage from going dark, and the whole head looks fresher and tastes better for much longer.

Marietta F. Walter
Hale, MI

Test Kitchen Tip

To select an artichoke, hold it in the palm of your hand. It's tender and fresh if it feels heavy for its size. If it feels light, it's probably dried out—choose another.

cooking up Crab cakes

Simple ingredients and simple techniques. These are the secrets to the best crab cakes you'll ever make.

Crab cakes don't have to be difficult. Actually, the more you tinker with them, the more you take away from their subtle flavor. Since crab is such a delicately flavored meat, ingredients like Old Bay seasoning, onions, celery, or bell peppers can overpower it. When making crab cakes, keep in mind the phrase "less is more."

With that said, there are five important factors to consider when making crab cakes. They are the type of crab, the filler (for body), the binder (how it's held together), the flavorings (so they don't overpower), and perhaps the most important—chilling.

Here's what you need to know to make the perfect crab cake creation right at home.

What crab to buy

I like using blue crabmeat because it's pretty easy to find in most markets. Besides, since crab cakes originated on the East coast, it seems only natural to use their indigenous crab. I also like using pasteurized crab—it's always available, ready to use, and safe to eat. Besides, once it's made into cakes, you'll be hard-pressed tasting the difference between fresh and pasteurized.

Pasteurized crab comes three ways: lump, backfin, or claw. I prefer lump because of the large pieces, but it's the priciest—about $12.00 per half pound (enough for 10 cakes). Moderately-priced backfin is shredded-looking and can contain shells, but still works well for cakes. Claw meat is the least expensive and tastes fine, but it tends to be darker than the other crabmeats. It all comes down to preference and price.

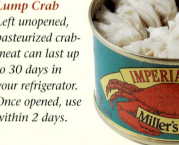

Pasteurized Lump Crab
Left unopened, pasteurized crabmeat can last up to 30 days in your refrigerator. Once opened, use within 2 days.

Crab cakin'

Once you've selected the type of crab, it's time to start making the cakes. Remember, less is more.

Filler

To create body, the crab must be blended with another ingredient, and bread crumbs work best. For a delicate, crisp texture, try the Japanese bread crumbs called panko. Because of its popularity, many grocery stores carry panko, but all Asian markets stock it.

While I recommend using panko, you can make your own. Remove the crust from a good white bread and process it to a coarse grind. Then put crumbs on a large pan and stale for a day.

Binder

Cream, cheese, mayonnaise, and eggs can bind crab cake ingredients. The best choice is egg. It's not greasy, adds richness, and makes a light binder that, when cooked, holds extremely well.

▲ Whisk dried spices into the liquids. This prevents overmixing when combining with the crab.

▲ Be sure to check the crabmeat for shells. They are easy to miss.

Flavoring

Forget the urge to "doctor" this recipe. You'll notice that only a handful of ingredients are used just to enhance the flavor of crab, not to mask it.

Mixing

To prevent crab from shredding too much, blend wet ingredients with the dried spices first. This minimizes mixing when the crab and bread crumbs are added. Once blended, liberally line a baking sheet with bread crumbs, then use a $1/4$ cup to measure out each cake. Press cake portion to $3/4$" high. Now sprinkle the top of each cake with bread crumbs.

Chilling

Chilling for at least an hour is critical so the delicate cakes don't fall apart. Wet ingredients naturally bind together during chilling—the eggs will tighten the cakes further during cooking.

CRAB CAKES
MAKES: 10 OR 11 CAKES
TOTAL TIME: 20 MINUTES + CHILLING

COMBINE:
14–16 oz. pasteurized lump crabmeat, drained
$1^1/2$ cups panko bread crumbs
2   T. minced fresh parsley
2   T. scallions, minced

WHISK TOGETHER; COMBINE:
4   eggs
1   T. lemon juice
1   t. dry mustard
1   t. Worcestershire sauce
$1/2$ t. cayenne
$1/2$ t. kosher salt

FORM CAKES WITH; CHILL:
1   cup panko bread crumbs

FRY IN:
Vegetable oil

SERVE WITH:
Tartar or Remoulade Sauce, *Page 8*

Combine crabmeat, panko, parsley, and scallions; set aside.

Whisk together eggs and next 5 ingredients. Combine crabmeat mixture with wet ingredients using your hands or a wooden spoon to keep crabmeat intact.

Form cakes with a $1/4$-cup measure. Transfer to a parchment-lined baking sheet covered with 1 cup crumbs. Press cakes into crumbs and sprinkle tops with more crumbs. Chill 1 hour.

Fry cakes in 2 T. oil over medium-high heat in a nonstick pan. Cook cakes in batches so the pan isn't crowded. Fry until golden brown, about 3–4 minutes per side. Drain on paper towels.

Serve with Tartar or Remoulade Sauce.

Use a $1/4$-cup measure to portion cakes. Form them on a parchment-lined baking sheet that is covered with panko—this coats the bottom. ▶

▲ *Press cakes down to $3/4$" and sprinkle tops with crumbs. This way you don't have to handle cakes too much.* **Chill** *for at least 1 hour.*

cooking Crab cakes

To cook the crab cakes, all you're shooting for is to fry them to a golden brown. This gives the eggs plenty of time to cook and bind.

For best frying results, keep in mind four rules. One, use a non-stick pan—you don't want these delicate cakes sticking. Two, fry in plain vegetable oil. Other fats taste too strong. Three, use a fork to place the chilled cakes into the frying pan. This way you don't knock off too much of the crumb coating. Finally, don't overcrowd the pan so it can maintain its heat when the cakes are added.

▼ *Use a fork to lift the chilled crab cakes into a nonstick pan. Fry over medium-high heat.*

▲ *Fry until golden brown. Drain on paper towels and hold in 200° oven if necessary.*

crab cake sauces

TARTAR SAUCE
MAKES 1¼ CUPS
TOTAL TIME: 10 MINUTES

WHISK TOGETHER:

1	cup mayonnaise
2	T. sweet pickle relish
1	T. capers
1	T. yellow onion, grated
2	t. white wine vinegar
1	t. Dijon mustard
	Salt and pepper to taste

BEFORE SERVING, STIR IN:

2	T. chopped fresh parsley
1	hard-boiled egg, chopped, *optional*

Whisk together first 6 ingredients, salt, and pepper.
Before serving, stir in parsley and hard-boiled egg.

REMOULADE SAUCE
MAKES 1 CUP
TOTAL TIME: 10 MINUTES

PROCESS:

½	cup red bell pepper, chopped
¼	cup scallions, chopped
¼	cup Dijon mustard
¼	cup mayonnaise
2	T. shallots, chopped
2	T. chopped fresh parsley
2	T. honey
1	T. fresh lemon juice
	Salt and pepper to taste

Process all ingredients in a food processor fitted with a steel blade until vegetables are finely chopped. Season with salt and pepper; chill until ready to use.

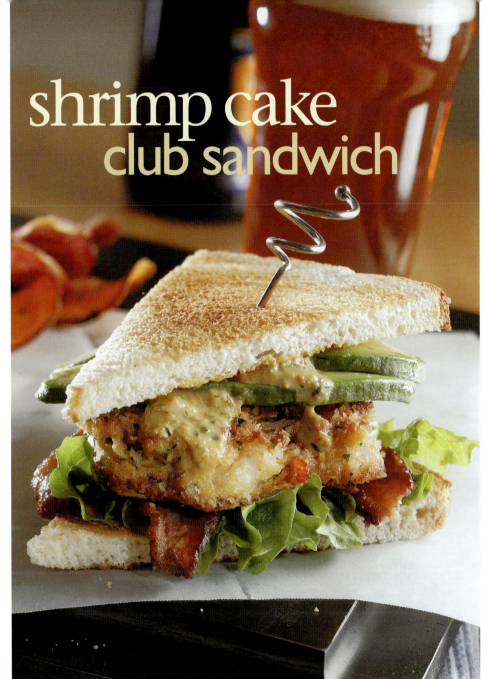

shrimp cake club sandwich

SHRIMP CAKE CLUB SANDWICH

MAKES 9 OR 10 CAKES
TOTAL TIME: 40 MINUTES + CHILLING

COMBINE:

1	lb. medium shrimp, peeled, deveined, roughly chopped
2	cups panko bread crumbs
2	T. scallions, minced
2	T. minced fresh parsley
2	T. minced fresh chives

WHISK TOGETHER; COMBINE:

4	eggs
1	T. fresh lemon juice
1	t. dry mustard
1	t. Worcestershire sauce
$1/2$	t. kosher salt
$1/2$	t. cayenne

FORM WITH; CHILL:

1	cup panko bread crumbs

FRY IN:

Vegetable oil

SERVE WITH:

Toasted bread, lettuce, cooked bacon strips, sliced avocado, and Remoulade Sauce, *Page 8*

Combine shrimp, panko, scallions, parsley, and chives.
Whisk eggs with the next 5 ingredients then combine it with the shrimp mixture.
Form and chill shrimp cakes as for crab cakes on Page 7.
Fry cakes in oil as on Page 8.
Serve on toast with lettuce, bacon, avocado, and remoulade.

▲ *Remove the vein by cutting down the length of the back and lifting it out with a knife.*

Cut the shrimp into chunks (the size of macadamia nuts). This will create a cake with a little bite to it. ▼

▲ *For sandwich, toast two slices of white bread. Cut into triangles for looks. Stack with lettuce, bacon, shrimp cake, avocado, and remoulade.*

Asian salad
Salmon cakes

These aren't your mother's Sunday salmon patties.
This is fresh salmon with new age punch!

Salmon is a strongly flavored fish that can handle plenty of seasoning. That's why these salmon cakes are loaded with simple, easy-to-find Asian ingredients. Actually, you probably have most of them sitting in your kitchen right now.

Other than the flavorful ingredients that you'll use, what makes these cakes different from your mother's patties is that you use fresh salmon—not canned. And don't fret the cost! You should be able to find it at your grocery store or a warehouse grocer (like Sam's Club) for about $4.50 a pound.

The key to these cakes is poaching the salmon—that is, to gently cook the fish in simmering (barely bubbling) water. Poaching is a good technique to use since it's easy to do and it preserves the natural flavors of the fish.

Fresh salmon

Make the cakes today, then fry and serve tomorrow with great results. A make-ahead recipe was never this easy or this good!

Poaching salmon

Poach the salmon in enough water to cover the fish. Use a salt-to-water ratio of one teaspoon salt to one quart water (most like the ocean). Heat this just until you start to see bubbles, about 200°. Add the fish, cover, and simmer (never boil) just until you can flake the fish—about 6 minutes per pound. Once the fish has poached, remove from water and chill in the refrigerator.

Shaping and serving

After the salmon has chilled, flake it with a fork then blend with all the ingredients. Salmon isn't as delicate as crab so don't worry too much about overmixing.

Once the cakes are made, be sure to chill them as you would regular crab cakes so they hold their shape while cooking. Now make the vinaigrette.

I serve the salmon cakes with an herbed salad, but you don't have to—a more traditional approach is just as good. Try rice and sauteed fresh spinach with garlic. But still use the fantastic vinaigrette over the cakes.

◄ *Poach fish in simmering salt water. Cover and cook until it flakes. A little acid (lemon) helps keep the flesh firm.*

Chill salmon after poaching, then flake it to prepare the salmon cakes. ►

make it a **menu**

ASIAN SALAD WITH SALMON CAKES
MAKES 12 CAKES, 6 SERVINGS; TOTAL TIME: 30 MINUTES + CHILLING

FOR THE ASIAN VINAIGRETTE—
WHISK TOGETHER; CHILL:
- 1/4 cup fresh lime juice
- 3 T. vegetable oil
- 2 T. low-sodium soy sauce
- 2 T. sugar
- 2 t. toasted sesame oil
- 1 t. fresh ginger, minced
- 1 t. crushed red pepper flakes
  Kosher salt to taste

FOR THE SALMON CAKES—
COMBINE:
- 1 lb. fresh salmon, poached, chilled, flaked
- 2 cups panko bread crumbs
- 1/3 cup scallions, minced
- 1/4 cup chopped fresh cilantro

WHISK TOGETHER; COMBINE WITH:
- 4 eggs
- 3 T. fresh lime juice
- 3 T. low-sodium soy sauce
- 2 T. rice vinegar
- 2 T. fresh ginger, minced
- 2 T. jalapeño, seeded, minced
- 1 T. sugar
- 1 t. kosher salt

FORM WITH; CHILL:
- 1 cup panko bread crumbs
- 1/4 cup sesame seeds

FRY IN:
- Vegetable oil

FOR THE SALAD—
TOSS WITH 6 T. VINAIGRETTE:
- 2 bags (5 oz. each) mixed baby greens
- 1/2 cup torn fresh basil leaves
- 1/2 cup torn fresh mint leaves

Whisk all vinaigrette ingredients together and chill until serving.
Combine salmon, panko, scallions, and cilantro.
Whisk together eggs, lime juice, soy sauce, vinegar, ginger, jalapeño, sugar, and salt. Combine with salmon mixture.
Form cakes as on Page 7, adding sesame seeds to crumbs; chill.
Fry cakes in oil as on Page 8.
Toss greens with vinaigrette and plate. Set two cakes on each salad and drizzle with more vinaigrette.

▲ *Combine all ingredients for cakes, then form, chill, and fry.*

▲ *Just before serving, toss greens with vinaigrette and top with two cakes. Drizzle cakes with more vinaigrette.*

allabout
Vinegar

When it comes to vinegar, endless choices can stupefy the most confident cook. Don't let it happen to you.

Not enough attention is paid to vinegar, and that's too bad because it's essential to a well-stocked kitchen. In just a splash, vinegar can heighten a dish's saltiness or tone down its sweetness. And it's just the thing to rev up soups or sauces that "need something" without excess sodium or calories. If the five basics are on hand (red and white wine, apple cider, balsamic, and rice) you've instantly expanded your scope of cooking.

Vinegar-making is a two-step fermentation process. The first occurs when yeasts feed on sugars, converting them to alcohol (also the first step in wine- and beer-making). In the second fermentation, bacteria feed on the alcohol and turn it into acetic acid. And that's when vinegar is made.

Today, high-tech equipment and controlled environments expedite that process, resulting in inexpensive vinegar decent enough for everyday use. But it's also worth exploring interesting, complex tasting vinegars from small producers. More costly, yes, but often very good. Avoid those fancy vinegars that feature fruit, herbs, or vegetables floating inside. They look pretty, but taste dreadful.

Store vinegar in a cool, dark place. Its shelf life is indefinite, but sediment may form—strain it. The vinegar is fine.

red wine

Surprisingly, many mass-market red wine vinegars are made from Concord grape juice—it creates a slightly sweeter product that's more in tune with American taste tendencies than all-red wine vinegars (some brands may be a blend of juice and wine). Those made with a specific wine variety (cabernet, chianti, etc.) are usually more expensive, yet the flavor is more complex. As with all vinegars, you may have to taste a few to find your favorite. A natural on Greek- and Italian-type salads, red wine vinegar is also great drizzled in bean soups or wine sauces.

white wine

Unless a white wine vinegar actually specifies the type of wine it's derived from (i.e. chardonnay, champagne), expect it to be made from white grape juice or a blend of juice and wine. Vinegars made from actual white wine are usually more flavorful. Use them in fish and chicken marinades, or blend with honey or sugar, then drizzle over melon. As for herb-infused vinegar (white wine or otherwise), the best tasting ones will be those you make yourself. Simply stuff several dill, tarragon, or thyme sprigs into a bottle of good-quality vinegar.

apple cider

It used to be that a majority of American homes kept a keg of apple cider vinegar in their cellars. Many people start their day with a glass of it, swearing by its nutritional benefits. But most cooks use it as a deglazing liquid for a pan sauce, or in pickling, as a better-tasting alternative to distilled white vinegar. It's also often added to baked beans. Unfiltered, unpasteurized cider vinegar is more flavorful than its clear amber cousin. Even better, though, are artisan-made cider vinegars from small producers.

the exotics

If you're looking to expand your vinegar collection, **www.zingermans.com** carries most of these vinegars—and more!

Cider Vinegar with Honey is both sweet and tangy. Blended with good olive oil, it's all you need for a simple, light vinaigrette. It's also good splashed on fruit salads, or used in a sauce for fish.

Banyuls Vinegar is made from a fortified wine (wine with added liqueur or spirits) from the same family as sherry and port. It is unique to the Banyuls region of southern France and quite rare. The flavor is light and clean—great on salads.

Chardonnay Vinegar is, obviously, a type of white wine vinegar. This brand, however, is exceptional and highly recommended. Pungent and fruity, it makes an excellent marinade base for chicken or shrimp.

Sherry Vinegar makes all the difference in bean or lentil soup, tomato sauces, mushroom sautes, and on roasted root vegetables. Well-aged sherry vinegar is tangy, yet rich, and a bit salty due to vinegar makers' proximity to the sea.

The good stuff comes from Spain and is aged 25–50 years using the "solera" system: Oak barrels are stacked in a pyramid with "young" vinegar in the bottom barrels and the oldest in the top barrel. As the vinegar ages, it's periodically drawn from lower barrels and transferred to higher ones, where it eventually reaches the top. At each drawing off, young vinegar is added to the lower barrels to continue the process. Although sherry vinegar is aged similar to balsamic, its flavor and consistency are quite different. They are not interchangeable.

Champagne Vinegar (not shown) can be tricky to find, but if you do locate it, buy it. It's milder than white wine vinegar, and makes a terrific salad vinaigrette mixed with a little honey. It's also nice in a beurre blanc or hollandaise.

balsamic

Authentic balsamic vinegar is out of most people's price range (see **Cuisine**, Issue 12), but there is a place in your kitchen for a good-quality, reasonably-priced balsamic—spend $10–$15 on a bottle from a specialty food shop. It's great for marinating meat and vegetables, super as a basting sauce for grilled foods, and can really give marinara a lift. And, odd as it sounds, it's awesome on sugared strawberries! Grocery store brands may claim to be "tradizionale" on the label, but they often contain sugar and caramel color, and are aged for days, not years.

rice

A "newcomer" on American store shelves, rice vinegar has been made and used in Asia for centuries (it's an essential flavoring in the rice used to make Japanese sushi). The flavor is light, mild, and low in acidity, about 4% (white wine vinegar is about 7%). It makes a great, light salad dressing (try it on mesclun), and is a standard ingredient in many Asian dipping sauces. Buy the "unseasoned" type of vinegar—it's more recipe-friendly. Rice vinegar with added sugar, salt, garlic, herbs, or chiles is superfluous. Add those flavors into recipes yourself.

new, improved
chopped
salads

Craving something above and beyond
the usual lettuce-and-tomato salad?
Here's your answer.

So what is it that makes a good
salad? Flavors and textures—
crunchy, sweet, salty, chewy. And
those are the keys to these two
chopped salads. Overflowing
with flavor and texture, they're
almost guaranteed to disappear
right down to the last lettuce leaf!

What, exactly, *are* chopped
salads? Not surprisingly, they're
made of ingredients that have all
been cut into bite-size pieces.
That way, each bite has a little
bit of every component in it,
emphasizing individual textures
and flavors. A few decades ago,
you couldn't read a cookbook or
magazine without running into
a recipe or two for chopped salad.

These two have a contemporary spin, yet are still true to the
spirit of original chopped salads.
Bagged lettuce and other "convenience" items (corn chips,
canned beans) are used without
shame. And tiny leaves of fresh
herbs scattered into the lettuce
provide hits of "surprise" flavor.

The salads here are also more
modern in presentation—layered
in big glass bowls or arranged in
rows on platters. It's a little thing,
but flashy presentation can make
the ordinary seem pretty special.

fajita salad

A twist on taco salad

Talk about needing a fresh start—taco salad in a stale tortilla shell has needed a facelift for quite some time. This fajita salad has the good things of its predecessor (like corn chips!), but steps out of the box with its sweet-spicy dressing and slices of seared flank steak.

The dressing pops on account of chipotle chiles (smoked red jalapeños) in adobo (a vinegar-based sauce). Find them in Latino sections of supermarkets. The dressing also doubles as a marinade for the flank steak.

Cook the steak to medium-rare for optimum flavor and texture, then thinly slice against the grain. This helps guarantee tender pieces of meat—critical in a salad.

FAJITA SALAD

Makes About 10 Cups
Total Time: About 1 Hour

FOR THE DRESSING—
COMBINE:
1/4	cup ketchup
1/4	cup fresh lime juice
2	T. honey
2	T. yellow onion, grated
2	T. vegetable oil
2	T. water
1	t. (or to taste) chipotle chile in adobo, minced
1/4	t. ground cumin
	Salt to taste

FOR THE FLANK STEAK—
MARINATE IN 1/4 CUP DRESSING:
1	lb. flank steak, trimmed

FOR THE SALAD—
PREPARE:
1	bag (10 oz.) mixed romaine/ leaf lettuce salad greens
1	cup grape tomatoes, halved
1	cup Cheddar cheese, grated
1	cup corn chips, coarsely crumbled
1	can (14.5 oz.) black beans, drained, rinsed
1/2	cup cilantro leaves
1/4	cup scallions, sliced

SEAR STEAK IN:
1	t. vegetable oil

GARNISH SALAD WITH:
Sour cream

Combine ingredients for dressing in a small bowl. Remove 1/4 cup for marinating flank steak; set remaining dressing aside.

Marinate steak in 1/4 cup dressing for at least 15 minutes or up to 2 hours. Chill if marinating the steak longer than 30 minutes, otherwise it may be marinated at room temperature.

Prepare ingredients for salad, keeping components separate. Heat oil for searing the steak in a large nonstick skillet over high heat. Remove steak from marinade (discard the excess); season with salt and pepper.

Sear steak on both sides until medium-rare, 3–4 minutes per side. Transfer meat to a cutting board and let rest 5 minutes, then thinly slice steak against the grain with a sharp knife.

To assemble, layer half the greens in a deep glass bowl (a 12-cup trifle bowl is perfect). On the lettuce, layer half of each of the tomatoes, cheese, chips, beans, cilantro, scallions, and steak slices. Drizzle with half the dressing, then layer the rest of the ingredients. Pile the other half of the steak slices in the center, and drizzle remaining dressing on top.

Garnish with a dollop of sour cream and serve.

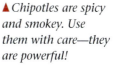

▲ *Chipotles are spicy and smokey. Use them with care—they are powerful!*

▼ *Sear marinated steak in a hot, non-stick pan. Take care that it doesn't scorch.*

▲ *Look at the structure of the steak before cutting, then slice it against the grain.*

▲ *Arrange ingredients in a large glass bowl to show off the tiers— the order isn't critical.*

new, improved
chopped
salads

Restaurant versions of Greek salads are always the same—tons of good ingredients but lacking in flavor. It's a real disappointment.

This salad, on the other hand, is everything a Greek salad should be and more. Over the top with texture and flavor, it's admittedly more work to throw together than an average dinner salad. But you won't regret it, nor will your guests. An empty serving platter is your reward.

A couple of ingredients *can* be left out of this salad without problem. If you do this, though, be sure to aim for balance: Since feta and olives are salty and soft, either could be omitted, but not both. You need at least one to keep flavor and texture in check.

Now, get the biggest platter you have and arrange everything on the lettuce in rows, Cobb salad-style. Drizzle the salad with dressing just before you serve it.

greek salad

GREEK SALAD WITH CHICKEN

Fresh or dried herbs are fine for the dressing. If using dried, be sure they were purchased within the last six months for freshness and cut back to 1/4 tsp. each.

MAKES ABOUT 12 CUPS
TOTAL TIME: 1 HOUR

FOR THE DRESSING—
COMBINE:
1/4 cup red wine vinegar
1/4 cup fresh lemon juice
3 T. extra-virgin olive oil
1 T. sugar
1 T. garlic, minced
1/2 t. minced fresh rosemary
1/2 t. minced fresh thyme
1/2 t. minced fresh oregano
    Pinch crushed red pepper flakes
    Salt to taste

FOR THE CHICKEN—
MARINATE IN 1/4 CUP DRESSING:
2 boneless, skinless chicken breasts (about 5 oz. each)

FOR THE CROUTONS—
BRUSH WITH OLIVE OIL; TOAST:
2 pita bread rounds

FOR THE SALAD—
PREPARE:
1 bag (10 oz.) mixed romaine/ escarole salad greens
2 cups tomatoes, diced
1 cup cucumber, seeded, diced
1 cup bell peppers (red, green, yellow mix), diced
1/2 cup kalamata olives, pitted, halved
1/2 cup feta cheese, crumbled
1/4 cup red onion, slivered
SEAR CHICKEN IN:
1 T. olive or vegetable oil
SPRINKLE SALAD WITH:
1/4 cup Italian parsley leaves
2 T. torn mint leaves

Combine ingredients for dressing in a small bowl. Remove 1/4 cup for marinating chicken; set remaining dressing aside.

Marinate chicken in 1/4 cup dressing for at least 15 minutes or up to 2 hours. Chill if marinating chicken longer than 30 minutes, otherwise it may be marinated at room temperature.

Brush pita bread with oil and toast on a baking sheet in a 400° oven for 10–15 minutes, or until crisp and browned. Break into croutons when cool.

▲*Bake oil-brushed pitas until crisp and golden. Let cool before breaking into bite-size pieces.*

▲*Before serving, sprinkle parsley and mint leaves over the salad, then drizzle with the vinaigrette.*

Prepare ingredients for salad, mounding the salad greens on a large platter and arranging other ingredients decoratively in rows on top. Heat oil for searing chicken in a large nonstick skillet over high heat. Remove chicken from marinade (discard the excess); season with salt and pepper.

Sear chicken in oil on both sides until cooked through, 4–5 min. per side. Transfer to a cutting board and let rest 5 minutes, thinly slice against the grain, and arrange slices on greens.

Sprinkle salad with herbs, then drizzle with dressing and serve.

Place greens on a large platter, then arrange remaining ingredients in rows on top. ▼

options

GREEK SALAD WITH SHRIMP

Marinate shrimp in dressing for 15 minutes. Just before serving the salad, saute them in 2 tsp. olive oil over high heat until cooked through, 3–4 min.

MARINATE IN 1/4 CUP DRESSING:
1/2 lb. medium (31–35 count) shrimp, peeled

basic**cuisine**

cleaning **leeks**

Leeks are bad news when it comes to holding onto the dirt they grow in. Not even spinach can rival a dirty leek. To clean one, first trim the top, cutting off most of the green part. (It's too fibrous to eat, but save it for seasoning stocks.) If the leek is to remain whole, split it in half almost down to the root, then rinse it thoroughly holding the leek vertically under cold running water. Try to spread the layers as far apart as possible so the dirt rinses away.

If you're going to chop up the leek, then go ahead and cut it into the desired shape, place pieces in a colander, and rinse completely.

vanilla **beans**

▲ Vanilla beans are used to flavor liquids such as milk, syrups, or fruit juices. To use, split the bean in half lengthwise down the center, add both halves to the liquid, and heat. Steep it in the liquid 20–30 minutes, then remove. For more intense flavor, scrape out the tiny seeds with the back of a knife and add them to the liquid as well. A bean can be reused once or twice—just rinse and dry.

cracking **eggs**

▲ Always crack eggs on a flat surface. Cracking them on a bowl's edge could push bacteria or tiny bits of shell into the egg.

◄ No matter how you use the eggs, always crack them into a bowl first. This way, you can clearly see any shell that might have broken off into the egg. Any bowl is fine but, obviously, white bowls won't work since the shell disappears against the background.

making **a roux**

tempering

▲ Tempering is used to combine eggs with hot liquids—it's a typical step in making custards and sauces such as crème anglaise. It allows heat-sensitive eggs to be added to hot liquids with less risk of scrambling when they're incorporated into the liquid. To temper, whisk a portion of a recipe's hot liquid ($^1/_4$ to $^1/_2$ the mixture is plenty) into the beaten eggs. This gradually raises the egg's temperature.

▲ Now pour the tempered eggs back into the remaining hot liquid and cook as directed in the recipe. For the smoothest custard or sauce, it's important to whisk the mixture constantly as it cooks—the eggs could still scramble if you're not careful. And be sure the heat is fairly low (medium or medium-low) for gentle cooking and low risk of scorching.

White roux

Blond roux

Brown roux

◄ A roux is fundamental to cooking—many sauces and soups are thickened by one.

A roux is simply equal parts fat (usually butter or oil) and flour. Slowly cooked over low heat, roux should be stirred constantly to prevent burning.

There are three classic roux based on color (determined by cooking time). **White** roux is cooked just long enough to remove the starchy taste in the flour. It has the most thickening power, but not much flavor. **Blond** roux is a light golden color, and **brown** roux has a nutty color and flavor, but thickens the least. ►

seasonalsoups

velvet cream soups

Most of us are used to heavy cream soups that stick with you for days, but these will impress you with their delicate smoothness.

Let's face it—cream soups do not qualify as spa food. They're full of fat and not exactly what you would see on a restaurant's "Lite Menu." But they *can* be lighter than what most of us are used to. By using three simple techniques to thicken these cream soups, you can shed some of the heaviness.

The first step is to puree vegetables with the broth. Besides helping thicken, it also adds deep flavor and body.

The second step is to make a light roux. Forget about using egg yolks or a heavy béchamel as in soups past.

Now, the last step, adding half-and-half, isn't totally low-cal, but the soup still has to be creamy. Half and half has about a third less fat than heavy cream, yet adds a fair amount of thickness and body. It's the same smooth, rich, velvet-like soup you've dreamed of without sacrificing flavor.

Making the base

In any soup, the base is where much of its flavor comes from. This one is no exception, and here the bland flavor of canned broth is kicked up with fresh vegetables—leeks, potatoes, broccoli, or asparagus. Pureeing them with the broth thickens and flavors the base; finishing with half-and-half makes it rich and creamy.

But before making the base, you have a choice to make—broccoli or asparagus soup? The stems of whichever you opt for, are used in the base and will be the dominant flavor in the soup. The asparagus tips or broccoli florets will be steamed, then added to the soup just before serving.

The remaining vegetables are included in the base for their flavor and texture. Leeks always work well in cream soups because of their mild onion-y flavor. New potatoes are best for this, not russets—they don't get mealy when blended like russets can. Finally, celery adds a sweet, mild flavor—and don't forget the leaves!

After the vegetables are simmered and soft, puree the base in a blender. Blending any hot liquid is dangerous—use caution! *Keep the batches small.* With the blender container only half full, *cover the lid with a towel*, and plant your hand firmly on top. *Always start on low*, then gradually increase the speed.

Straining the base may seem painstaking, but it makes all the difference in achieving a velvety texture. Set a medium-mesh sieve over a large bowl and press the pureed vegetables and broth through with a spatula.

▼ *Carefully puree vegetables and broth on low speed. Gradually increase speed as base smooths out.*

▲ *Strain pureed vegetables and broth through a sieve. Discard remains; set base broth aside.*

▼ *Melt butter, add flour, then stir in half-and-half. When thick, add the strained soup base.*

SOUP BASE FOR ASPARAGUS OR BROCCOLI CREAM SOUP

MAKES 8 CUPS
TOTAL TIME: 45 MINUTES

FOR ASPARAGUS SOUP—
PREPARE:
1   lb. asparagus, *Page 22*
FOR BROCCOLI SOUP—
PREPARE:
1   head broccoli, *Page 23*
FOR THE SOUP BASE—
COOK, PUREE, AND STRAIN:
      Asparagus or broccoli stems
4   cups low-sodium chicken
      or vegetable broth
2   cups leeks, trimmed,
      chopped, rinsed (white
      and light green parts)
1 1/2 cups red new potatoes,
      peeled, cubed
1   cup packed fresh parsley
1/2   cup celery, leaves and ribs,
      chopped
MELT:
5   T. unsalted butter
WHISK IN AND COOK:
1/4   cup all-purpose flour
STIR IN:
3   cups half-and-half
ADD AND SIMMER:
      Strained soup base
2   T. dry sherry
1   T. fresh lemon juice

Prepare the asparagus or broccoli stems.

Cook stems and remaining vegetables, broth, and parsley in a stockpot over high heat. Bring to a boil, reduce heat, and simmer until vegetables are tender, 15 minutes. Puree base in a blender until smooth. Strain and set aside.

Melt butter in the stockpot over medium-low heat.

Whisk in flour and cook 2 minutes, stirring constantly.

Stir in half-and-half. Simmer 4–5 minutes over medium heat, stirring constantly until thickened.

Add strained soup base, sherry, and lemon juice.

asparagus
cream soup

A lighter, more diet-friendly cream soup base opens up a world of possibilities. Spring's asparagus and ever-popular broccoli make two of the most flavorful soups you'll eat.

The hardest thing with these soups is choosing which vegetable to use. Asparagus, the quintessential spring vegetable, is tempting, but broccoli, the produce aisle's old stand-by, is good too. Thankfully, the soup will be great whatever you decide.

Aside from the base, the key to great flavor is in the chunks of vegetables. We've all had our share of overcooked vegetables in cream soup. The solution is to first steam the tips (or florets), then add them to the soup just before serving. Sure it's a bit more work, but it guarantees bright green, crisp vegetables.

Now, these soups are not one-dimensional. They're built so you can add other ingredients without much hassle. Check out the options with each recipe to see what sounds good—the possibilities are endless.

ASPARAGUS CREAM SOUP
MAKES 8 CUPS

PREPARE:

1   recipe Soup Base for Cream Soup made with asparagus stems, *Page 21*

BEFORE SERVING, ADD TO SOUP:
Steamed asparagus tips, see *below*
Salt and white pepper to taste

SERVE WITH:
Parmesan Croutons

▲ *Trim off woody portion of asparagus spears (about 1" from bottom) and discard. Chop center portion of spears and use in soup base. Steam tips for 3 minutes; add to the soup before serving.*

PARMESAN CROUTONS
MAKES 2 CUPS
TOTAL TIME: 15 MINUTES

TOAST IN 400° OVEN FOR 10 MINUTES:

2   cups French bread, cut into $1/4$" cubes

MELT IN SAUTE PAN:

2   T. unsalted butter

ADD:

$1/2$ t. paprika
$1/4$ t. kosher salt
Toasted bread cubes

TOSS WITH:

$1/2$ cup Parmesan cheese, grated

options

STIR IN 1–2 ITEMS:
Grated Parmesan
Chopped fresh chives
Cooked crabmeat
Chopped hard-boiled eggs
Sauteed mushrooms
Strips of prosciutto

broccoli
cream soup

CHIVE-BUTTER CROSTINI

MAKES 8 SLICES
TOTAL TIME: 15 MINUTES

TOAST IN 400° OVEN FOR
10 MINUTES; COOL:
- 8   slices baguette-type bread, 1/2" thick

COMBINE:
- 1/4   cup unsalted butter, softened
- 2   T. chopped fresh chives
- 1   T. lemon zest, minced
- 1/4   t. kosher salt

SPREAD MIXTURE ON:
- Toasted bread

BROCCOLI CREAM SOUP

MAKES 10 CUPS

PREPARE:
- 1   recipe Soup Base for Cream Soup made with broccoli stems, *Page 21*

BEFORE SERVING, ADD TO SOUP:
- Steamed broccoli florets
- Salt and cayenne to taste

SERVE WITH:
- Chive-Butter Crostini

options

STIR IN 1–2 ITEMS:
- Julienned or diced ham
- Grated Swiss cheese
- Shredded cooked chicken
- Cooked wild rice
- Toasted almonds
- Crumbled cooked bacon

▲Remove broccoli florets from stem; set aside to steam. Trim tough outer layer of stems with a knife, then finish with a peeler. Chop and use in base.

▲Cut florets into bite-sized pieces and steam 4 minutes. Add to soup just before serving.

chef**at**home: *Howard Helmer*

making omelets

Howard Helmer's message is simple: Making an omelet should *not* be intimidating. It's fast, easy, and anyone can do it!

Enthusiasm exudes from Howard Helmer as he demonstrates how to make an omelet. He repeats his unique "dig a hole and fill it" technique as he whips out 40-second omelets one after another, proving that omelet-making is indeed as easy as it looks! Even beginners can do it in less than two minutes. Once you learn the technique, you'll never be at a loss for a quick, wonderful meal.

Howard's most emphatic omelet advice is "Please, *please* don't overcook the eggs!" It pulls the moisture out, leaving the omelet tough and dry. And leave the three-egg omelets to the restaurants—two eggs are perfect.

Giving us three different recipes, Howard teaches the basic omelet technique, a jazzy tortilla omelet wrap, and a creamy French variation.

*The world's fastest omelet maker, Howard Helmer has twice earned the **Guinness Book** record, cooking up a whopping 427 omelets in just 30 minutes. His many television appearances include Oprah, Good Morning America, and The Food Network.*

*As National Representative for the American Egg Board, Howard criss-crosses the country each year demonstrating cooking techniques for both professional and home cooks. Visit **aeb.org** for incredible egg information, safety facts, and recipes.*

Howard Helmer omelet lesson

Making an omelet isn't complicated, but there is a technique to learn.

Equipment: Omelets require just two tools—a skillet and spatula. Use a 10-inch *nonstick* skillet (slope-sided) so the eggs don't cling. A narrow turning spatula made of plastic or wood won't scratch the pan.

Liquid: An omelet can be made with eggs alone, but adding a little liquid loosens the egg so it moves freely in the pan. The *type* of liquid is up to you. Water produces a light omelet, while dairy products make the flavor and texture richer.

Fat: Butter is melted in the skillet for the sole purpose of adding flavor to the omelet. The nonstick skillet and spray ensure easy release.

Heat: The key to a tender omelet is quick cooking over high (but not scorching) heat. High heat is not an egg's enemy—it's too much *time* over the heat that tightens the proteins, squeezing all the moisture out.

Pulling: Howard's "dig a hole and fill it" technique works like this: Pull the eggs from the outer edge to the center of the pan, tilting as you go so raw egg covers the empty surface. Repeat this process, pulling from each side of the pan. When a small mound forms in the center and the edges are set, roll excess liquid to the outer edges. It's ready to fill when the egg no longer runs. It may appear moist, but residual heat will firm up the omelet as it makes its way to the table.

Filling and folding: Howard says anything goes for fillings. The omelet method will still be the same.

With eggs set but still moist, add the fillings to one side of the omelet, opposite and perpendicular to the handle. Now use a spatula to fold the unfilled half over the filled half. Grasp the pan's handle and "roll" the omelet out onto a plate.

▲ *Melt butter in a briefly preheated pan. Add eggs as soon as butter begins to bubble. Don't let butter brown—it affects flavor and color.*

▲ *Pull eggs from outer edge to center of the pan, tilting so raw egg fills the hole.*

▲ *Add fillings to front half of omelet when egg is still wet, but not runny.*

◄ *Lift skillet, scooting omelet until it hangs an inch over the edge, resting on a plate. Quickly invert onto plate so the underside of the omelet is up.*

HERB & THREE-CHEESE OMELET

MAKES ONE OMELET
TOTAL TIME: 5 MINUTES

WHIP:
- 2 eggs
- 1 T. half-and-half, milk, or water
- 1 T. chopped fresh chives (or other fresh herb)
- Salt and pepper to taste

MELT:
- ½ T. butter

POUR IN EGG MIXTURE; ADD:
- 6 T. grated cheeses (3 T. Swiss, 2 T. Cheddar, 1 T. Parmesan)

Whip eggs with liquid, chives, salt, and pepper. Make sure all the white is fully incorporated.

Melt butter over high heat in a 10" nonstick skillet coated with cooking spray. Heat until bubbly.

Pour egg mixture into skillet, pulling them toward the center from each side. Remove from heat when eggs no longer run but are still quite moist.

Add cheeses to top half of omelet, fold, then invert onto a plate. Let rest 1 minute before serving.

Gently lift omelet half to fold. Don't worry if it tears—it won't show. ▼

chef at home: *Howard Helmer*

▲ *In a preheated skillet, warm tortilla 5–10 seconds on each side.*

▲ *Cook omelet following steps on Page 25, without folding; fill and slide onto tortilla.*

TORTILLA OMELET WRAP

The tortilla makes this omelet an especially hearty breakfast or lunch. Serve with salsa, or avocados and tomatoes tossed with lime juice.
MAKES ONE OMELET; TOTAL TIME: 10 MINUTES

WHIP:
2   eggs
1   T. half-and-half, milk, or water
     Salt and pepper to taste

WARM:
1   10-inch flour tortilla

MELT:
½   T. butter

POUR IN EGG MIXTURE; TOP WITH:
⅓   cup Monterey Jack cheese, grated
⅓   cup cooked ham, diced
2   T. red bell pepper, diced
2   T. scallions, diced
1   T. jalapeño, seeded, diced

SLIDE ONTO:
     Warmed tortilla

CUT AND SERVE WITH:
     Salsa or avocado-tomato relish

Whip eggs, liquid, and seasonings.
Warm tortilla in skillet; set aside.
Melt butter in a 10" nonstick skillet coated with cooking spray over high heat. Heat until bubbly.
Pour in egg mixture. Pull eggs toward the center from each side. Remove from heat when eggs no longer run but are still quite moist.
     Top with filling ingredients, sprinkling them over entire omelet.
Slide omelet onto warmed tortilla. To roll, first fold bottom edge of tortilla up 1", then fold sides in 1". Begin rolling, ending seam side down. Let rest for 1 minute, then cut omelet in half.
Cut and serve with salsa or avocado-tomato relish.

▲ *Fold bottom and side edges in, then roll up omelet and tortilla together.*

▲ *Carefully cut wrap in half at an angle. To serve, lean one half on top of other so cut side is visible.*

Stirred French omelet

The previous two omelets have large curds because of the gentle pull and fill technique you've been using. It creates a firm, sturdy omelet that's easy to fill.

However, if you like an omelet with a smoother, tender texture, try this French omelet. The pan, butter, and eggs remain the same. It's *after* you add the eggs that the real action begins.

Simultaneously shake the pan and stir the eggs vigorously with a spatula. You will notice immediately that the curds are much smaller. Just like the other omelets, as soon as the eggs no longer run, the cooking is finished. Now add the fillings and fold out onto a plate. *Voilà.*

▲ *Shake the pan while making small, quick stirring motions.*

▲ *Roll excess liquid around to the edges of the omelet.*

◄ *Add fillings to front half of the omelet when eggs are still moist, but not runny. Fold and serve.*

FRENCH OMELET WITH SPINACH & SWISS CHEESE

MAKES ONE OMELET
TOTAL TIME: 5 MINUTES

WHIP:
2   eggs
1   T. half-and-half, milk, or water
     Salt and pepper to taste
MELT:
1/2 T. butter
POUR IN EGG MIXTURE; ADD:
1/3 cup Swiss cheese, grated
1/3 cup sauteed spinach, drained
GARNISH WITH:
1   T. sour cream
     Strip of lemon peel

Whip eggs, liquid, and seasonings.
Melt butter in a 10" nonstick skillet coated with cooking spray over high heat. Heat until bubbly.
Pour egg mixture into skillet. Immediately begin shaking the pan while making small, quick stirring motions. Remove from heat when eggs no longer run but are still quite moist.

Add cheese and spinach to top half of omelet. Fold in half and invert onto a plate. Tuck the thin edges under the omelet if desired. Let rest for 1 minute.
Garnish with a dollop of sour cream and a strip of lemon peel.

braising
lamb shanks

It's springtime, and for cooks that also means lamb time. Get ready to dig in to these shanks for the perfect salute to the season.

People who don't like lamb fall into two camps. There are those whose only "lamb" experience actually involved gamey-tasting, older mutton. Then there are those who've never had lamb (or mutton) and are afraid to try it.

Well, if you aren't quite sold on lamb's good points, this is for you. To me, shanks can't be beat in terms of flavor, economy, and ease. As for presentation, see Page 31—it doesn't get much better!

What are shanks?

A lamb's shanks are the "shins" of their front (foreshanks) and back legs (hind shanks). If possible, get hind shanks—they're a bit larger and more meaty. Odds are, though, that your butcher won't give you a choice between them. But that's fine since they can be used interchangeably.

Buying shanks

By law, all lamb is from animals under a year old, typically five to seven months. When buying lamb (any cut, not just shanks) look for meat that's pinkish-red in color, not deep red, like beef. The darker hue indicates that the animal was older, so the meat may be slightly tougher. But that's not too big a deal since lamb, being young, is naturally tender.

Age is also revealed at the bones. Moist, pink, porous, somewhat translucent bones are signs of young lamb—shanks with white, dry bones are older.

Shanks vary in size depending on their age and location (front or back legs). Typically, they are 1–1$^{1}/_{2}$ pounds—plan on one shank per person.

Like beef, lamb can be frozen with good results, so don't shy away from the freezer section in your quest. That's good to know, too, if lamb shanks are on sale—stock the freezer!

If possible, buy American-raised lamb. Colorado ranchers produce some of the mildest tasting lamb around. Imports from New Zealand are good, but some may find it a bit gamey.

Before braising

Faithful *Cuisine* readers know braising—it's used a lot, especially with tough cuts of meat. Although lamb *meat* is tender, lamb *shanks* are tough due to tissues in them that connect muscle to bone. Long, slow simmering is required to melt the tissues and tenderize the meat.

Before braising, trim off most of the fat, but don't remove the thin, white membrane that stretches over the muscles. It helps hold the shank together as it cooks, yet will melt and turn tender during braising.

A *large*, heavy stockpot or roaster is crucial here—shanks are big and inflexible. Expect to stack them on top of each other. Avoid cast iron as it may react with acidic items (tomatoes, wine) in the braising liquid, causing an off flavor. Get the pan really hot for searing, and don't forget to turn on the exhaust fan!

1 Sear shanks in pairs, browning them well all over. Remove shanks from pan and set aside.

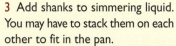

2 Saute onions, garlic, and jalapeño until soft. Add remaining ingredients (except those for glaze) and bring to a simmer.

BARBECUE-STYLE LAMB SHANKS
MAKES 4 SERVINGS; TOTAL TIME: ABOUT 3 HOURS

FOR THE SHANKS—

SEAR IN 3 T. OLIVE OIL; REMOVE:
4   lamb shanks, trimmed (about 1 lb. each)

SAUTE IN 2 T. OLIVE OIL:
2   cups yellow onion, diced
3   T. garlic, minced
1   jalapeño, seeded, minced

ADD; BRAISE SHANKS IN:
1   can (14.5 oz.) crushed tomatoes in puree (1 3/4 cups)
1   can (14 oz.) low-sodium beef broth
1   cup dry red wine
1/2   cup ketchup
1/4   cup brown sugar
2   T. prepared yellow mustard
2   T. apple cider vinegar
2   T. Worcestershire sauce
2   t. minced fresh rosemary
1   t. ground cumin
2   bay leaves

FOR THE GLAZE—

COMBINE; GLAZE SHANKS WITH:
1/4   cup honey
3   T. chipotle chiles in adobo, minced
    Juice and minced zest of 1 lime

SERVE WITH:
    Cheddar Cheese Grits, Page 33

Sear trimmed shanks in oil in a large stockpot or Dutch oven over high heat, see *Figure 1*. Sear them two at a time, otherwise the pan will be too crowded to brown them properly. Once browned (about 5 minutes per side), transfer shanks to a platter. Pour off any residual fat in the pan and return the pan to the burner.

Saute onion, garlic, and jalapeño in 2 T. oil over med.-high heat, scraping up any brown bits in the pan, see *Figure 2*. Cook until onion is soft, about 8 minutes.

Add remaining ingredients and bring to a simmer. Return shanks to the pan (it's okay if they stack on top of each other), cover, and bring liquid to a boil, see *Figure 3*. Reduce heat to maintain a low, gentle simmer, adjusting the heat as needed. Cook shanks 1 hour, checking periodically to make sure the liquid is gently bubbling. After 1 hour, turn and rearrange the shanks, see *Figure 4*, then cover and simmer another hour.

Combine glaze ingredients while shanks braise; set aside.

Preheat oven to 400° with rack in the middle. After braising two hours, transfer shanks to a parchment-lined baking sheet, brush with some of the glaze, and roast in the oven for 5 minutes, see *Figure 5*. Turn, glaze the other side, and roast another 5 minutes.

Meanwhile, skim off and discard any fat floating on top of the braising liquid, see *Figure 6*. Increase heat to high and bring sauce to a boil to reduce slightly. **Serve** glazed shanks on grits with sauce ladled over, see *Figure 7*.

3 Add shanks to simmering liquid. You may have to stack them on each other to fit in the pan.

Bring the shanks and liquid to a boil, reduce heat, cover, and simmer for 1 hour, paying attention to how rapidly the liquid is bubbling.

cuisinetechnique

Behind braising

Once braising has begun, there's not much more you need to do. But keep an eye on a few items as the shanks do their thing.

Simmering

The liquid in the pot must maintain a simmer—it shouldn't be too cool or too hot. Most people tend to boil it too hard, which doesn't allow the tissues to melt slowly and gently. A rapid boil causes the meat to cook faster than the tissues can melt. Then when the tissues have dissolved properly, the meat has dried out.

Turning

Second, don't forget to turn the shanks after the first hour of braising. Turning assures that the ones on top have a chance to simmer in a good amount of sauce. Take care when doing this—the meat will be starting to come away from the bone and is easily pulled off. As the shanks cook, they'll shrink and should fit a little better in the pan.

Glazing and finishing

Lamb shanks aren't usually glazed, but this sweet-spicy-tart coating sets these apart from the rest. The glaze also gives the meat a classy-looking finish. It is optional, but glazing is a minor investment that yields big results.

While the shanks glaze in the oven, take the time to skim off the fat on the surface of the braising liquid. There will be quite a lot—shanks are fatty, even after the excess has been trimmed. Simmer the sauce a few minutes to thicken it and intensify flavors, then adjust seasonings with salt and pepper before serving.

Making ahead

Like many soups and stews, lamb shanks are good the first day, even better the second. If you want to make these ahead, finish the shanks to the point of glazing, cool completely (place the pot in a sink full of ice water), then chill. The next day, spoon off the fat solidified on top and bring everything to a simmer. Cook until heated through, then glaze and finish as above.

4 After braising an hour, gently rearrange shanks so the bottom ones are on the top. Cover and simmer shanks another hour.

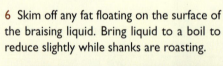

6 Skim off any fat floating on the surface of the braising liquid. Bring liquid to a boil to reduce slightly while shanks are roasting.

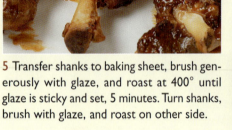

5 Transfer shanks to baking sheet, brush generously with glaze, and roast at 400° until glaze is sticky and set, 5 minutes. Turn shanks, brush with glaze, and roast on other side.

7 Serve shanks on a mound of cheese grits. Or take a look at Pages 32 and 33 for other great side dish options.

sides for
lamb shanks

Side dishes usually don't get a second thought.

But these are so good, it's agonizing choosing just one.

sides

Rosemary Buttered Noodles, *Page 32*

Cheddar Cheese Grits, *Page 33*

Gremolata Mashed Potatoes, *online extra*

Lamb shanks and side dishes have a sort of symbiotic relationship. Both could exist on their own and do fine, but together, they are far greater than the sum of their parts. It's like Thanksgiving—turkey isn't the same without stuffing!

The three side dish options here cover a lot of territory—noodles, corn, and potatoes. There's something for everybody. Of the three, the noodles take the least amount of time and effort, although none are hard. Don't forget, there's a lot of "down" time to kill while the shanks are simmering.

Now, I'll confess that I don't usually settle on one side dish when making lamb shanks. I can't—each is so good, it kills me to decide. So that's why, on my table, it's buttered noodles and cheese grits. Overkill? Probably. Regrettable? No way.

Rosemary buttered noodles

ROSEMARY BUTTERED NOODLES

Curly egg noodles are best for this dish, but you could also use pasta. Penne, gemelli, and rotini are good choices.

MAKES ABOUT 4 CUPS
TOTAL TIME: ABOUT 20 MINUTES

FOR THE BREAD CRUMB TOPPING—
TOAST IN 1 T. OLIVE OIL:
1   cup bread crumbs (from firm white sandwich bread)
SEASON WITH:
     Salt and cayenne to taste

FOR THE NOODLES—
COOK ACCORDING TO PACKAGE DIRECTIONS:
8   oz. dried egg noodles
MELT; TOSS NOODLES IN:
4   T. unsalted butter
2   t. minced fresh rosemary
TOP WITH:
     Grated Parmesan cheese
     Coarse sea salt
     Ground black pepper to taste
     Prepared toasted bread crumbs

Toast bread crumbs for the topping in a skillet over medium-high heat, stirring constantly. Cook until golden brown and crisp, 8–10 minutes. Remove from heat.
Season crumbs with salt and cayenne to taste; set aside.
Cook noodles as directed on the package. Drain, but do not rinse.
Melt butter over medium-high heat in the same pan that was used to cook the noodles. Add the rosemary and cook just until fragrant, about 1 minute. Do not allow the butter to brown. Add drained noodles to the pan and toss to coat with the butter, then transfer to a serving dish.
Top noodles with Parmesan, sea salt, and black pepper. Sprinkle bread crumbs over the top and serve.

Toast bread crumbs in a small skillet until golden. Stir continually to keep them from scorching. ▶

Melt butter in the pot the noodles boiled in, then add rosemary. Stir in cooked, drained noodles. ▼

▲ *Transfer noodles to a serving platter and finish with cheese, salt, pepper, and bread crumbs.*

Saute onions, then garlic. Add milk; bring to a boil. Watch so it doesn't boil over. ▶

▲*Gradually whisk grits into hot milk mixture. Cook until grits are thick, stirring constantly.*

Stir in cheeses until melted. Just before serving, stir in scallions. ▶

cheddar
cheese grits

CHEDDAR CHEESE GRITS

To hold grits for serving, place them in a double boiler set over simmering water and pour a layer of milk on top of the grits. Then, when ready to serve, stir the milk into them along with the scallions and seasonings.

MAKES ABOUT 4 CUPS
TOTAL TIME: 20–30 MINUTES

SAUTE IN 2 T. UNSALTED BUTTER:
$1/2$ cup yellow onion, diced
4   cloves garlic, minced
ADD; BRING TO A BOIL:
4   cups whole or 2% milk
GRADUALLY WHISK IN:
1   cup instant white grits
OFF HEAT, STIR IN:
1   cup Cheddar cheese, grated
$1/2$ cup Parmesan cheese, grated
STIR IN:
       Sliced scallions
       Salt, pepper, and Tabasco
       to taste

Saute onion in butter in a large saucepan over medium heat. Cook until soft, about 5 minutes. Add garlic and cook just until fragrant, about 1 minute.
Add milk and bring to a boil.
Gradually whisk grits into boiling milk, stirring constantly to prevent lumps. Cook, stirring often, until desired consistency is reached, about 5 minutes for thick but not stiff grits. They will thicken even more upon standing.
Off heat, add cheeses and stir until melted.
Stir in scallions and seasonings before serving. If grits are thick, thin them with hot milk or water.

38

online **extra**

For another braised lamb shank recipe and side dish option, visit our web site at **www.CuisineAtHome.com**

faster **with** fewer
chicken breasts

Got a package of chicken breasts and half an hour? Then you're well on your way to a great-tasting dinner. No excuse for take-out now!

TARRAGON-CREAM CHICKEN

Flexibility is the secret here. If you don't have prosciutto, use bacon and drain well, or just omit it. You may also substitute chicken broth for the wine.
MAKES 4 SERVINGS; TOTAL TIME: 30 MINUTES

SEASON:
4   boneless, skinless chicken breast halves

DUST CHICKEN WITH:
½   cup all-purpose flour

SAUTE CHICKEN IN; REMOVE:
2   T. olive oil

ADD:
8   oz. white mushrooms, halved if large
3   oz. prosciutto, sliced

ADD:
1   cup dry white wine *or* low-sodium chicken broth
1   cup heavy cream

RETURN TO PAN:
    Browned chicken

STIR IN:
2   t. minced fresh tarragon
1   t. apple cider vinegar

GARNISH WITH:
    Minced fresh chives

SERVE OVER:
    Toasted bread

CHICKEN PARMESAN

This classic Italian dish starts out with two breast halves split in half—four pieces. Once flattened, they easily make four servings.
MAKES 4 SERVINGS; TOTAL TIME: 30 MINUTES

FLATTEN; SEASON:
2   boneless, skinless chicken breast halves, split

DIP CHICKEN INTO:
2   eggs, beaten

DREDGE IN:
½   cup Italian-seasoned bread crumbs

SAUTE IN:
2   T. olive oil

COMBINE; POUR OVER:
1   jar (26 oz.) marinara sauce
½   cup low-sodium chicken broth

SPRINKLE WITH:
1   cup mozzarella cheese, grated
¼   cup Parmesan cheese, grated

SERVE WITH:
    Cooked angel hair pasta

Flatten chicken breasts with a mallet to ¼" thick. Season with salt and black pepper. **Dip** into eggs.

Dredge chicken in bread crumbs.

Saute chicken in olive oil in a large skillet coated with nonstick cooking spray. Cook over medium-high heat until lightly browned, about 3–5 minutes per side.

Combine the marinara and broth then pour over chicken. Bring to a boil, cover, and reduce heat to low. Simmer 5 minutes; turn chicken.

Sprinkle chicken with both cheeses. Cover and simmer 5 minutes, or until cheese is melted.

Serve with cooked pasta.

Season chicken with salt and black pepper.

Dust each breast with flour, shaking off any excess.

Saute chicken in olive oil over medium-high heat in a saute pan coated with nonstick cooking spray. Cook until lightly browned on both sides, 5–7 minutes

total. Remove chicken, set aside, and keep warm.

Add mushrooms and prosciutto to the pan. Cook until mushrooms soften and begin to brown, 2–3 minutes.

Add wine (or broth) and heavy cream.

Return chicken to pan, reduce heat and simmer until sauce thickens slightly, about 8 minutes.

Stir in tarragon and vinegar; cook 1 minute.

Garnish with chives.

Serve chicken over slices of toasted bread.

CHICKEN & ARTICHOKES

A simple and refreshing array of spring flavors and ingredients make this a fast, company-worthy dinner.
MAKES 4 SERVINGS; TOTAL TIME: 30 MINUTES

COMBINE FOR DRESSING:
1/4	cup olive oil
1/4	cup fresh lemon juice
2	T. honey
2	t. garlic, minced
1	t. dried thyme
1/2	t. kosher salt
1/2	t. crushed red pepper flakes

SEASON; SAUTE IN 2 T. OLIVE OIL:
4	boneless, skinless chicken breast halves

ADD AND REDUCE:
1	can (13.75 oz.) whole artichoke hearts, drained, halved
	Prepared dressing

TOP CHICKEN WITH:
1	lemon, thinly sliced

SERVE OVER:
Cooked orzo

GARNISH WITH:
Chopped fresh parsley

Combine the oil, lemon juice, honey, garlic, thyme, salt, and pepper flakes in a small bowl for the dressing.

Season chicken breasts with salt and black pepper. Saute in 2 T. oil in a large saute pan coated with nonstick cooking spray. Cook over medium-high heat until lightly browned on both sides, 3–5 minutes per side. Reduce heat to medium, cover, and cook 5 minutes. **Add** artichokes and dressing. Simmer and reduce about 3 minutes.

Top chicken with slices of lemon; cook 2 minutes, or until dressing thickens.
Serve over cooked orzo.
Garnish with chopped fresh parsley.

PINEAPPLE-SPICED CHICKEN

A spicy blend of heat, cinnamon, and pineapple puts a hint of the islands on the family dinner table.
MAKES 4 SERVINGS; TOTAL TIME: 30 MINUTES

SAUTE IN 2 T. OLIVE OIL:
1	medium red onion, sliced

ADD; COOK AND REMOVE:
2	cups fresh pineapple, diced

COMBINE FOR RUB:
1	T. all-purpose flour
2	t. ground cinnamon
2	t. chili powder
2	t. kosher salt
1	t. ground cumin
1	t. black pepper
1/4	t. cayenne

Saute onion in oil in a large skillet sprayed with nonstick cooking spray. Cook over medium-high heat 2 minutes. **Add** pineapple and cook 2 minutes. Remove pineapple mixture from pan; set aside. **Combine** the rub ingredients. **Coat** both sides of chicken breasts with the rub mixture. Brown chicken in oil over medium-high heat, about 3 minutes per side.

COAT; BROWN IN 1 T. OLIVE OIL:
4	boneless, skinless chicken breast halves

ADD AND SIMMER:
	Pineapple-onion mixture
1/3	cup pineapple juice (6 oz.)
3	T. brown sugar

SERVE OVER:
Cooked couscous

GARNISH WITH:
Fresh cilantro leaves

Add pineapple-onion mixture, juice, and sugar. Bring to a boil, reduce heat, cover, and simmer 4 minutes. Turn chicken and simmer, covered, an additional 4 minutes.
Serve over couscous.
Garnish with cilantro leaves.

wares
which whisk?

The primary purpose of whisks is to aerate, blend, mix, and whip. But choose the right one for the job.

Whisks come in a dizzying array of types, styles, and sizes made from a variety of different materials. So how do you know which one to use? It all comes down to understanding the function of each type of whisk and what constitutes a good one.

Types: After testing a large cross-section of whisks (55 of them!), we found they break down into six general categories, each meant to perform a specific function. Page 37 explains the whisk types and their purposes. But gimmicky variations aren't included—like whisks with wire spheres inside the head or stainless steel balls on the end of straight wires. We found them all inferior, offering no value.

Length: Whisks are measured from end to end. You'll find all lengths, but a standard 12" whisk is the best size for all-around home cooking. Short whisks have their place for specific jobs, and bigger sizes are most beneficial for large quantities.

Wire material: In today's market whisks are made with a variety of materials, but stainless steel wires are still the best way to go. Although silicone-coated, nonstick-coated, and nylon whisks have emerged for use with nonstick cookware, none of them performed nearly as well as basic stainless steel. We also found them to be unnecessary because whisks don't have open tines that damage surfaces.

Wire strength: It's all about balance. Wires should be thick enough to hold their shape and stand up to the task, but thin enough to have some give or liveliness— that's what provides good whipping action. Put a whisk to the test by gently pulling on a wire. It should move back into place on its own. Extra thick wires are primarily for commercial purposes or dough.

▲ *Nonstick, silicone-coated, and nylon wires are available but not preferred.*

Handles: Made of stainless steel, hard plastic, chrome plated brass, or wood, handle material is largely a matter of personal preference.

What's important here is the way the wires are attached to the handle. They should be sunk into epoxy or a filled, solid handle. This ensures that it's watertight (for sanitary purposes) and that the wires are secure.

▲ *Wires need to be anchored in either epoxy or a filled handle.*

One-whisk kitchen: If I could have just one whisk in my kitchen, it would have to be a French whisk. It handles most everyday tasks admirably and is more versatile than a balloon. Good models will last for years and are available from around $8 all the way up to $30. Each brand is slightly different, but we particularly liked whisks made by Best, Rösle, and Matfer.

▲ *Some whisks have loops at the top. If wires are high quality, loops serve no purpose.*

Choose the right whisk for the job.
A Whisk Reference Guide

Balloon whisk

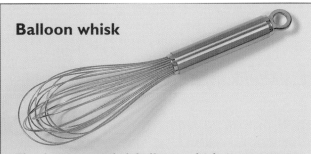

The large, rounded balloon whisk is meant to incorporate air and increase the volume of light ingredients like cream or egg whites. Size of the head varies between brands—look for a large diameter, with as many wires as possible. There's also a balloon variation that has a pronounced bulbous head. It's also effective, but not superior.

French whisk

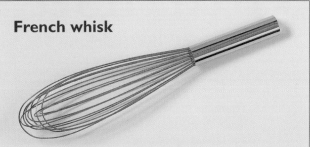

The narrow French whisk (also called a sauce or egg whisk) does a little of everything. It smooths custard, sauce, and gravy, and can beat eggs, incorporate dry ingredients, and even whip cream if necessary. Its narrow tip reaches into places the bigger balloon whisk cannot. While some task-specific whisks may perform a single job better, this is the most practical whisk.

Flat whisk

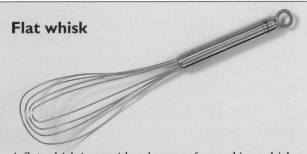

A flat whisk is considered more of a working whisk than a mixing whisk. Use it for deglazing, when you need to work the bottom of a pan. When pressed down, the stable interior wire stays in contact with the pan and acts as a scraper while the other wires stir. It covers a much wider surface area of the pan than a French whisk is able to.

Coil whisk

Several versions of the coiled whisk exist, but all have a tinned steel coil looped around a sturdy frame. The best models have a hinged frame that allows half of the coil head to bend, making it able to conform to the sides of any pan or bowl and reach into the edges. It's particularly good for sauces, gravies, and shallow pan work, but also whisks eggs with ease.

Twirl whisk

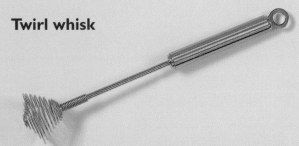

Made from one piece of coiled wire, the head of the twirl whisk benefits from double whisking action. The head springs up and down working the liquid as the whisk rotates, making it ideal for smoothing gravy and sauce, and whisking eggs. Look for a very flexible wire head with a lot of spring. It will bend and meet the angles of bowls and pans, reaching the edges.

Saucepan whisk

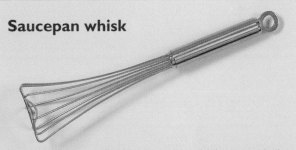

Bent wires form a flat head on this whisk, particularly suiting it for use in saucepans or large pots of soup, stew, or sauce. It's able to connect with the edges of a pan base while stirring the contents. While well suited for this specific duty, the saucepan whisk is not a multitasker. It isn't helpful in shallow pans, and the angled corners don't allow it to whip cream or eggs.

Tiramisù

Tiramisù, dream dessert of the '90s, has seen better days. Badly in need of a redo, this one actually lives up to its "pick me up" promise.

Tiramisù [tih-ruh-mee-SOO] has been so overplayed, it's hard to know what "good" should taste like. The problem is its simplicity: ladyfingers (small sponge cakes) dabbed with coffee and liqueur, then layered with custard. Perceiving it as too "basic," people turn around and garb it up with weird variations or over-the-top presentations. Then suddenly, the flavor has vanished.

But not here. This version actually tastes *better* than it looks! Building it in a standard springform pan makes it beautiful to look at, but that really won't matter much once you taste it—this is awesome. Another bonus: It's a dessert that *has* to be made a day in advance. No last minute fussing required.

Cooking up the custard

The problem with so many tiramisù is that the custard isn't good. But that's where the bulk of the flavor is, so it really needs to be special.

This custard is fairly standard in terms of ingredients, with a couple of exceptions. Vanilla beans aren't a staple in a lot of cupboards, but I urge you to use one here. It adds an intensity that can't be matched by vanilla extract alone. If possible, buy beans in bulk at a natural food store, looking for those that are plump and pliable. Dried up beans (like ones in many grocery stores) are hard to work with and lack flavor.

Mascarpone [mahs-kahr-POH-neh] is a very rich Italian cream cheese available in many grocery or specialty food stores. Check the date stamp as it is quite perishable and not unusual to get an expired container. If you can't find mascarpone, substitute it with the same amount of cream cheese. The custard won't taste *exactly* the same, but it'll be fine. Just do not omit the cheese—it's needed for body.

FOR THE CUSTARD—
HEAT:
2	cups whole milk
1	cup sugar
1	vanilla bean, split, scraped, see *Basic Cuisine, Page 18*
	Pinch salt

WHISK TOGETHER:
4	eggs
1/3	cup all-purpose flour

POUR CUSTARD OVER:
8	oz. mascarpone
2	T. unsalted butter, chilled

STIR IN; CHILL:
1/4	cup dark rum or Marsala
1	T. vanilla extract

TO ASSEMBLE—
PREPARE:
4	3-oz. pkgs. soft, plain (*not* cream-filled) ladyfingers
1 1/2	cups strong coffee

DUST WITH:
Cocoa powder

SERVE WITH:
Fresh strawberries

Heat milk, sugar, vanilla pod and seeds, and salt in a large heavy saucepan over medium heat. Warm just until sugar dissolves.

Whisk eggs in a mixing bowl until blended, then gradually add the flour. It tends to clump—whisk until most lumps have dissolved.

Temper about 1 cup hot milk into the egg mixture (see Basic Cuisine, Page 18), then add the egg mixture to the pan. Cook, whisking constantly, until custard is thick. Boil 1 minute to eliminate the flour's starchy taste.

Place mascarpone into the bowl you mixed the eggs in and smash with a spatula to soften. **Pour** hot custard over mascarpone and butter; stir to blend. **Stir in** rum and vanilla. Cover custard with plastic, pressing it onto the surface to prevent a skin from forming. Chill until cold. **Prepare** the ladyfingers, coffee, and springform pan, see *Page 40*. Assemble tiramisù as illustrated on Pages 40 and 41. Chill cake overnight to set up. When ready to serve, remove the outer ring and plastic wrap. **Dust** top of tiramisù with a generous amount of cocoa powder. **Serve** in wedges with berries.

Mascarpone can be found in small tubs in the cheese section of grocery stores. It is expensive, but the flavor is incomparable. ▼

◄ *Temper a bit of hot milk into egg mixture, then add eggs to the remaining milk.*

▲ *Cook custard until thick. Whisking constantly helps minimize lumps.*

▲ *Pour hot custard over mascarpone and butter. Stir until well blended, add rum and vanilla, then chill until cold.*

Tiramisù in the round

1 **Preparing the framework**
Line a 9" springform pan by laying two pieces of plastic wrap crosswise on a work surface (colored wrap is for photo purposes only). Place the pan's base in the center on top of the plastic.

Gather the outer pieces of the wrap and place in the center of the base. Securely attach the outer ring, then lift out the wrap to line the sides.

2 **Building the walls**
Stand ladyfingers around sides so they fit snugly—if needed, halve 1 or 2 to fill in. Also place them snugly (flat side down) on bottom to cover as much of the base as possible.

3 **Constructing the layers**
Brush sides and bottom with coffee and spread 1 1/4 cups custard on bottom layer. Top custard with a second ladyfinger layer, dab with coffee, then spread with 1 1/4 cups custard. Add a third ladyfinger layer, coffee, and remaining custard.

4 **Putting on the "roof"**
On the last custard layer, arrange some ladyfingers in a daisy pattern, brush with coffee, then place more ladyfingers between the "petals." Fill center with torn ladyfingers, brush with coffee, and chill.

loaf pan option

The unveiling

5 **Unwrapping**
To unmold, release the side of the pan and lift it away from the base. Pull plastic down and away from sides of cake, and lift base away from the plastic. Transfer tiramisù to a serving platter while still on the base—*do not* remove it. It is too fragile to move from the base.

◄ Prepare the custard as on Page 39 (you will not use it all for this option); have ready 3 packages of ladyfingers. Spray a 9x5x3" (approximately) loaf pan with nonstick spray, then line the bottom and sides with plastic wrap.

Place ladyfingers along sides of the pan, then on the bottom (round side down), making sure they fit snugly. Brush with coffee and top with a layer of custard (about 1 cup). Layer with ladyfingers, coffee, and custard two more times, ending with a layer of ladyfingers. Wrap and chill. ►

6 **Final touches**
Just before serving, dust the cake with a good amount of cocoa powder. If done too far ahead, the cocoa will soak up moisture and darken in spots—just redust those areas. Slice tiramisù into wedges and serve with strawberries.

◄ To unmold, remove top layer of plastic and invert pan onto serving platter. Gravity should pull the tiramisù out of the pan. Remove plastic wrap.

Before serving, dust tiramisù with cocoa powder, then slice. If you cut between each ladyfinger lining the top for each slice, this tiramisù serves 7–8. ►

from **our** readers

Q&A
questions & answers

ROASTING OR BAKING?
What does "roasting" mean? How is it different than baking?
Gene Davidson
St. Louis, MO

The biggest factor that sets roasting apart from baking is high oven temperature. It causes food to truly roast, resulting in a crusted, caramelized exterior with deep flavor. That high temperature offers an extra bonus—shorter cooking time!

But there are other factors that create roasting. It requires some fat, either natural or added. And whether cooking meats or vegetables, use low-sided dishes or pans and leave uncovered. High sides and lids encourage steaming instead of roasting.

VANILLA MINUS ALCOHOL
Is it possible to purchase vanilla extract without alcohol in it?
Vyctoria Ullah
Wallingford, CT

No, it is not possible to purchase *pure* vanilla extract without alcohol. Pure vanilla extract must follow a standard of identity that requires it contain at least 35% alcohol.

However there are a couple of options. Many (though not all) of the imitation vanillas are alcohol-free—you'll have to read the labels. There is also a product called Cookbook Vanilla that uses real vanilla bean extractives, but contains no alcohol. It's available at Trader Joe's grocery stores.

PLASTIC WRAP
I've heard of people using plastic wrap in the oven. Is it safe?
Kim Murphy
Fort Wayne, IN

We checked with the leading manufacturers and they all gave the same resounding answer, "We do *not* recommend it!"

Plastic wrap is primarily meant for food storage in the refrigerator. Each brand has a slightly different softening or melting point, but all will break down and melt onto dishes or food if used in the oven. Most brands say their wrap can be used in the microwave as long as it's vented by peeling back the wrap for steam to escape.

KEEPING BUTTERMILK
How long can buttermilk be kept in the refrigerator? Can it be frozen?
Lucienne Mathieu
Marlborough, CT

The dairies we spoke with said that because buttermilk is cultured and low in acid, it should last well past the printed date. If properly refrigerated, you can use it up to two weeks after the date.

And yes, buttermilk can be frozen—that's good since recipes usually call for only a cup or two. To freeze, measure buttermilk into one cup portions in freezer

BROWNIE TEMPERATURE
Is the 425° temperature correct for the Palm Beach Brownies in Issue 36 ? I tried it and the edges burned.
Gloria Gallagher
Sunnyvale, CA

Yes, the 425° oven temperature is correct in the recipe for Maida Heatter's Palm Beach Brownies. Maida says that baking at a high temperature allows the inner brownie to stay moist.

But we should have included the note Maida adds with the recipe in her *Book of Great Desserts.* "When you remove the cake from the pan you might see burned and caramelized edges. (You might not—it depends on the pan.) If you do, you can leave them on or cut them off. I have friends who say this is the best part. I cut them off, but can't resist eating them."

We've had good results baking on the middle rack at 400°.

containers. Thaw in the refrigerator and be sure to shake before using. Freezing could alter the texture slightly, but it should not affect baking outcomes.

BRINING LIQUID

Can the brining liquid from the pork chops in Issue 33 be safely stored and reused?

Jeanne Hill
Locust Grove, VA

The USDA Meat and Poultry division says no. While it's true that the brine would only touch raw meat that will later be cooked, the USDA says there are just too many variables involved. It's not worth taking the chance that remaining bacteria in the brine will be transferred to other meats. They recommend discarding the brining liquid after use.

NUTRITIONAL FACTS

Do you have plans to provide nutritional information along with your recipes, including fiber content?

Lisa Johnson
Shawnee, KS

You'll find complete nutritional information for all of the recipes from each new issue on our website **CuisineAtHome.com**. Just click on Online Extras to lead you to Nutrition Facts.

We began providing these figures with Issue 35, but have recently added the dietary fiber content as well.

MUSTARD THAT'S PREPARED

I often see "prepared" mustard listed in recipes. Is it something I make or can I buy it?

Leigh Crawford
Saugerties, NY

When a recipe calls for prepared mustard, it just means the common yellow mustard typically used on hot dogs. The reason it is "prepared" is because other ingredients are mixed (prepared) with the dry mustard or seeds to create it. Technically, other mustards, like Chinese or Dijon, are prepared as well but recipes will most likely specify them by name.

LEMONGRASS

What is lemongrass and how should it be used?

Robert Ross
Jackson, MS

Long an essential ingredient in Asian cuisine, lemongrass is a reedy, grass-like stalk with a slightly bulbous base. It has an aromatic lemon scent and flavor, without the tartness of lemon.

Lemongrass is most often minced for use in everything from marinades and dressings,

PASTA QUESTION

Should I use the same amount of fresh pasta as I would dried?

Patricia Scherzinger
Silverton, OR

Fresh pasta is lighter than the denser dried pasta, so use this rule of thumb: 1 pound dried equals $1\frac{1}{4}$ to $1\frac{1}{2}$ pounds fresh, depending on the pasta brand.

to chicken and fish. First remove outer layers on the bottom third of the stalk to reveal the tender core, then mince. Or bruise and crush the stalk with the back of a knife, cut it into two-inch lengths, and add the pieces to soups, stews, or curries. The stalk is tough, however, so remove the pieces before serving.

Refrigerate up to six weeks in a plastic bag. Or wrap in foil, freeze, and break off pieces to use straight from the freezer. But don't bother with dried lemongrass—it has little flavor.

SPROUTED GARLIC

Can garlic cloves be used once they have started to sprout?

Edward M. Clemenco
San Jose, CA

Our friends at the Gilroy Garlic Festival say that once garlic has sprouted it can still be used, as long as the clove itself is still crisp. But be sure to cut the green sprout away—it can be bitter. Some garlic lovers actually believe the garlic has a milder flavor after it has sprouted.

grand**finale**

tiramisù
with raspberries

INDIVIDUAL TIRAMISÙ WITH RASPBERRIES

Build these tiramisù in clear glass serving vessels to show off the layers of cake, custard, and berries. Four-ounce coffee cups are perfect. It's fine if the cups don't match— that adds to their charm!

MAKES SIX 4-OZ. TIRAMISÙ
TOTAL TIME: ABOUT 1 HOUR + CHILLING

PREPARE FOR ASSEMBLY:
1/2   recipe custard for Tiramisù, Page 39
2   pkgs. (3 oz. each) soft ladyfingers
1 1/2 cups frozen raspberries in syrup, thawed, lightly crushed
1   cup strong coffee

DUST WITH:
    Cocoa powder

Prepare 1/2 the recipe of custard and remaining assembly items as listed on Page 39. Cool custard before assembling tiramisù.

To assemble, place about 1 tsp. berries in the bottom of each cup, then top with a ladyfinger that's been torn in half. Brush with coffee, spread with 1 tsp. berries, then top with 2–3 T. custard. Arrange two or three more pieces of torn ladyfingers on the custard, brush with coffee, and layer one more time. On the last custard layer, overlap two or three whole ladyfingers across the top. Brush with coffee, cover with plastic, and chill 4–24 hours.
Dust tops of each tiramisù with cocoa just before serving.

▲*Spoon some of the raspberries in the bottom of serving dishes. Halve ladyfingers and arrange two pieces on the berries.*

▼*Brush cake with coffee and top with additional berries. Spoon custard on top and continue layering.*

Cuisine at home®

Southern style
Pulled Pork
Perfected!

White Chocolate
Cheesecake
to die for

Seared Steaks
Steak House
results at home

3 sensational
Summer
Soups

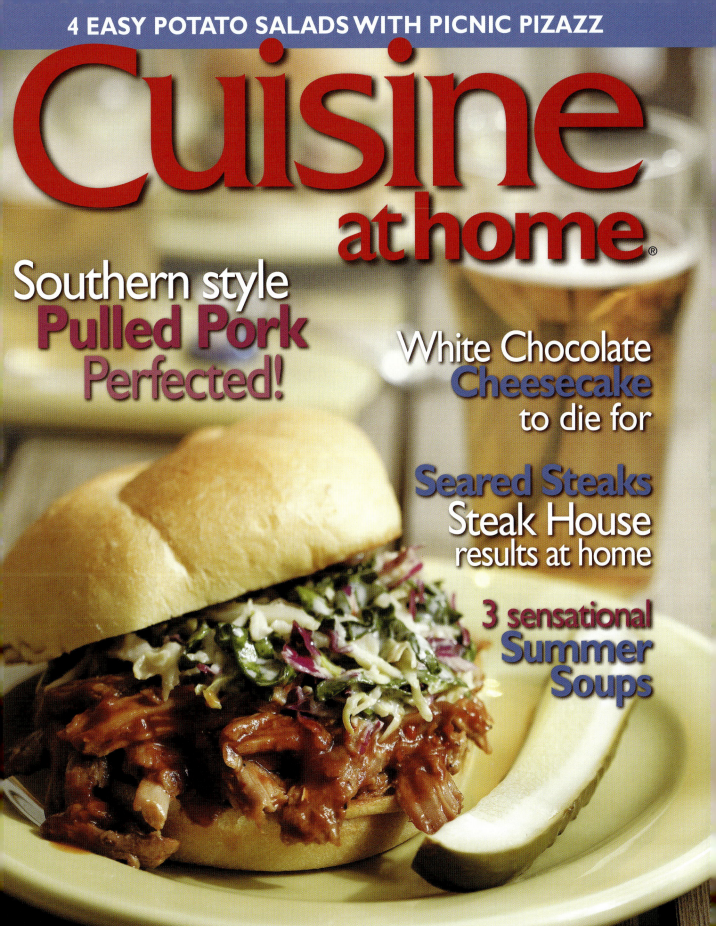

Issue No. 39 June 2003
A publication of August Home Publishing

Cuisine at home.

Publisher
Donald B. Peschke

Editor
John F. Meyer

Senior Editor
Susan Hoss

Associate Editor
Sarah Marx Feldner

Assistant Editor
Sara Ostransky

Test Kitchen Director
Kim Samuelson

Art Director
Cinda Shambaugh

Assistant Art Director
Holly Wiederin

Graphic Designer
April Walker Janning

Image Specialist
Troy Clark

Photographer
Dean Tanner

Contributing Food Stylist
Jennifer Peterson

AUGUST HOME
PUBLISHING COMPANY

Corporate:

Corporate Vice Presidents: Mary R. Scheve, Douglas L. Hicks • *Creative Director:* Ted Kralicek • *Professional Development Director:* Michal Sigel *New Media Manager:* Gordon C. Gaippe • *Senior Photographer:* Crayola England *Multi Media Art Director:* Eugene Pedersen • *Web Server Administrator:* Carol Schoeppler • *Web Content Manager:* David Briggs • *Web Designer:* Kara Blessing *Web Developer/Content Manager:* Sue M. Moe • *Controller:* Robin Hutchinson *Senior Accountant:* Laura Thomas • *Accounts Payable:* Mary Schultz • *Accounts Receivable:* Margo Petrus • *Research Coordinator:* Nick Jaeger • *Production Director:* George Chmielarz • *Pre-Press Image Specialist:* Minniette Johnson • *Electronic Publishing Director:* Douglas M. Lidster • *Systems Administrator:* Cris Schwanebeck *PC Maintenance Technician:* Robert D. Cook • *H.R. Assistant:* Kirsten Koele *Receptionist/Administrative Assistant:* Jeanne Johnson • *Mail Room Clerk:* Lou Webber • *Office Manager:* Natalie Lonsdale • *Facilities Manager:* Kurt Johnson

Customer Service & Fulfillment:

Operations Director: Bob Baker • *Customer Service Manager:* Jennie Enos *Customer Service Representatives:* Anna Cox, Kim Harlan, Cheryl Jordan, April Revell, Deborah Rich, Valerie Jo Riley, Tammy Truckenbrod • *Buyer:* Linda Jones *Administrative Assistant:* Nancy Downey • *Warehouse Supervisor:* Nancy Johnson *Fulfillment:* Sylvia Carey

Circulation:

Subscriber Services Director: Sandy Baum • *New Business Circulation Manager:* Wayde J. Klingbeil • *Promotions Analyst:* Patrick A. Walsh • *Billing and Collections Manager:* Rebecca Cunningham • *Renewal Manager:* Paige Rogers • *Circulation Marketing Analyst:* Kris Schlemmer • *Circulation Marketing Analyst:* Paula M. DeMatteis • *Art Director:* Doug Flint • *Senior Graphic Designers:* Mark Hayes, Robin Friend

www.CuisineAtHome.com

talk to *Cuisine at home*
Questions about Subscriptions and Address Changes? Write or call:

Customer Service
2200 Grand Avenue,
Des Moines, IA 50312
800-311-3995,
8 a.m. to 5 p.m., CST.

Online Subscriber Services:
www.CuisineAtHome.com
Access your account • Check a subscription payment • Tell us if you've missed an issue • Change your mailing or email address • Renew your subscription • Pay your bill

Cuisine at home® (ISSN 1537-8225) is published bi-monthly (Jan., Mar., May, July, Sept., Nov.) by August Home Publishing Co., 2200 Grand Ave., Des Moines, IA 50312. *Cuisine at home*® is a trademark of August Home Publishing Co. ©Copyright 2003 August Home Publishing. All rights reserved. Subscriptions: Single copy: $4.99. One year subscription (6 issues), $24.00. (Canada/Foreign add $10 per year, U.S. funds.)

Periodicals postage paid at Des Moines, IA and at additional mailing offices. "USPS/Perry-Judd's Heartland Division automatable poly". Postmaster: Send change of address to *Cuisine at home*®, P.O. Box 37100 Boone, IA 50037-2100. *Cuisine at home*® does not accept and is not responsible for unsolicited manuscripts. PRINTED IN CHINA

editor's letter

There's nothing that gets me more lathered up than the smell of a smoking grill, especially after enduring months of "holing up" for the winter. The anticipation of smoked meat is just a little too intense for me to handle this early in the " 'cue" season—my mouth even starts to water at the first sniff of burning lighter fluid!

But I shouldn't be surprised by these reactions. They're normal for anyone who has experienced the "yin" of a stark winter and the "yang" of warm summer days. It's not only the season opener for barbecue but a time to reacquaint yourself with all those friends who also laid low waiting out the cold. There's not a better way to kick off summer than with a Southern tradition called a pig pickin'. You have to try this because it's a hoot—here's how it works.

Normally, a whole pig is roasted, but for you first-timers, start with pork shoulder. The meat is smoked and slow-roasted until it practically falls off the bone. Keep the meat warm, ice down plenty of beverages, and set the picnic table with an assortment of BBQ sauces and a wide array of side dishes. Leave the center of the table open for the smoked pork.

With everything in place, your friends gathered and *standing* around the table, plop the smoked pork shoulders right in the middle of everything. Now you're ready to eat! Everyone starts picking at the pork, pulling off bite-size pieces with their fingers— yes, use your fingers! Then simply dip those tender morsels into a favorite BBQ sauce and "pop"... right into your mouth.

It's not dinner, but a happening—a pig pickin' happening. The interaction of eating and socializing becomes every bit as important as the food and process itself. The recipe begins on Page 18 and tells you everything you need to know about roasting a pork shoulder to fall-off-the-bone perfection. It'll be up to you to bring the fun, enthusiasm, and spirit of friendship. Have a blast with your new tradition!

table of contents

from **our** readers

tips
and techniques

Quick Toast

To toast coconut quickly, microwave it. Spread 1 cup shredded coconut on a 10" microwavable plate. Microwave on high 3–4 minutes, stirring at 30 second intervals, until lightly browned. Coconut's high oil content helps keep it from burning.

Julia Glynn
Alexandria, VA

Storing Ice Cream

To prevent ice crystals from forming on ice cream, place a piece of waxed paper or plastic wrap directly on the surface. Press it firmly onto the ice cream so that it forms a tight seal. Cover with the lid and return to the freezer.

Katie Kyles
St. Augustine, FL

Vanilla Powdered Sugar

To flavor powdered sugar with vanilla, store a split vanilla bean in it. Keep the bean in the sugar for at least two weeks to impart a strong vanilla flavor, then sprinkle the sugar over pastries and desserts. Icing made with vanilla-flavored powdered sugar is whiter in color—there's no need to add dark vanilla extract!

Kathy Sayler
Hagerstown, MD

Microwave Dehydrator

When fresh parsley and cilantro are in season, stock up, then dry them in your microwave!

Wash the herbs and spin dry in a salad spinner. Place the clean leaves on a paper towel-lined plate, then microwave to dry. Ovens vary in power, but microwave the herbs on high for two minutes, fluff the leaves, then cook another 1–2 minutes.

Be sure the leaves are totally dry and crisp before storing, otherwise they could mold. Cool completely, then store in an airtight jar or plastic bag.

Nancy Knobel
Fontana, CA

Editors note: Whole basil leaves dried this way stay bright green! One to two minutes on high, rotating halfway through, is perfect.

Slick Slicing

To prevent potatoes from sticking to the knife while slicing, spray the blade with cooking spray before and during slicing. This keeps starch from building up on the blade.

Janet Curry
Houston, TX

Thin Is In

I like thinly shredded cabbage in coleslaw, but using a knife for shredding is difficult, even if the blade is really sharp. So, to shred cabbage thinly, first cut the head in half and remove the core. Then cut the halves into quarters. With a Y-shaped peeler, start "peeling" the flat surfaces of each cabbage quarter to create thin shreds. When the quarters get too small to shred with a peeler, just use a knife to finish the job.

Monica Velgos
Cambridge, MA

Paper Liner

To keep condensation off of lettuce, line a storage container with paper towels. Add cleaned lettuce leaves and top with another paper towel layer. The paper absorbs excess moisture. This works with fruits and other vegetables too.

Amy Carpenter
Austin, TX

Great Shakes

Use a small grated Parmesan cheese shaker (like the ones used in pizza parlors) to hold kosher salt for cooking or use at the dinner table. The bigger holes work well for dispensing the large kosher salt crystals.

Marian Schaer
Clinton, CT

Test Kitchen Tip

Don't toss the stems from fresh herbs like parsley and cilantro. Finely chop them and use to flavor sauces, soups, and stews. Reserve the leaves for garnishing.

Freezing Bananas

When you have a surplus of ripe bananas, wrap them airtight and place in the freezer. Peel with a knife and use in smoothies, or thaw and use in muffins and breads.

Laura Marx
Wauwatosa, WI

Grease Trapper

To degrease stock, skim the surface of the liquid with a loosely crumpled piece of plastic wrap—it attracts grease like a magnet. Repeat the process with new plastic until the fat is gone.

Jan Plunk
Silsbee, TX

Oiling Foods

To prevent sticky, baked-on oil buildup on baking sheets, brush the food with oil instead of applying oil directly to the pan. This also helps prevent the oil's tendency to bead up on the pan.

Sarah Sandahl
Rochester, NY

Ricing Guacamole

For perfectly textured guacamole, use a potato ricer. Place large chunks of avocado into the ricer and press right into a bowl. Scrape the outside of the ricer with a spatula, then stir in remaining ingredients.

Sue Rush
Prescott, AZ

Mashed Mint

To get the most flavor from fresh mint, bruise the leaves. Place the sprigs in a plastic bag and smash them with a meat mallet. This releases their oils—perfect for lemonade and iced or hot tea.

April Thrun
San Francisco, CA

share your **tips** with *Cuisine at home*
and techniques

If you have a unique way of solving a cooking problem, we'd like to hear from you, and we'll consider publishing your tip. Just write down your cooking tip and mail it to *Cuisine at home*, Tips Editor, 2200 Grand Ave., Des Moines, IA 50312, or contact us through our email address shown below. Include your name, address, and daytime phone number. If we publish your tip, we'll give you a year's subscription of *Cuisine at home* to be used by you or a friend.

Email: CuisineAtHome@CuisineAtHome.com
Web address: CuisineAtHome.com

Steak House Searing

A $50 meal in your own dining room?

It's so easy, you may never eat out again!

Nothing beats a meal at a swank steak house, but dropping a huge wad of cash on dinner out isn't always an option. Luckily, steak house steaks *can* happen at home.

At the forefront for success are good, *thick* tenderloin filets. Buy them already cut, or trim a tenderloin yourself. It's not hard and, if you're feeding a lot of people, is often more economical.

Once you have the steaks, use this practically foolproof two-part technique to cook them to perfection. First, sear the filets on the stove over fairly high heat. This creates a deep brown crust that's key to the meat's flavor and texture. Next, use an old restaurant trick and transfer the filets to the oven to finish cooking.

The result? Steaks so awesome you'd swear you were eating out—except for the sinful of dinner dishes!

Look at labels
*"Peeled" means fat has been removed from the tenderloin— that's fine. "Butt" means the package contains thick, oddly shaped butt pieces. Do **not** buy it!*

SEARED BEEF TENDERLOIN FILETS

MAKES SEVEN OR EIGHT 8-OZ. FILETS
TOTAL TIME: ABOUT 40 MINUTES

TRIM, CUT, AND SEASON:
1   6-lb. whole beef tenderloin
SEAR FILETS IN:
2   T. olive or vegetable oil
SERVE WITH:
      Bernaise Sauce and Boursin Creamed Spinach, *Pages 8–9*

Preheat oven to 425° with a rack in the center.

Trim tenderloin and cut into filets; season with salt and pepper. Heat an ovenproof pan over medium-high heat for 5 minutes.

Sear filets in oil on one side for 4–5 minutes. Turn them over, place the pan in the oven, and roast to desired doneness, *see chart, right*. Allow filets to rest 5 minutes before serving.

Serve with sauce and spinach.

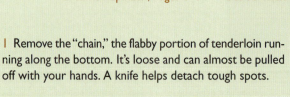

1   Remove the "chain," the flabby portion of tenderloin running along the bottom. It's loose and can almost be pulled off with your hands. A knife helps detach tough spots.

Trimming and cooking

Trimming a tenderloin is no big deal, but you *have* to buy the right thing: a whole, untrimmed, six- to eight-pound tenderloin.

Read labels (see left) and inspect packaging carefully. It's not unusual to find big pieces packed together to resemble a whole tenderloin. Do *not* buy it like this—the pieces are uneven and make misshapen filets. I've found whole tenderloins at grocery warehouses like Sam's Club for $10–$12 a pound. Butchers may also carry them but, at $15–$20 a pound, pre-cut filets are a better (and easier) choice.

To trim a tenderloin, first remove the "chain," a ropy piece of meat and fat, *Figure 1* (it looks like scrap but, trimmed of fat, is great in stews). Now remove the silverskin surrounding much of the tenderloin, *Figure 2*. It's super-

2 Trim away the membrane (silverskin) and fat covering the tenderloin.

tough and won't melt with cooking. Finally, remove the "butt" and "tail" (use them in sautes or stir-fries), then cut the large center portion into filets, *Figure 3*.

Cooking the filets is the easy part—sear them, then finish in the oven. The ticket to searing is a *hot* pan, so first heat a heavy, ovenproof skillet or saute pan on the stove for five minutes. If searing more than four filets, use two pans. After heating the pan, add oil and sear the filets well on one side, *Figure 4*. Don't forget to turn an exhaust fan on now—it can get smoky! Resist the urge to

3 Remove the thick butt and thin tail sections, then cut the center piece into 2"-thick filets—you should get 6–8 steaks.

move the filets, as constant contact with the pan creates that crust. Turn the steaks over, *Figure 5*, then finish them in the oven.

Use the chart below to determine doneness times. Don't rely on internal temperature—thermometer holes cause juices to leak. And be sure to let the steaks rest before serving, *Figure 6*.

4 Sear filets in hot saute pan for 5 minutes over medium-high heat.

5 Turn filets over and transfer to oven. Roast 5–9 min. to desired doneness, *right*.

6 Allow filets to rest for 5 min. before serving. This helps redistribute juices through the meat.

Doneness

RARE
Sear: 5 minutes
Roast: 5 minutes
Rest: 5 minutes

MEDIUM-RARE
Sear: 5 minutes
Roast: 7 minutes
Rest: 5 minutes

MEDIUM
Sear: 5 minutes
Roast: 9 minutes
Rest: 5 minutes

On the Side

In order to be great, a good steak needs a sauce and a side dish. These updated classics fit the bill perfectly.

If you're going to make tenderloin filets on Pages 6–7, it's imperative to pull out all the stops with these sides. Bernaise sauce (a hollandaise jazzed up with tarragon) is a classic with filets, so simple you won't believe it's a fancy French sauce.

Creamed spinach is standard steak house fare—and usually pretty mediocre. But this one made with creamy Boursin [boor-SAHN] cheese breathes new life into the dish. The recipe doesn't make much, but a little goes a long way!

BERNAISE SAUCE

MAKES 1½ CUPS
TOTAL TIME: ABOUT 20 MINUTES

BRING TO A BOIL; REDUCE:
¼ cup white wine vinegar
¼ cup dry white wine
3 T. shallots, minced
1 T. chopped fresh tarragon

OFF HEAT, ADD:
2–3 T. water
4 egg yolks

GRADUALLY DRIZZLE IN:
1 cup (2 sticks) unsalted butter, melted

STRAIN; SEASON WITH:
Juice of half a lemon, salt, white pepper, and cayenne to taste

Bring vinegar, wine, shallots, and tarragon to a boil in a small saucepan over medium-high heat. Boil until liquid is evaporated, about 5 minutes.
Off heat, add water, then whisk in egg yolks until frothy.
Gradually drizzle in butter, whisking constantly to incorporate. Sauce should be thick, but thin it with a little water if needed. If it's too thin, return it to low heat and whisk constantly until thickened.
Strain sauce through a medium-mesh strainer into a heatproof cup. Season with lemon juice, salt, white, and cayenne peppers.

Whisk egg yolks into reduced wine-water mixture. ▼

▲ *Gradually drizzle in butter, whisking constantly until thick.*

Hold the sauce ▶
To keep the Bernaise warm for serving, place the cup into a pan of warm water set over low heat. Stir often to keep sauce smooth.

BOURSIN CREAMED SPINACH

You can find Boursin (a soft herb and garlic cheese spread) in the deli section of most grocery stores.

MAKES ABOUT 2 CUPS
TOTAL TIME: ABOUT 1 HOUR

SAUTE IN 1 T. UNSALTED BUTTER:
1/2   cup yellow onion, diced
ADD:
2   T. all-purpose flour
GRADUALLY WHISK IN:
1   cup whole or 2% milk
1/2   cup heavy cream
STIR IN:
1   pkg. (5.2 oz.) Boursin cheese
ADD:
1   pkg. (10 oz.) frozen chopped
      spinach, thawed, squeezed
      dry of excess moisture
2   T. Parmesan cheese, grated
1   t. lemon zest, minced
      Salt, white pepper, cayenne,
      and nutmeg to taste
COMBINE; TOP SPINACH WITH:
2/3   cup coarse fresh bread
      crumbs (made from two
      slices firm white bread)
1   T. unsalted butter, melted
1   T. olive oil
      Salt and black pepper to taste

▲ *Stir Boursin into sauce a little at a time until fully incorporated and smooth.*

Cover spinach with a thick coat of crumbs. Bake while you prepare the steaks. ▶

▲ *Add spinach, Parmesan, zest, and seasonings to cheese sauce.*

Preheat oven to 425°; coat a shallow 2-cup baking dish with nonstick spray and set aside.
Saute onion in butter in a large saucepan over medium heat. Cook until onion is soft, 5 min.
Add flour and stir to coat onion. Cook about 1 minute.
Gradually whisk milk and cream into onion mixture, stirring constantly to prevent lumps. Simmer sauce for 1 minute.
Stir in Boursin a little at a time until melted and smooth. Remove saucepan from heat.
Add spinach, Parmesan, lemon zest, and seasonings. Transfer spinach to prepared baking dish.
Combine crumbs, butter, oil, and seasonings. Top spinach with crumbs, packing them to adhere. (Dish may be covered and chilled at this point to be baked later.) Place dish on a baking sheet and bake until crumbs are golden and sauce is bubbly, 20–25 minutes.

Steak au Poivre
with Brandy Cream Sauce

This steak house standard may seem run-of-the-mill, but its easy elegance is worth revisiting. Like maybe for dinner tonight?

Tenderloin filet is a great steak, but my favorite has got to be steak au poivre [oh PWAHV-r]. It's a big, flavorful strip steak (one feeds two people!) coated with a pungent peppercorn crust that's tamed by a rich cream sauce.

The key lies in the pepper coating. Black and white peppercorns, plus a few mustard seeds, give this crust more depth than one made of straight black peppercorns. Take care not to crush them too much—like fresh garlic, pepper gets stronger and hotter as it's ground.

Just *one* side of the steaks is coated. Doing this tempers the pepper's heat a little and provides a clean side for searing (as with the tenderloin, *Page 7*). That searing step imparts flavor to the meat and creates a base on which to build the brandy cream sauce.

STEAK AU POIVRE WITH BRANDY CREAM SAUCE

TOTAL TIME: ABOUT 30 MINUTES

FOR THE STEAKS—
COARSELY CRUSH:

2	T. whole black peppercorns
1	T. whole white peppercorns
2	t. whole yellow mustard seeds

COAT; SEAR IN 2 T. OIL:

2	1-lb. strip steaks, 2" thick

FOR THE SAUCE—
SAUTE IN 1 T. UNSALTED BUTTER:

1/4	cup shallots, minced

STIR IN; REDUCE:

1/2	cup heavy cream
1/4	cup brandy
1	T. Dijon mustard

FINISH WITH:

1	T. fresh lemon juice
1	t. minced fresh thyme
	Salt and cayenne to taste

Preheat oven to 425°, rack in center.
Coarsely crush peppercorns and mustard seeds for the steaks in a resealable freezer bag using a meat mallet, skillet, or rolling pin. Spread the coating onto a plate.
Coat one side of the steaks with an even layer of the peppercorn mixture. Liberally season the other side with salt; set aside until ready to sear.

Heat a large ovenproof saute pan over medium-high heat for 5 minutes, as on Page 7. Add oil then sear steaks, peppercorn side up, until brown and crusty, 4–5 minutes. Carefully turn steaks over, place pan in the oven, and roast to desired doneness, *Page 7*. Transfer to a platter and allow steaks to rest while making sauce.
Saute shallots in butter for the sauce over medium heat until soft, using the pan the steaks were in.
Stir in cream, brandy, and mustard. Simmer until thickened, 3–4 minutes.
Finish sauce with lemon juice, thyme, salt, and cayenne. Serve immediately with the steaks.

When crushing the peppercorns, aim for a texture similar to Grape Nuts cereal. A meat mallet is great for this job, but a rolling pin or the bottom of a small, heavy skillet works just fine too. ▶

◀ Spread the coating onto a plate, then press one side of a steak into it; fill in any bare spots by hand. Now season the uncoated side with salt.

For a great seared crust, heat the saute pan for 5 minutes before adding the steaks, peppercorn side up. Sear for 5 minutes, or until a deep brown crust forms.

Don't move the steaks around during searing—constant contact with the pan's surface creates the best crust. Carefully turn the steaks over and transfer to the oven to finish. ▶

◀ After roasting, remove steaks and let them rest while you make the sauce. Use the same pan the steaks were in, but don't forget—it's really hot! Saute the shallots in butter until soft, then add the brandy, cream, and mustard.

Reduce sauce, finish with lemon juice, thyme, and seasonings, then pour it right over the steaks. It will blend with any juices from the steaks for one more layer of flavor. ▶

faster **with** fewer

potato salads

With summer upon us, potato salad season isn't far behind! These four are guaranteed to spark up your picnics.

CLASSIC POTATO SALAD

"Marinating" the potatoes in pickle juice is key to this salad's flavor. Take care not to overcook the potatoes—test them often.
MAKES 5 CUPS; TOTAL TIME: ABOUT 30 MINUTES

1 1/2	lb. white potatoes, unpeeled, cubed
2	eggs
1/4	cup sweet pickle juice
1/2	cup mayonnaise
1/2	cup sweet gherkins (whole baby pickles), chopped
1/2	cup celery, diced
1/4	cup scallions, chopped
2	T. chopped fresh parsley
1	T. prepared yellow mustard
1	t. sugar
	Salt, pepper, and cayenne to taste

Boil potatoes and eggs in salted water to cover. Cook just until potatoes are tender, 12–15 minutes. Drain; set eggs aside to cool.

Toss hot potatoes with pickle juice in a bowl; cool to room temperature. Peel and slice eggs into 1/4"-thick rounds.

Combine remaining ingredients in a separate bowl. Gently stir in potatoes and eggs. Serve salad cold or at room temperature.

WARM GERMAN POTATO SALAD WITH KIELBASA

Roasting the potatoes gives this traditional tangy-sweet salad a more complex flavor. The kielbasa makes it hearty.
MAKES 6 CUPS; TOTAL TIME: ABOUT 30 MINUTES

1 1/2	lb. red potatoes, sliced into 1/4"-thick rounds
1	T. olive oil
	Salt and pepper to taste
1/2	lb. smoked kielbasa, sliced into 1/4"-thick rounds
1	T. olive oil
1/2	cup yellow onion, diced
1/3	cup apple cider vinegar
2	T. olive oil
2	T. brown sugar
1	T. Dijon mustard
2	t. minced fresh thyme
1/2	cup celery, diced
	Salt and pepper to taste

Preheat oven to 450° with rack in lower third. Coat baking sheet with nonstick spray.

Toss potatoes with oil, salt, and pepper on the prepared baking sheet. Arrange in a single layer and roast for 10 minutes. Stir potatoes and continue roasting until browned and cooked through, about 10 more minutes.

Saute kielbasa in 1 T. oil in a large skillet over medium-high heat. Brown on both sides, about 5 minutes.

Add onion and saute until soft and lightly browned, 3 minutes.

Stir in vinegar, 2 T. oil, sugar, mustard, and thyme; simmer 3–4 minutes. Keep warm while potatoes roast.

Add celery, salt, and pepper to kielbasa mixture just before potatoes are done— not too soon or celery will lose its green color. Drizzle warm dressing over potatoes and toss gently with a spatula to coat. Serve salad warm.

SPICY SWEET POTATO SALAD

Be sure the grill is on medium to low heat. Otherwise the dressing could burn due to the sugar in the jelly.

MAKES 4 CUPS; TOTAL TIME: ABOUT 30 MINUTES

3   strips thick-sliced bacon, diced
1/2   cup red onion, slivered
1/4   cup hot jalapeño jelly
2   T. apple cider vinegar
     Salt to taste
1 1/2 lb. sweet potatoes, peeled, cut into 1" cubes
1/4   cup chopped fresh cilantro
1–2 jalapeños, sliced
2   T. scallions, sliced
     Lime juice to taste

Stir in potato cubes to coat with sauce; transfer to the prepared foil. Gather ends and sides of foil and fold to close.

Preheat grill to medium (or the oven to 450° with rack in the center). Arrange two large sheets of foil in a "+" pattern; lightly coat with nonstick spray.

Saute bacon in a skillet over medium heat until crisp. Pour off fat; leave bacon in the pan.

Add onion and saute until soft and brown, about 5 minutes.

Whisk in the jelly, vinegar, and salt; simmer until smooth.

Place bundle on the grill (or on a baking sheet and then in the oven); cook until potatoes are tender, 20–25 minutes. Transfer to a serving dish.

Before serving, top potatoes with cilantro, chiles, scallions, and lime juice. Serve salad warm or at room temperature.

CAESAR POTATO SALAD

Use store-bought croutons or make your own for this salad. The sieved egg garnish is optional, but pretty.

MAKES 6 CUPS; TOTAL TIME: ABOUT 30 MINUTES

1 1/2 lb. red potatoes, unpeeled, cubed
1   egg
1/4   cup fresh lemon juice
3   T. extra-virgin olive oil
2   T. Parmesan cheese, grated
1   T. Dijon mustard
2   t. sugar
1   t. garlic, minced
1/2   t. anchovy paste, *optional*
     Generous amount of black pepper
1   cup romaine leaves, cut into strips
1   cup salad croutons
     Sieved hard-boiled egg

Boil potatoes and egg in salted water to cover. Cook just until potatoes are tender, 12–15 minutes. Drain; set egg aside to cool.

Combine lemon juice, oil, Parmesan, mustard, sugar, garlic, anchovy paste, and pepper in a bowl while potatoes cook.

Toss hot potatoes in dressing and let sit for 10 minutes. Add romaine and croutons.

Garnish with bits of hard-boiled egg that's been pushed through a sieve. Serve salad warm or room temperature.

savory summer
Soups

summer
soup
menu

Mulligatawny Soup

Toasted pita bread

Pineapple sherbet

Soup in the summer? Not a typical combination, but it makes an ideal light meal for the season.

Putting away winter wool sweaters is a rite of passage this time of year. Appetites are also inclined to "pack up" the stews, chili, and soups of winter. Lighter, brighter flavors of salads, sandwiches, or *anything* off the grill are much more appealing.

But it's time to rethink that. Soup *does* work in warmer weather. First, it's light—a bowl of soup and some bread is often all you need to keep going. Second, soups are quick to make and don't require an oven. Finally, they're a perfect way to use some of the spectacular vegetables that are starting to flood the produce aisles and farmers markets. So go ahead and fire up that soup pot. You've waited all winter for this!

Mulligatawny Soup

If you're still dubious about eating soup in warm weather, think about this: These three soups all originate from fairly warm geographical areas. For instance, this mulligatawny [muhl-ih-guh-TAW-nee], or "pepper water," is from southern India. Not exactly the frozen tundra.

This soup is fairly spicy, but that's a good thing. It'll actually help cool you down. For a tamer dish, use less cayenne, back off on the jalapeño, or use a mild curry powder. Heat levels vary with brands—you may have to experiment.

But don't eliminate the heat altogether. Coconut milk helps buffer spiciness, as do the rice, cilantro, and Mango-Apple Salad.

MAKES ABOUT 8 CUPS
TOTAL TIME: 50 MINUTES

FOR THE SALAD—
COMBINE AND SET ASIDE:
1 mango, peeled, diced
1 Granny Smith apple, diced
   Juice of 1 lime

FOR THE SOUP—
SAUTE IN 3 T. VEGETABLE OIL:
2 lb. boneless, skinless chicken thighs, cut into 2" pieces, seasoned with salt and pepper

ADD AND SAUTE:
1 cup yellow onion, sliced
3 T. curry powder
2 T. garlic, minced
2 T. fresh ginger, minced
2 jalapeños, seeded, minced
$1/4$ t. cayenne

STIR IN; SIMMER:
4 cups low-sodium chicken broth
1 cup tomatoes, seeded, diced
$1/4$ cup chopped fresh cilantro

MELT; WHISK IN:
2 T. unsalted butter
2 T. all-purpose flour
2 cups strained soup broth

FINISH WITH:
1 can (14 oz.) lite coconut milk

SERVE AND GARNISH WITH:
   Cooked basmati rice
   Mango-Apple Salad
   Toasted coconut

Combine mango, apple, and lime juice for the salad; set aside.
Saute chicken in oil in a soup pot over medium-high heat, about 5 minutes, stirring constantly.
Add onion, curry, garlic, ginger, jalapeño, and cayenne; saute until onion is soft, 4–5 minutes.
Stir in broth, tomatoes, and cilantro. Bring to a boil, reduce heat, and simmer 10 minutes.
Melt butter in a medium saucepan, then whisk in flour. Add about 2 cups strained soup broth and whisk to combine (return solids back to the soup pot). Simmer flour mixture for 1 minute, then stir into soup. Cook soup 2 minutes to thicken.
Finish with coconut milk.
Serve soup over basmati rice, garnished with Mango-Apple Salad and toasted coconut.

▼ *Peel mango, slice lobes from both sides of pit, then dice for the salad.*

Saute chicken until cooked through. Add onion, garlic, ginger, jalapeños, and spices. Cook until onion softens. ▶

▲ *Strain soup broth into the flour-butter mixture. Simmer 1 minute to thicken.*

Stir thickened broth mixture back into pot; simmer 2 minutes. ▼

Peanut Soup with Mustard Greens

Peanuts are a staple in African cooking and make an intriguing base for this soup—in the form of peanut butter. Mustard greens add kick, but if you prefer, use spinach (just don't saute it first).

MAKES 8 CUPS
TOTAL TIME: 40 MINUTES

menu

Peanut Soup with
Mustard Greens

Sweet potato salad

Brownies

SAUTE IN 2 T. VEGETABLE OIL:
1   cup yellow onion, diced
ADD:
1/2   cup carrot, diced
1/2   cup celery, diced
1/4   cup red bell pepper, diced
1   T. garlic, minced
1   T. chili powder
1   t. kosher salt
1/2   t. cayenne

ADD AND SIMMER:
4   cups low-sodium chicken
     broth
2   cups cooked chicken breast,
     shredded
1   can (14.5 oz.) diced tomatoes
STIR IN:
1/2   cup creamy peanut butter
1/4   cup dry instant couscous
SAUTE IN 2 T. OLIVE OIL:
4   cups mustard greens,
     stemmed, chopped
     Salt to taste
GARNISH WITH:
     Chopped dry roasted
     peanuts and chopped
     scallions (green parts only)

Saute onion in oil in a soup pot over medium-high heat until softened, about 4 minutes.
Add carrot, celery, bell pepper, garlic, and seasonings. Cook about 4 minutes, stirring often.
Add broth, chicken, and tomatoes. Bring to a boil, reduce heat to low, and simmer 10 minutes.
Stir in peanut butter and couscous. Cover, remove from heat, and allow to sit 5 minutes.
Saute mustard greens in oil in a large saute pan over high heat. Cook, stirring frequently, just until wilted, 3–4 minutes. Season greens with salt; stir into soup.
Garnish each serving with peanuts and scallions.

For easy cleanup, coat cup with nonstick spray before measuring in the peanut butter. ▼

▲ *Saute greens over high heat, tossing frequently. Season with salt, then add to the soup.*

Peel and devein shrimp. Slice shrimp in half lengthwise—it'll curl up like a corkscrew when cooked. ▼

▲ *Add okra, scallions, reserved shrimp and bacon before serving. Let sit 5 minutes off heat.*

Louisiana Shrimp Gumbo

Gumbo gets its name from the African word for okra, a standard gumbo ingredient which helps to thicken the soup. But don't cook okra long—it will turn stringy.

menu

Shrimp Gumbo

Corn muffins

Key lime pie

MAKES 8 CUPS; TOTAL TIME: 1 HOUR

SLICE IN HALF:
| 1 | lb. medium shrimp (31–35 count), peeled, deveined |

FRY:
| 6 | strips (½ lb.) thick-sliced bacon, diced |

SAUTE IN 2 T. DRIPPINGS; REMOVE:
Prepared shrimp

SAUTE IN 3 T. DRIPPINGS:
1	cup yellow onion, diced
½	cup celery, diced
½	cup red bell pepper, diced
1	T. garlic, minced

COMBINE; STIR IN:
¼	cup all-purpose flour
1	t. dried oregano
1	t. dried thyme
1	t. dried basil
1	t. kosher salt
1	t. black pepper
1	t. cayenne

DEGLAZE WITH:
3	T. fresh lemon juice
2	T. dry sherry
1	T. Worcestershire sauce

ADD:
3	cups bottled clam juice
1½	cups low-sodium chicken broth
½	cup converted-style rice

STIR IN:
| 1 | cup frozen sliced okra |
| ¼ | cup scallions, chopped Reserved shrimp and bacon |

GARNISH WITH:
Chopped celery leaves

Slice shrimp in half lengthwise.
Fry bacon until crisp in a large soup pot over medium-high heat.

Remove, drain on paper towels, and set aside. Pour off bacon drippings, reserving 5 T. Return the pot to the burner.

Saute shrimp in 2 T. drippings for 3 minutes over medium heat, stirring constantly. Remove shrimp and set aside.

Saute onion, celery, bell pepper, and garlic in 3 T. drippings for 3–4 minutes, stirring constantly.

Combine flour and seasonings; stir into vegetables. Cook 2 minutes, stirring constantly.

Deglaze with lemon juice, sherry, and Worcestershire, scraping up bits from the bottom of the pot.

Add the clam juice, broth, and rice. Bring to a boil, cover, reduce heat to low, and cook 20 minutes.

Stir in okra, scallions, shrimp, and bacon. Remove from heat and let sit for 5 minutes.

Garnish with celery leaves.

Barbecued Pulled Pork

Grilling outside is one of those simple pleasures in life.

But slow-roasting pork until it's fall-off-the-bone tender

yet still juicy, hits another level. It's XTREME barbecue!

It doesn't matter whether you're putting on a pig pickin' or just serving sandwiches, pork has to be barbecued to perfection. That's not as easy as it seems. You have to consider four key concepts to successful pork cookery.

First, make sure you buy the right cut. It should have plenty of fat to flavor the meat as it slow-roasts. Second, the fat has to melt away enough so the meat isn't greasy, but not so much as to dry it out—a delicate balance. Third, flavor comes from a good rub, sauce, and plenty of smoke. Finally, like for most of us, rest does wonders—give it plenty!

BARBECUED PORK RUB
FOR ONE 8-LB. PORK SHOULDER

COMBINE:
- 1/4 cup kosher salt
- 1/4 cup black pepper
- 1/4 cup chili powder
- 1 T. dried oregano
- 1 T. dried thyme
- 1 t. cayenne

COAT:
- 1 8 lb. pork shoulder (Boston butt)

Combine all rub seasonings.
Coat the shoulder with the rub, massaging it into the meat.

Grilling set up

Before the pork hits the fire, both the meat and the grill have to be just right. So from your first step into the grocery store to actually lighting the grill, success will be in planning and preparation.

Cut of meat: Go for about an eight-pound pork shoulder, but read the sidebar "Buying Shoulder" before shopping. Selecting a tender, high quality cut of pork (like loin) will result in disaster! A tougher cut that has plenty of fat and connective tissues will withstand the long exposure to the heat.

Indirect heat: Grilling indirectly is for cuts of meat that take a long time to cook (it's like baking in the oven). Set up the grill so that half has fire and the other half does not. Cooking is done on the area where there is no fire underneath, but there's still plenty of heat.

This can be done easily on both gas or charcoal grills. For a gas grill, simply turn one burner on medium-high, keeping the other burner turned off. For a charcoal grill, when the briquets have turned white, rake them around the sides and cook the meat in the middle of the grate.

Smoke: Whether you use a gas or charcoal grill, you'll need smoke for authentic barbecue flavor. Creating it on a charcoal grill is a no-brainer—just add pieces of water soaked wood directly onto briquets. Aromatic woods like hickory, apple, mesquite, or cherry deliver plenty of that real barbecue flavor you want.

But gas grills are a different story. Ashes from the burning wood could clog the burners, so wrap pieces of dry wood in an aluminum packet shaped like a beggar's purse—this allows smoke to escape easily. Then put the packet on the grilling grate directly over the fire.

PORK BOSTON BUTT CRYOVAC

BUYING SHOULDER

Should you buy pork shoulder or pork butt? Buy either one because they are identical. Confused? While it sounds like they're at opposite ends of the pig, in reality, they're the same.

The term "butt" actually refers to the barrels used in colonial days to store and ship the less desirable cuts of pork earmarked for curing. This cut is similar to beef chuck and has to be cooked slowly in order to appreciate its wonderful flavor.

Can't find a shoulder? No problem. It's a common cut and your butcher should be able to order it easily.

1 Place chunks of wood in a foil pack—use two layers. Bundle packet leaving a hole at the top so smoke can escape.

2 Coat shoulder with rub. No need to let it sit—it'll have plenty of time to absorb flavors on the grill.

3 Preheat one side of grill to med.-high. Place smoke packet over the fire, drip pan under unlit side.

4 Place pork over drip pan and grill for 3 hours. Check every hour to make sure there's plenty of smoke.

grilling for pulled pork

I'm going to insult every barbecuing purist with this method of grilling—but it works. This unorthodox step entails wrapping the shoulder in aluminum foil after it smokes, then letting it finish cooking on the grill.

Smoking: Before wrapping, smoke the shoulder for three hours for real pit barbecue flavor. Monitor this stage every hour to insure there's continual smoke. Make more packets and add them if needed.

Rotating: Rotate the meat three times for even cooking. Don't rotate anymore than this because the grill can lose too much heat each time the lid is opened.

Wrapping: Wrapping the pork shoulder in aluminum foil is not standard operating procedure for the true pitmeister, but it serves our purpose for a several reasons. First, true barbecue is supposed to use only dry heat which concentrates flavor as moisture is taken away. But by wrapping, the natural juices are recycled back into the meat, creating plenty of moisture and flavor.

Second, wrapping shortens the cooking time. Smoking a shoulder using traditional methods can take up to ten hours, but this method cuts the time in half.

Finally, using this method is forgiving. Once wrapped, you can practically forget it. Cook to an internal temperature of 180° so the fat renders but pork remains juicy.

5 Smoking takes 3 hours. Add wood packets as needed to keep plenty of smoke circulating.

6 Once smoking is complete, wrap pork in two layers of foil, crimping edges to seal in moisture. Return to grill; cook 2 hours.

Don't worry about this red ring around the meat. It's not undercooked but rather a natural reaction to the smoke. ▼

7 After 2 hours, insert thermometer into thickest part of meat. You want to hit 180°.

8 Keep foil around the meat and let rest off heat for 30 minutes. It's now ready for pulling with fork or fingers.

Root Beer
BBQ sauce

The best sauces for pork are vinegar-based. Try this one that's slightly sweetened with root beer.

Sound bizarre? Maybe, but this root beer sauce packs plenty of punch.

Vinegar is the best base since it cuts through fattier meats like this cut of pork. Adding a root beer syrup (it's easy to make) provides the unusual flavors of sassafras, cherry, wintergreen, and ginger extracts.

39

online extra

Want more sauces? Visit www.CuisineAtHome.com for more recipes for great barbecue sauces.

ROOT BEER BBQ SAUCE
MAKES 3 1/2 CUPS; TOTAL TIME: ABOUT 1 1/2 HOURS

REDUCE:
1   2-liter bottle root beer

ADD AND SIMMER:
1 1/2 cups apple cider vinegar
1/2   cup ketchup
1/4   cup yellow mustard
2   T. lemon juice
1   T. Worcestershire sauce
1   T. Tabasco
1   t. kosher salt
1   t. black pepper

FINISH WITH:
2   T. unsalted butter

Reduce root beer to 1 cup over medium heat in a large saucepan (it takes about one hour).

Add vinegar, ketchup, mustard, lemon juice, Worcestershire, Tabasco, salt, and pepper. Stir well to combine. Simmer 20 minutes.

Finish with butter to give the sauce extra body and flavor.

Reduce 2 liters of root beer down to one cup. The syrup should coat the back of a spoon. ▶

Pulled Pork
sandwich

Anything grilled is good, but nothing holds a candle to the king of all barbecue recipes—the pulled pork sandwich with slaw.

A pretty bold statement for what appears to be just another BBQ dish. But it's true—this sandwich has it all. Layers of complex flavors and classic pairings.

Sounds like a snooty wine description, doesn't it? It may be a bit much for barbecue, but it does have a hint of truth. Biting spices are massaged into the pork before cooking. Aromatic woods infuse hints of smoke. Piquant sauce dresses the tender meat. If that's not enough, all this is piled onto a grilled buttered bun and topped with a tangy, colorful coleslaw, providing a delicate tension between hot and cold. Not bad for a barbecue sandwich!

menu

Pulled Pork
Sandwich with
Spinach Coleslaw

Classic Potato
Salad

Orange sorbet

Special coleslaw

I realize that there are opposing camps regarding coleslaw preparation and consumption. They can be divided into two categories: Vinegar- or mayonnaise-based, and on the sandwich or on the side?

The correct answers for this recipe are to use vinegar for flavor and a touch of mayonnaise to bind it. Then, put the slaw on the sandwich (at least just this once).

It's a simple recipe that's clean and refreshing. I added sliced fresh spinach for color so it makes quite a statement, even if it's not on a sandwich!

SPINACH COLESLAW
MAKES 10 CUPS
TOTAL TIME: 10 MINUTES

WHISK TOGETHER:
- $1/2$ cup mayonnaise
- $1/2$ cup vegetable oil
- $1/2$ cup white wine vinegar
- $1/4$ cup sugar
- $1 1/2$ t. dry mustard
- 1 t. kosher salt
- $1/2$ t. cayenne

ADD:
- 1 bag (1 lb.) coleslaw mix
- 1 bag (10 oz.) shredded red cabbage
- 1 bag (6 oz.) fresh spinach, thinly sliced

Whisk together all ingredients except cabbages and spinach. **Add** the cabbages and spinach. Toss and let coleslaw sit 30 minutes before serving.

Bundle spinach leaves together and slice into thin strips. ▼

PULLED PORK SANDWICH
MAKES 8 SANDWICHES
TOTAL TIME: 15 MINUTES

COMBINE:
- 8 cups Pulled Pork, chopped
- 1 cup barbecue sauce

GRILL:
- 8 kaiser-style buns, buttered

ASSEMBLE EACH SANDWICH WITH:
- 1 cup pork mixture
- $1/2$ cup Spinach Coleslaw

Combine pork with sauce. **Grill** the buttered buns, or toast them in a saute pan. **Assemble** sandwiches on buns with pulled pork and coleslaw.

Make sandwiches with pulled or chopped pork. It's best to chop while meat is still warm. ▶

◄ *Toss the warm pork with a little sauce. Warm foods tend to absorb flavors easily.*

◄ *Butter the buns and then toast them on the grill. You can also brown them in a saute pan.*

wares
BBQ sauces

Forget the national supermarket sauces—in our test, regional varieties won hands down!

Opinions about barbecue sauce tend to be very strong. So at the risk of ruffling some barbecue feathers, I'm going to come right out and say that there isn't just *one* ultimate barbecue sauce. But some are better than others.

Types: Barbecue sauces are made with one of three bases: tomato, vinegar, or mustard. While often interchangeable, each performs specific tasks best.

Tomato sauces are often fairly thick, cling well, and are usually applied during the last few minutes of grilling. Vinegar sauces range from watery to medium-thick. The thinner the sauce, the less it adheres to grilled meat. It's especially good mixed with pulled pork or for dipping. Mustard sauces range from thick to thin and require a real affinity for mustard.

Ingredients: Beyond the base, several common components go into most sauces. Count on a sweetener, a sour, seasonings, some kind of "bite" or heat, and aromatics. Sometimes a surprise ingredient is also added that sets it apart from other sauces.

Before taste testing, I assumed the sauces would fall into some predictable categories that would correlate with the ingredient lists. My prejudice figured sauces with corn syrup leading the list would land in the "no" pile, tomato paste would *always* outperform ketchup, and the longest ingredient lists would taste artificial.

But repeated blind tastings of 38 sauces revealed no pattern whatsoever! It seems the only hard and fast rule for ingredients is *balance*. While it's okay to taste a specific ingredient, a particular flavor shouldn't overwhelm or offend (like liquid smoke).

Choosing: Start with sauces from your own region—they're affordable and sold at your grocery store. Then expand to other areas and flavors, beginning with our six regional picks that range from tart to smoky-sweet. All our picks can be mail ordered.

National vs. Regional Sauces

My original intent was to test and rate the top national brands. But I found only six that are distributed to grocers across the entire nation, and they all tasted harsh and uninteresting. It seems that in trying to appeal to *all* people in *all* parts of the country, they've ended up with sauces lacking in character.

I soon realized the more interesting story (and taste) is in the smaller, regional sauces. They're far more distinct, flavorful, and fun—real representations of barbecue in their area. And they usually have an interesting story to boot!

With literally hundreds of sauces available (some good and some not-so-good), these six recommendations are only a small representation of the great options available.

These regional BBQ sauces received four stars (or "Worth the cost of shipping!") in the Cuisine Test Kitchen.

Vick's Flaming Pig Sauce

Developed over 20 years in Red Springs, North Carolina, Vick's Flaming Pig Sauce has a vinegar base that's tart (but not too strong) with a sweet, spicy aftertaste. Its smooth balance of flavors makes it an ideal introduction to the vinegar sauce field. Versatile enough to cover all barbecue bases, the shimmering liquid has a beautiful consistency good for basting, mixing, or dipping. Order at **ironq.com** or **flamingpigsauce.com**.

Southern Comfort Classic

Not your typical sauce, Southern Comfort Classic Barbeque Sauce is laced with little bits of herbs, spices, and onions, and almost has the appearance of salsa. Made with no preservatives, it is lightly sweet with a clean tang and just a little bit of spiciness. And naturally, the ingredient list includes Southern Comfort. Made in Charleston, South Carolina, it's available at **ironq.com**, and specialty and grocery stores.

Bone Suckin' Sauce (Original)

Phil Ford developed this sauce in 1987 while trying to copy his mother's recipe for a western North Carolina-style sauce. But it was his sister-in-law that named it and prodded retail launching in 1992. The smooth sauce has honey sweetness with a tangy twist of tomato and vinegar. Go to **ironq.com** to purchase, or for a store locator map, see **BoneSuckin.com**.

Sweet Baby Ray's

Created in the Chicago area, Sweet Baby Ray's is a great all-around traditional barbecue sauce. The thick sauce is quite sweet but well balanced with a mild smoky flavor that doesn't overwhelm. Available in more than 16,000 grocery stores covering more than half the states in the nation. For locations go to **sweetbabyrays.com**, or call **(877) 729-2229** to order (only in cases of 12).

American Spoon Memphis Style

There's no need to be skeptical about a Memphis-style BBQ grilling sauce that is made in Petoskey, Michigan. American Spoon Foods has created a sauce avid vinegar lovers will appreciate. Rather thin in texture, it has mustard undertones that kick up some bite. It's perfect for mopping and dipping, but handles grilling duties also. Order at **spoon.com**.

Big Bob Gibson Bar-B-Q

Big Bob Gibson's is a BBQ restaurant in Decatur, Alabama with a colorful history. Known since 1925 for their unique Original White Sauce, lately they've been winning awards for their relatively young Red Sauce. Compatible spices with kicks of vinegar and light smoke combine for deep flavor in this medium-thick sauce. To place an order, read their history, or see restaurant locations, check out **bigbobgibson.com**.

clarifying butter

making crème fraîche

Clarifying butter is a process used to separate the milk solids from the oily butterfat in butter. You've probably experienced putting whole butter into a hot pan—it quickly turns brown. That browning is the milk solids cooking. They just can't tolerate higher heats.

To get the butter taste without the browning, clarify butter. Slowly melt whole butter over low heat. You'll eventually see three layers form. The top layer is foamy and made up of water and milk—skim it off and discard. The deep yellow middle layer is the butter-fat—pour this off into a container. This is the clarified butter you want to use for sauteing. What's left in the bottom are the milk solids—pitch them.

▲ *Add buttermilk and lemon juice to cream. Let sit at room temperature, then chill. Use when thick.*

Many recipes call for crème fraîche, a thick, tangy French cream similar to sour cream, but smoother and richer. Its body and thickness comes from natural bacteria in unpasteurized cream. But since this is an unpasteurized process, we have to improvise in the States by using the natural fermenting agents in buttermilk. Mix 1 cup heavy cream, ¼ cup buttermilk, and 1 tablespoon lemon juice. Cover and let sit at room temperature 6–8 hours, then refrigerate. Crème fraîche is great for cooking because of its rich flavor and stability—it doesn't break when heated, unlike sour cream.

melting **chocolate**

To melt dark, milk, and white choco-
lates for dipping or recipes, use a
double boiler set over barely simmering
water (a heatproof bowl nested over a
saucepan makes a great double boiler).
Take the chocolate off the heat *before*
all lumps are totally gone—they'll melt
as the chocolate sits. Microwaving
on high power works too,
but stir the chocolate
every 30 seconds to keep it
from scorching.

    If using a double boiler,
it's critical that no water or
steam gets in the chocolate.
Just a drop will cause the
chocolate to "seize," or
stiffen, and render it useless.

*Chop the choco-
late into small
pieces for quick,
even melting.* ▼

deglazing **a pan**

After sauteing or roast-
ing, look at the bottom
of the pan. Those dark
food particles stuck to
the bottom are caramel-
ized drippings from meat
juices. This is called
"fond," a French term
loosely meaning bottom
or foundation. Fond is loaded with
flavor, and can be used to make gravy
or added to sauces. The best way to
capture these flavorful deposits is by
deglazing. Add any liquid like wine,
stock, or water to the pan and start
scraping vigorously while bringing the
liquid to a boil. This is your "foundation
of flavor" for sauce or gravy.

▲*Deglaze the pan
with liquid, then
scrape the bottom
to loosen the fond.*

Garlic

Garlic is a study in contradiction. Its aroma can be blindly offensive or overpoweringly alluring, while its flavor can be sharply harsh or sweet as creamy butter.

Sound confusing? Garlic is a bit of an enigma, but doesn't have to be if you know what it's about. The key is in how you dissect this savory subject—literally.

Stinking compounds

Pick up a bulb of garlic and take a whiff. Not much odor, is there? That's because its chemical make-up must be altered before it tastes or smells like garlic.

Garlic contains two compounds that are separated from each other by thin cell walls. Not to get too scientific, but these compounds are called *alliin* and *allinase*. On their own, they are fairly unremarkable, but when joined, they are 100% pure, turbo-charged garlic.

Elephant garlic is a member of the leek family. Use it when you want an onion flavor with just a hint of garlic.

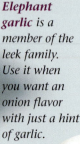

The more these two compounds are mixed together, the more potent the garlic flavor becomes. For example, crushed garlic is a lot stronger than sliced. Take a look at the chart on the next page. See what I mean?

You'll really see this in action if you try the 40-clove chicken on Page 30. Since the garlic cloves are whole, the alliin and allinase don't mix. The result is a mellow chicken dish that tastes more like butter than garlic.

Different garlics

There are over 600 varieties of cultivated garlic out there, and those can be divided into two species: hard-neck and soft-neck. This may be useful information if you're playing Trivial Pursuit, but the reality is that most of us are only exposed to one kind at

the grocery store—the "artichoke soft-neck." They tend to be on the larger side with plenty of cloves (14–20 cloves per head).

But don't get this confused with "elephant garlic." While true garlic is part of the lily family, elephant garlic is actually a relative of the leek. Yes, it looks like garlic on steroids (twice the normal size), but don't expect twice the flavor. You'll get more of an onion-y taste with mere hints of garlic.

What to buy

While garlic is available year-round, the new crop comes in about June and July. This is when garlic is at its best.

Look for bulbs that are firm and plump with no signs of shrinkage. Go for the ones with big, fat cloves which indicate freshness (garlic tends to shrivel as it ages). And finally, don't refrigerate fresh garlic. Store it in an open container in a cool, dark place away from other foods.

Working with Garlic

By understanding the structure of garlic, you can work with it more effectively. A firm push with the hand begins the process so you can easily peel the cloves. Then you can vary its strength simply by the way you prepare it. Remember, the more that the alliin and allinase come together, the stronger the flavor will be.

Break the bulb by first rubbing your hands around it to remove the papery outer layers. Position the bulb at a slight angle, stem pointed into the work surface. With the heel of your hand, press the root of the bulb down and away from you, breaking the bulb into cloves.

Peel a clove by first trimming off the brittle root end. From there, gently twist the clove between your fingers to loosen the skin until it can be peeled off. Unfortunately, the fresher the garlic, the harder the cloves are to peel.

Mildest Flavor—Whole Clove

Using whole cloves is by far the mildest way to cook with garlic. When simmered or roasted, they can be spread like butter.

Mild Flavor—Sliced Clove

Compound interaction is minimized when garlic is sliced. Its mild flavor is great with sauteed spinach.

Medium Flavor—Chopped Clove

Garlic intensifies when chopped, getting stronger as it gets smaller. Coarsely chopped, it's nice in lighter sauces like fresh marinaras.

Full Flavor—Minced Clove

"Rock" a knife back and forth through chopped garlic and you'll eventually mince it. Minced garlic is perfect in stir-fries.

Intense Flavor—Smashed Clove

The strongest garlic flavor comes when the cloves are smashed. Use it in marinades for high-impact flavoring.

GARLIC BREAD
(The Real Way)

This isn't the typical foil-wrapped, oven-baked garlic bread. Turn a baguette into a real treat with good extra-virgin olive oil and a fresh garlic rubdown.

TOTAL TIME: 10 MINUTES

Cut baguette diagonally to create long slices.
Brush each piece liberally with extra-virgin olive oil, coating both sides.
Toast in a pan like you would cook French toast, carefully browning each side.
Rub one side of toasted bread with a fresh whole clove of garlic. Serve immediately.

▲ *Brush both sides of bread with **good** olive oil and toast.*

▲ *Rub pieces of toasted bread with cloves of fresh garlic.*

40-clove garlic chicken

If a little bit is good, too much is better! All this garlic can turn sweet and mellow.

Garlic has a bad reputation for its dominant flavor and odor. I'm sure you know people who refuse to eat it for those reasons. But here's a dish that'll make those with the most garlic-sensitive palates think twice.

Chicken and garlic are slowly simmered with fresh herbs to create a mildly flavored, but rich-tasting main course. The secret to its mellow flavor is whole cloves—not crushed or minced. This prevents the compounds from combining to create those strong garlic traits.

But what's so cool is that the cooked cloves can be spread onto a toasted baguette like butter, then served with the tender chicken.

menu

40-Clove Garlic Chicken

Lemon Rice Pilaf

Toasted baguette

Glazed baby carrots

40-CLOVE GARLIC CHICKEN

Most 40-clove recipes use a whole chicken. I've used thighs so they can easily simmer partially submerged in the mild garlic and fresh herb sauce.

MAKES 6 CHICKEN THIGHS WITH SAUCE
TOTAL TIME: 1 HOUR

COMBINE:
1/3 cup all-purpose flour
2 T. paprika
1 T. kosher salt
1 T. black pepper

BROWN IN 3 T. OLIVE OIL; REMOVE:
6 chicken thighs, dusted in flour mixture

ADD AND SAUTE:
40 cloves garlic, peeled
3 ribs celery, diced
1 medium yellow onion, sliced

ADD AND BRAISE:
1 cup dry white wine
1 cup chicken broth
2 sprigs fresh rosemary
2 sprigs fresh thyme
2 bay leaves
  Browned chicken thighs

SERVE WITH:
  Lemon Rice Pilaf, *right*
  Toasted baguette slices

Dust thighs in seasoned flour and brown in oil. Remove from pan. ▼

Add garlic, celery, and onion. Cook, stirring constantly, until onion and garlic are lightly browned. ▶

Preheat oven to 375° with rack in the center.

Combine flour, paprika, salt, and pepper in a large plastic bag. Coat chicken in seasoned flour. Shake off excess flour. Heat oil in a large ovenproof saute pan over medium-high heat.

Brown chicken on both sides; remove from pan.

Add garlic, celery, and onion; saute until lightly browned.

Add wine, broth, and herbs, then arrange browned chicken on top, skin side up; bring to a simmer. Cover the pan; transfer to the oven and braise 45 minutes.

Serve with Lemon Rice Pilaf and toasted baguette slices.

▲ *Deglaze with wine and broth. Add herbs and thighs. Bring to a simmer, cover, and braise in oven.*

39

online extra

For a pilaf alternative, visit **www.CuisineAtHome.com** for one of *Cuisine at home's* Mashed Potato recipes.

make it a menu

LEMON RICE PILAF

Lemon is a complementary flavor to garlic and fresh herbs. Add it right at the end so its flavor isn't diminished during cooking.

MAKES 6 CUPS
TOTAL TIME: 25 MINUTES

SAUTE IN 2 T. VEGETABLE OIL:
1 cup yellow onion, diced

ADD; STIR TO COAT:
1 1/2 cups converted-style rice

STIR IN, BRING TO A BOIL; COVER:
3 1/2 cups water
1 T. unsalted butter
2 t. kosher salt
1 bay leaf
1/4 t. cayenne

STIR IN:
  Zest of 1 lemon, minced
  Juice of 1 lemon

Saute onion in oil in a large saucepan just until softened.

Add rice and continue sauteing until it starts to turn golden.

Stir in water, butter, salt, bay leaf, and cayenne. Bring to a boil, cover, and reduce heat to low. Cook until liquid is absorbed, 20 minutes. Remove from heat.

Stir in lemon zest and juice. Allow rice to steep a few minutes before serving.

▲ *Add lemon zest and juice to cooked rice. Stir, cover, and steep a few minutes.*

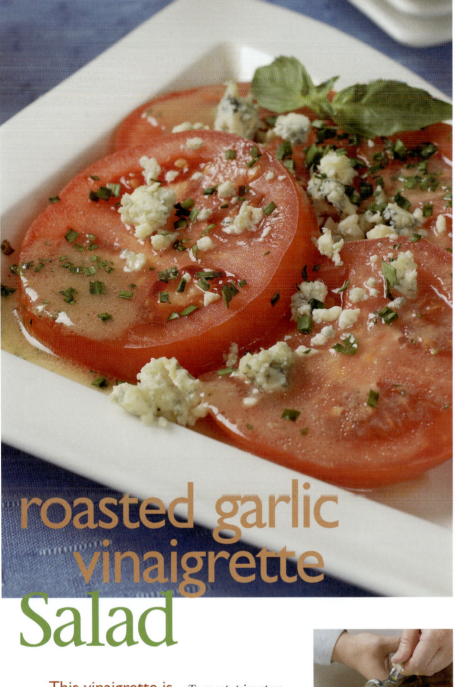

roasted garlic vinaigrette Salad

This vinaigrette is perfect over a salad of fresh tomato slices. But try drizzling it over grilled asparagus or chicken—fantastic!

To roast, trim stem ends off garlic, place on foil, and drizzle with olive oil. Wrap, place in an ovenproof dish, and roast for 30 minutes at 425°. ▶

◀When bulbs are cool enough to handle, squeeze out cloves. Do this while the bulbs are still warm— the cloves will come out easier.

ROASTED GARLIC VINAIGRETTE

Roasted garlic is mild and can be used in many ways. Besides this vinaigrette, try it in softened butter or in mashed potatoes.

MAKES 2 CUPS
TOTAL TIME: 45 MINUTES

PROCESS:
Roasted garlic cloves from 3 bulbs
$3/4$ cup white wine vinegar
$1/3$ cup fresh lemon juice
2 T. honey
1 T. Worcestershire sauce
1 t. kosher salt
$1/4$ t. ground white pepper

GRADUALLY DRIZZLE IN:
$3/4$ cup vegetable oil

STIR IN:
1 t. chopped fresh thyme

Process roasted garlic and remaining ingredients (except oil and thyme) in a food processor.
Gradually drizzle oil in a steady stream with processor running.
Stir in the thyme. Refrigerate until ready to use. For a thinner dressing, add additional vinegar or lemon juice.

TOMATO-HERB SALAD

MAKES 4 SALADS
TOTAL TIME: 10 MINUTES

DIVIDE:
4 large tomatoes, thickly sliced
$1/4$ cup blue cheese, crumbled
1 T. minced fresh basil
1 T. minced fresh chives

DRIZZLE WITH:
Roasted Garlic Vinaigrette

Divide all ingredients among four salad plates.
Drizzle tomatoes with some of the vinaigrette. Serve with sliced baguette if desired.

chef at home: *Rick Bayless*

summer
tostada party

Award-winning chef-restaurateur, cookbook author, and television personality, Rick Bayless has introduced Americans to authentic regional Mexican cuisine.

*Six years of culinary research in Mexico was the foundation for Rick and his wife Deann's Chicago restaurants, the casual **Frontera Grill,** and **Topolobampo,** one of America's only fine-dining Mexican restaurants. Among his many awards and honors, he was named the James Beard Foundation's 1995 National Chef of the Year. And his most recent book, **Mexico One Plate At A Time,** is the companion to his popular PBS series.*

*To learn more about Rick's books, restaurants, television show, and Mexican products, visit his entertaining and informative web site at **fronterakitchens.com.***

It's perfect party fare! A fiesta of textures and tastes, tostadas offer something for everyone.

Rick Bayless believes at least one meal a week should be a real pull-out-the-stops celebration for family and friends. And build-your-own tostadas are just the ticket to get everyone involved.

Tostadas are really just simple, hand-held meals. It's the toppings that turn them into celebratory fare. With fried tortillas as the base, Rick introduces us to authentic toppings that show off the playful flavors of Mexico.

He teaches us how to make Shrimp Seviche—lime-marinated shrimp in a spicy, ketchupy sauce. Chicken Tinga features a rich chipotle salsa you'll want to make again and again. And the Mashed Black Beans are so full of flavor you won't believe they started from a can! Best of all, Rick's recipes are easy to follow, use readily available ingredients, and can be made ahead—so you can join the party!

chefathome: *Rick Bayless*

Seviche 101

Seviche or ceviche? Well, it depends on who you ask. But both spellings are pronounced the same way [seh-VEE-chee] and mean the same thing—very fresh seafood that's "cooked" just by soaking in citrus juice. And it's the juice that also provides the bright, fresh flavor seviche is known for.

The technique for seviche uses the acid in the juice to do the cooking, just as heat would. But shrimp require a slightly different method. They're cooked with heat before soaking in lime juice, because it takes too long for the lime to penetrate the thick shrimp and they end up tough. This pre-cooking technique is perfect for anyone squeamish about cooking with lime alone.

Poaching fresh shrimp is the best choice for flavor and texture. But purchasing cooked shrimp is an acceptable alternative (if frozen, thaw before using).

SHRIMP SEVICHE

Seviche is best made the same day it's served. Marinate the shrimp, then add the remaining ingredients up to a few hours in advance.

MAKES 4 CUPS; TOTAL TIME: ABOUT 1 HOUR

TOSS TOGETHER:
1   lb. shrimp (41–50 count), poached
1/2 cup fresh lime juice (2–3 limes)

RINSE AND ADD:
1/2 cup white onion, diced

ADD:
1   small ripe avocado, cubed
1/2 cup ketchup
1/2 cup cucumber, peeled, seeded, diced
1/2 cup jicama, peeled, diced
1/3 cup chopped fresh cilantro
2   T. olive oil
1–2 T. Tabasco or Mexican hot sauce
1/2 t. kosher salt

SERVE ON:
   Tostadas, *Page 35*

GARNISH WITH:
   Tangy Romaine, *Page 35*
   Lime wedges
   Fresh cilantro sprigs

Toss shrimp and lime juice together in a glass bowl. Cover; chill 1 hour.
Rinse onion under cold water in a strainer. Add to marinated shrimp and lime juice.
Add avocado, ketchup, cucumber, jicama, cilantro, olive oil, and hot sauce. Toss and season with salt. Refrigerate if not serving immediately.
Serve seviche on tostadas.
Garnish tostadas as desired.

menu

Shrimp Seviche
Tostadas

Served with:
Tangy Romaine,
lime wedges,
fresh cilantro

Choosing and frying tortillas

In Mexico, tostadas are always made from corn tortillas. They're sturdy and offer more flavor than flour tortillas.

Choosing tortillas: Buy thin tortillas with visible flecks of ground corn. If they're dry and slightly stale, all the better. They'll absorb little oil and fry into crisp tostadas.

Frying: Oil temperature should be 350°—cooler yields greasy tostadas, while hotter delivers a burnt flavor. Test with a thermometer or by dipping the edge of a tortilla into the oil. It should sizzle vigorously, not calmly or explosively. If the oil is smoking, it's way too hot.

Keep the tortilla submerged by pushing it down into the oil with tongs every few seconds. To insure a light, crispy tostada, no areas should bubble above the level of the oil.

TOSTADAS

The word tostada refers both to tortillas after they're fried, and to the whole assemblage—crisp tortilla, toppings and all.

Makes 10 Tostadas
Total Time: 20 Minutes

Heat:
1/2" vegetable oil
Fry:
10 6" corn tortillas

Heat oil to 350° in a heavy skillet over medium heat.
Fry tortillas one at a time, slipping into oil, then flipping with tongs after 15 seconds. Continue to fry, pushing into oil every few seconds. When bubbling has subsided and tortilla has darkened a bit (1–1 1/2 minutes total), remove and drain on paper towels.

Tortillas can be fried up to two hours before serving.

TANGY ROMAINE

Layer tostadas with sliced romaine tossed in vinegar and oil.

Makes 6 Cups
Total Time: 5 Minutes

Combine:
1/4 cup apple cider vinegar
2 T. extra-virgin olive oil
Add and Toss:
6 cups romaine, thinly sliced
Season with:
1/2 t. kosher salt

Combine vinegar and oil in a large bowl.
Add the romaine, tossing to coat.
Season with salt.

Chile sense

Chipotle-Cascabel salsa is the deeply flavored, spicy base for Chicken Tinga. The rich taste, texture, and color comes from the chiles and roasted vegetables.

The salsa involves the authentic technique of toasting then rehydrating dried chipotle [chi-POHT-lay] and cascabel chiles. An easy but good alternative is to use canned chipotle chiles in adobo (a vinegary tomato sauce). Skip the toasting and soaking steps, and puree six canned chipotles with the roasted vegetables.

menu

Chicken Tinga
Tostadas *with*
Chipotle-Cascabel Salsa

Black Bean Tostadas
(*or serve Mashed Black
Beans on the side*)

Serve with:
Avocado, grated cheese,
Tangy Romaine, fresh cilantro

CHIPOTLE-CASCABEL SALSA
Makes 2 Cups; Total Time: 1 Hour

TOAST:
3   dried chipotle chiles, stemmed
3   dried cascabel chiles, stemmed
SOAK IN:
    Very hot tap water
BROIL:
½   lb. tomatillos, husked (3–4)
½   lb. Roma tomatoes (3–4)
ROAST:
1   large white onion, cut in ¼"
    thick slices, separated into rings
6   whole garlic cloves, peeled
PUREE:
    Rehydrated, drained chiles
    Roasted vegetables
STIR IN:
1½ t. chopped fresh thyme
½   cup water
SEASON WITH:
1   t. kosher salt
½   t. sugar

Adjust oven racks to top and middle positions. Preheat broiler to high.
Toast chiles in a heavy skillet over medium heat, pressing and stirring until they darken in spots, 2–3 min.
Soak chiles in hot water for 20 minutes (set a smaller bowl on top to keep chiles submerged), then drain.
Broil tomatillos and tomatoes on a baking sheet on upper rack until softened and blackened in spots, 5–6 minutes. Turn and broil 5–6 minutes more, until soft and equally dark. Reduce oven temperature to 425°.
Roast onion and garlic on a baking sheet on the middle rack. Stir occasionally until garlic is soft and onion richly browned, about 15 minutes.
Puree the chiles with the roasted vegetables (along with any juices from the baking sheet) in a blender or food processor until smooth.
Stir in thyme and water.
Season with salt and sugar.

MASHED BLACK BEANS

Canned black beans work great (as well as red or pinto). They can be made a few days in advance, then warmed before serving. Thin with a little water if necessary.

MAKES 3 CUPS
TOTAL TIME: 15 MINUTES

HEAT:
¼   cup vegetable oil
ADD AND COOK:
1   large white onion, chopped
STIR IN:
6   garlic cloves, minced
ADD; MASH:
2   cans (15 oz. each) black
     beans, rinsed and drained
THIN WITH:
½–1 cup water
SEASON WITH:
½   t. kosher salt

Heat oil in a nonstick skillet over medium heat.
Add onion and cook until golden, stirring often, about 7 minutes.
Stir in garlic and cook 1 minute.
Add beans and mash coarsely with a potato masher, mixing in onion and garlic at the same time.
Thin beans with enough water to give them a soft consistency that barely holds its shape in a spoon.
Season with salt. Cover and keep warm until serving.

CHICKEN TINGA

Shredded rotisserie chicken from the supermarket is an easy time saver here. Tinga, which means shredded meat, can be made a day or two ahead, then warmed before serving.
MAKES 5 CUPS; TOTAL TIME: 30 MINUTES

PUREE:
1½ cups Chipotle-Cascabel Salsa,
     Page 36
1   can (15 oz.) whole tomatoes
2   T. apple cider vinegar
SAUTE IN 1 T. VEGETABLE OIL:
1   large white onion, thinly sliced
ADD AND SIMMER:
     Salsa mixture
STIR IN:
4   cups cooked chicken, shredded
SEASON WITH:
1   t. kosher salt
SERVE ON:
     Tostadas, *Page 35*
GARNISH WITH:
2   ripe avocados, sliced or cubed
½   cup Parmesan, Romano or
     Mexican queso añejo cheese,
     grated
     Tangy Romaine, *Page 35*
     Chopped fresh cilantro

Puree salsa, tomatoes (with juice), and vinegar in a blender or food processor until smooth; set aside.
Saute onion in oil in a large skillet over medium heat until crisp-tender, about 5 minutes.
Add salsa mixture to onions and simmer until thickened, 5–10 minutes, stirring often.
Stir in the chicken; cool slightly.
Season with salt.
Serve warm Tinga on tostadas.
Garnish tostadas as desired.

white chocolate
cheesecake

It's pretty as a picture, but there's nothing dainty about this cheesecake—rich, smooth, creamy, and totally irresistible.

Cheesecake is one of those desserts that brings people to their knees. Even after the richest dinner, most people can manage to get down a couple of bites. And a lot of times, the cheesecake just isn't that great.

But here's one you won't want to pass up. Sweet yet tangy, dense and creamy—almost like the filling of a fine chocolate truffle. Believe me, it's worth every single calorie.

Desserts this delicious *and* good-looking are often perceived as hard to make. Not here. The crust is just crushed cookies and graham crackers, and the cake itself is made of cream cheese, eggs, sugar, and white chocolate for added richness. The flavor of the chocolate is prominent, so buy good-quality bars. And don't be intimidated by the swirl—it's a cinch to do. So go ahead, dig in!

Cheesecake tips

Here are a few pointers to get you started on this great cheesecake.

The Pan: A 9" springform pan is ideal, but 8 or 10" ones will work too (baking time may need adjusting). Springform pans make unmolding easy, but if you don't have one, use a cake pan with straight sides. Just beware—removing the cake isn't easy.

The Cream Cheese: Regular or low-fat cream cheese may be used here (bricks only, not the whipped stuff in tubs). Don't even think about non-fat cream cheese—it tastes bad and is pointless in cheesecake. But no matter what, be sure the cheese is room temperature for a smooth batter.

The Swirl: A fresh strawberry sauce is the basis for the swirl. This time of year is the berries' prime season so choose the reddest, ripest fruit for maximum flavor. The sauce must be chilled before swirling—if it's warm, it won't be thick enough to swirl well.

Chocolate crumb crusts tend to stick—a few graham crackers in the crust help prevent that. Even so, press the crumbs in rather lightly, about 1/2–1" up the sides of the pan. ▼

WHITE CHOCOLATE CHEESECAKE WITH STRAWBERRY SWIRL

Makes One 9" Cheesecake
Total Time: 60–80 Minutes + Chilling

FOR THE SAUCE—
PROCESS; SIMMER:
10	oz. fresh strawberries, hulled, quartered
3	T. sugar
2	T. strawberry preserves
	Juice of 1/2 lemon

COMBINE; WHISK IN:
2	T. water
2	t. cornstarch

FOR THE CRUST—
PROCESS:
7	chocolate wafer cookies, crumbled
3	whole graham crackers, crumbled
2	T. sugar
	Pinch salt

ADD:
3	T. unsalted butter, melted

FOR THE CHEESECAKE—
MELT; SET ASIDE:
8	oz. white chocolate, chopped

BLEND:
3	pkgs. (8 oz. each) cream cheese, room temperature
3/4	cup sugar

ADD:
3	eggs
	Melted white chocolate
1	t. vanilla extract
	Juice of 1/2 lemon

SWIRL IN:
1/4	cup cold strawberry sauce

Process berries, sugar, preserves, and lemon juice for the sauce in a food processor until smooth. Transfer to a saucepan; bring to a boil over medium-high heat.

Combine water and cornstarch in a small bowl until smooth; whisk into berry mixture. Simmer to thicken slightly, about 1 minute, see *Figure 1, Page 40*. Transfer to a bowl, cover, and chill until cold.

Preheat oven to 300° with rack in the center. Coat a 9" springform pan with nonstick spray.

Process cookies, crackers, sugar, and salt for crust in a food processor until fine.

Add butter as machine is running. Pat crumbs on bottom and up sides of pan.

Melt chocolate for the cheesecake over a double boiler and set aside, see *Figure 2*.

Blend cream cheese and sugar with a mixer until smooth, scraping the sides of the bowl periodically.

Add eggs one at a time, mixing well after each addition. Blend in melted chocolate, vanilla, and lemon juice, see *Figure 3*. Pour batter into prepared pan, then drizzle with 1/4 cup strawberry sauce, see *Figures 4 & 5*.

Swirl sauce into batter to create a marbled pattern, see *Figure 6*. Place pan on a baking sheet and bake until edges are set and puffed but center is still jiggly, 60–80 minutes; do not overbake. Turn off oven, crack door open with a wooden spoon, and cool cake inside 1 hour. Remove from oven and cool completely. Cover cake with a towel and chill overnight, see *Figure 7*. Slice cheesecake, see *Figures 8 & 9*, and serve with remaining strawberry sauce.

Cheesecake—
making it

Since there aren't many ingredients in this cheesecake, substandard ones, like cheap white chocolate, are very noticeable.

Most grocery stores carry Ghirardelli or Lindt brands, and they're fine here. *Do not* use the bars of white "coating" chocolate. It's waxy, flavorless, and nothing you want to eat—especially here.

1 Blend strawberries, sugar, preserves, and lemon juice. Bring mixture to a boil; whisk in cornstarch and water. Simmer to thicken, then chill.

2 Melt chocolate in a double boiler over barely simmering water. Remove from heat before totally melted—it'll smooth out as it sits.

3 Blend cream cheese and sugar in a large bowl; add eggs one at a time, mixing well after each. Blend in white chocolate, vanilla, and lemon juice.

4 Pour batter into the crumb-lined pan; smooth top of the cake with a spatula or knife.

5 Drizzle ¼ cup cold sauce over the cake. It won't pour smoothly so don't worry if it's not perfectly even all the way around.

6 To swirl, drag a skewer or knife tip through the sauce to marble it with the batter. Don't over-swirl—you'll just get pink cheesecake! Bake.

Cheesecake— baking it

The trickiest part of making cheesecake is figuring out when it's done. Cheesecake is really a thick custard and requires special treatment.

The first key is gentle baking. Although the cake spends a good hour in the oven, the low temperature helps make it creamy.

Second, avoid overbaking the cake. Too long in the oven makes the texture dry and crumbly, and often causes the top to crack.

It won't be easy but force yourself to turn off the oven when the center is still jiggly and underdone. The cake will keep cooking as it cools in the turned-off oven. Chilling overnight also firms it up.

7 Prop the oven door open and cool the cake inside for an hour, then cool to room temperature. Cover the cake with a towel and chill overnight. Unlike plastic wrap, the towel prevents condensation from dripping onto the cake.

8 Run a knife around the edge of the chilled cake to loosen, then release the sides.

9 Cut the cake with a thin-bladed knife dipped into hot water (do not wipe dry). Before each cut, clean the blade to prevent smearing.

Pool some of the remaining strawberry sauce on serving plates, then top with a slice of cheesecake.

from **our** readers

Q&A
questions & answers

REFREEZING SHRIMP

Is it safe to use defrosted shrimp in a recipe you intend to freeze?

Margaret Aldridge
Canandaigua, NY

Sure—and that's true for all seafood, not just shrimp. While you do need to immediately cook thawed seafood to prevent the spread of bacteria, after it has been defrosted and thoroughly cooked, it's safe to freeze again.

FONDANT

What is fondant and how is it used?

Jim & Kim Trenter
St. Paul, MN

▲ *Saturated fats*

Unsaturated fats ▲

FAT FACTS

In layman's terms, can you please explain the difference between saturated and unsaturated fat.

Allene B. Griffin
Macon, GA

The simplest way to answer your question is to say that saturated fats are bad for your heart and are most likely to be solid at room temperature. Unsaturated fats often remain liquid and are much better for you.

Saturated fats are commonly found in animal products. Butter,

lard, whole milk, and meat are examples. The FDA recommends that less than 10% of your daily caloric intake comes from saturated fats, since research has shown they raise LDL (or "bad") cholesterol.

Unsaturated fats, on the other hand, are most often found in plant foods such as avocados, olives, walnuts, and sesame seeds, and seafoods such as mackerel, tuna, salmon, and sardines. These fats have actually been shown to lower LDL cholesterol, so eat up! (In moderation, of course.)

▲ *Petit fours [PEH-tee fohrs] are beautifully decorated bite-sized cakes that traditionally use poured fondant for the icing.*

Fondant is a sugar-based preparation that's commonly applied to cakes as an alternative to frosting. It was originally used in England to help keep fruitcakes fresh longer. This method still holds true, since bakers often use "fondant frosting" as the backdrop for elaborately decorated cakes that take days to prepare.

There are two types of fondant: poured and rolled. As its name implies, poured fondant has a liquid consistency that allows you to actually pour the

icing over things—petit fours are a common example.

Rolled fondant, though, is much thicker, *see photo below.* It's rolled out like dough and then draped over cakes. Think of it like a whole sheet of frosting.

While it *is* possible to make fondant, even professionals will opt for the ready-to-use, pre-packaged stuff (try the brand Wilton, available from **Sweet Celebrations**, (800) 328-6722). With all the intricate details that fondant encourages, wouldn't you rather spend time focusing on that?

◀ *Rolled fondant is rolled out like dough and then gently placed over the cake.*

INDEX

Is there an updated Cuisine at home *index available? If so, how can I get access to it?*

Jack G. Hays
Birmingham, AL

The latest edition of our Comprehensive Index (Issues 1–36) is available only to subscribers when they renew their subscription. The 16-page supplement is bound into the next issue of *Cuisine at home* that's sent after the renewal is processed.

BAKING SODA

Does baking soda go flat? Can it be tested before using so it doesn't ruin a recipe?

Kathy Dolan
Ventura, CA

The folks at Arm & Hammer tell us that baking soda is a very stable product that has an almost unlimited shelf life. If the soda is kept in a cool, dry place it has the potential to retain its leavening properties for several months, even years!

But if in doubt, you *can* test it for effectiveness. Pour some vinegar or lemon juice into a cup and add a spoonful of baking soda. If it fizzes, it's still active.

CHOPPED ONIONS

Is there a good way to keep chopped, raw onions for a few days?

Olga Preston
Cambridge, MA

Store extra onions in the refrigerator in an airtight container or resealable plastic bag—emphasis on airtight. An onion's odor becomes stronger once it's been chopped, and fats like to absorb odors. If your baggie isn't as secure as you thought, you'll definitely know it the next time you reach for a cold glass of milk or spread butter on your toast!

INFUSED OIL SAFETY

Is there a danger of botulism with homemade oil infusions?

Judy Garner
Paris, TN

In short, YES! Most vegetables, fruits, herbs, and spices are naturally susceptible to botulism because they're grown in soil, where the *c. botulinum* spores originate. While the spores themselves don't pose a threat, leaving them at room temperature and in an oxygen-free environment (like oil) does.

As a result of these discoveries, the FDA has placed a strong recommendation on any homemade oil infusions. Any infusion

MOLD AND CHEESE

Once mold appears on cheese, is it okay to cut around it, or is the whole chunk bad?

Martha M. McCardell
Stamford, CT

According to the Food Safety and Inspection Service, whether or not you can cut away moldy cheese depends on the type of cheese you're dealing with.

If it's a soft cheese (i.e. cream cheese, Brie, Camembert), you're out of luck. All soft cheeses with mold growing on them should be completely discarded.

But if it's a hard cheese, (i.e. Parmesan, Cheddar, Swiss), cut entirely around and behind the mold until you can no longer see any obvious change. Make sure not to cut into the mold itself or the spores may spread to wherever the knife cuts next. Of course, if there's still any doubt, just throw the cheese out!

created at home should be made fresh for each use, storing extras in the refrigerator for no longer than one week.

Unfortunately, gone should be the days of this popular craft sale commodity. Instead, why not try sampling one of the many commercially infused oils out on the market today?

SALT TO TASTE

Why do your recipes usually say "salt to taste" instead of telling exactly how much to use?

Linda Firestone
Somerville, NJ

As a flavor enhancer, salt is a touchy subject. Some people love it; some have to avoid it like the plague. Personal preference and dietary restrictions play large roles in the amount of salt people choose to enjoy. "Salt to taste" is a way for recipes to appease everyone.

As an exception, specific measurements will be provided in a recipe where the salt's presence is critical for a successful outcome, such as with a brine or in many baked goods.

TUXEDO STRAWBERRIES

Select rich red strawberries without white "shoulders" or blemishes. For the best results, use medium-sized, heart shaped fruit.

MAKES 10 STRAWBERRIES
TOTAL TIME: ABOUT 30 MINUTES

WASH AND DRY:
10   strawberries with tops
MELT; DIP BERRIES IN:
4   oz. white chocolate, chopped
MELT; DIP BERRIES IN:
4   oz. semisweet chocolate, chopped

Line a baking sheet with parchment paper.
Wash strawberries and dry them thoroughly.
Melt white chocolate over double boiler or in microwave, *Page 27*. Dip berries to cover, place on baking sheet, and chill until hard.
Melt semisweet chocolate. Dip sides of berries to resemble a tuxedo jacket. Dot chocolate "buttons" on the white chocolate with a wooden skewer dipped in semisweet chocolate. Chill until ready to serve. For the best flavor, serve within 5 or 6 hours.

tuxedo strawberries

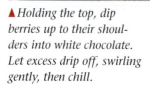

▲ *Holding the top, dip berries up to their shoulders into white chocolate. Let excess drip off, swirling gently, then chill.*

When white chocolate is hard, dip sides of berries in semisweet chocolate to look like jacket lapels. ▼

Dot shirt with two or three buttons. Chill until chocolate is hard. ▼

Cuisine at home®

Pizza
from the Grill
Crisp, Smoky, Perfect

Stuffing
Chicken Breasts
the easy way

Sizzlin' Salmon
Sweet, Hot, Intense

Issue No. 40 August 2003
A publication of August Home Publishing

Cuisine at home.

Publisher
Donald B. Peschke

Editor
John F. Meyer

Senior Editor
Susan Hoss

Associate Editor
Sarah Marx Feldner

Assistant Editor
Sara Ostransky

Test Kitchen Director
Kim Samuelson

Art Director
Cinda Shambaugh

Assistant Art Director
Holly Wiederin

Senior Graphic Designer
April Walker Janning

Image Specialist
Troy Clark

Photographer
Dean Tanner

AUGUST HOME
PUBLISHING COMPANY

Corporate:

Corporate Vice Presidents: Mary R. Scheve, Douglas L. Hicks • *Creative Director:* Ted Kralicek • *Professional Development Director:* Michal Sigel *New Media Manager:* Gordon C. Gaippe • *Senior Photographer:* Crayola England *Multi Media Art Director:* Eugene Pedersen • *Web Server Administrator:* Carol Schoeppler • *Web Content Manager:* David Briggs • *Web Designer:* Kara Blessing *Web Developer/Content Manager:* Sue M. Moe • *Controller:* Robin Hutchinson *Senior Accountant:* Laura Thomas • *Accounts Payable:* Mary Schultz • *Accounts Receivable:* Margo Petrus • *Research Coordinator:* Nick Jaeger • *Production Director:* George Chmielarz • *Pre Press Image Specialist:* Minniette Johnson • *Electronic Publishing Director:* Douglas M. Lidster • *Systems Administrator:* Cris Schwanebeck *PC Maintenance Technician:* Robert D. Cook • *H.R. Assistant:* Kirsten Koele *Receptionist/Administrative Assistant:* Jeanne Johnson • *Mail Room Clerk:* Lou Webber • *Office Manager:* Natalie Lonsdale • *Facilities Manager:* Kurt Johnson

Customer Service & Fulfillment:

Operations Director: Bob Baker • *Customer Service Manager:* Jennie Enos *Customer Service Representatives:* Anna Cox, Kim Harlan, Cheryl Jordan, April Revell, Deborah Rich, Valerie Jo Riley, Tammy Truckenbrod • *Buyer:* Linda Jones *Administrative Assistant:* Nancy Downey • *Warehouse Supervisor:* Nancy Johnson *Fulfillment:* Sylvia Carey

Circulation:

Subscriber Services Director: Sandy Baum • *New Business Circulation Manager:* Wayde J. Klingbeil • *Promotions Analyst:* Patrick A. Walsh • *Billing and Collections Manager:* Rebecca Cunningham • *Renewal Manager:* Paige Rogers • *Circulation Marketing Analyst:* Kris Schlemmer • *Circulation Marketing Analyst:* Paula M. DeMatteis • *Art Director:* Doug Flint • *Senior Graphic Designers:* Mark Hayes, Robin Friend

www.CuisineAtHome.com

talk to Cuisine at home
Questions about Subscriptions and Address Changes? Write or call:

Customer Service
2200 Grand Avenue,
Des Moines, IA 50312
800-311-3995,
8 a.m. to 5 p.m., Central Time.

Online Subscriber Services:
www.CuisineAtHome.com
Access your account • Check a subscription payment • Tell us if you've missed an issue • Change your mailing or email address • Renew your subscription • Pay your bill

Cuisine at home® (ISSN 1537-8225) is published bi-monthly (Jan., Mar., May, July, Sept., Nov.) by August Home Publishing Co., 2200 Grand Ave., Des Moines, IA 50312. **Cuisine at home**® is a trademark of August Home Publishing Co. ©Copyright 2003 August Home Publishing. All rights reserved. Subscriptions: Single copy: $4.99. One year subscription (6 issues), $24.00. (Canada/Foreign add $10 per year, U.S. funds.)

Periodicals postage paid at Des Moines, IA and at additional mailing offices. "USPS/Perry-Judd's Heartland Division automatable poly". Postmaster: Send change of address to **Cuisine at home**®, P.O. Box 37100 Boone, IA 50037-2100. **Cuisine at home**® does not accept and is not responsible for unsolicited manuscripts. **PRINTED IN CHINA**

editor's letter

Grilling is practically a cooking art form for me, as well as countless other barbecuing afficionados. So when the time came to redo my backyard patio, I didn't consider it work at all, but rather a labor of love that would eventually lead to the perfect platform for heightened grilling enjoyment. After weeks of work and enough aches and pains to fill two wheelbarrows, the patio is complete and looking fantastic—ready to test drive some of this issue's hot summer recipes.

The one recipe that turned out even better than I had hoped was the pizza—yes, it's grilled and it is exceptional. Many of the best pizzerias use extremely hot coal-fired ovens to produce an unforgettable crust that's crispy, charred, and smoky. I felt the grill would come closest to replicating some of those qualities, and it did. You'll be thrilled with the results, especially if you lace this thin-crusted pie with fresh mozzarella, Oven-Roasted Tomato Sauce, and basil—a perfect scenario in which less is more. Besides the pizza's spectacular flavor, grilling it becomes a patio party as everyone will want to get into the act and make their own.

Salmon is always good no matter how it's prepared, but like so many foods, grilling makes it sensational. For a different slant, I cured it briefly with sugar and salt for a more intense flavor. Was that ever a winner! It hits perfection status when basted with the hot, sweet flavors of an awesome Chipotle-Cherry Glaze. But if you're looking for something more mainstream, try the stuffed chicken breast. It's a simple technique that can be done ahead for a quick family supper or a more elaborate dinner party.

Nothing beats the summer heat like homemade ice cream, and nobody does ice cream better than Ben & Jerry's. Eric Fredette, one of Ben & Jerry's renowned "Flavor Gurus," shares with us the art of making their quality concoctions. He even created an over-the-top *Cuisine* flavor just for you—"When Turtles Go Brownie."

So get outside and start cooking. You'll quickly find, as I have, that your patio adds just the right "spice" to any recipe.

table of contents

from **our** readers

tips
and techniques

Skewer Safety

To store metal skewers safely, I stick the corks from wine bottles over the ends. That way, I am able to store them in a drawer without worrying about someone getting hurt. It's a great way to use my collection of corks too.

Janet Pelichowski
Ft. Collins, CO

Cooling Rack Dicing

When I have to dice a lot of hard-boiled eggs for salads (egg, macaroni, potato), I use a cooling rack with square grids. Peel the eggs, then press them through the rack directly into a bowl. It saves time and the eggs come out perfectly chopped. Clean-up is a breeze too—especially with a nonstick rack.

Becky (Bee) Conrad
West Mifflin, PA

Slick Silk Removal

To remove the silk from fresh sweet corn, simply dampen a sturdy paper towel with water. Draw the moist paper towel down the length of the corn and the silks will cling to the paper.

Joan Dolence
Knoxville, TN

Neutralize Garlic Odor

I have a foolproof method for removing garlic odor from your hands. First, rinse your garlicky hands with water, then rub them over a stainless steel faucet or sink surface—anything made of stainless steel. The active compound in garlic which produces its strong odor is neutralized by the nickel in stainless steel.

Peter Hyzak
Ponte Vedra Beach, FL

Flour Duster

I keep a shaker container filled with flour in my kitchen to use for dusting everything from meat to sauces. It's also great for flouring my work area when rolling out pie and pizza doughs.

Joyce Hill
Dallas, TX

Easy Greasing

To grease a pan without greasing your fingers, insert your hand into a plastic bag like a glove. Hold the butter or shortening in your bag-lined hand and smear it inside the pan.

Sarah Buckley
Minneapolis, MN

Stop the Splattering

I love bacon, but not the grease that gets everywhere when I cook it. To cut back on the splattering, sprinkle a little flour in the pan before frying. It really works!

Ethlyn Grienpentrog
Wauwatosa, WI

Dry Measuring

When measuring dry ingredients like cocoa, flour, or powdered sugar, place the measuring cup in a shallow plastic bowl before filling it. Any overflow is caught in the bowl and easily poured back into the bag or box without mess or waste.

Sue Martinez
Burlington, NC

Editor's note: We often use a paper plate in this same way—makes cleanup easy!

Clingy Dressing

To help salad dressing cling to lettuce, first rinse the greens and dry them in a salad spinner. Then place them in a bowl, sprinkle with grated dry cheese (such as Parmesan), and toss to coat. The salad dressing will cling to the cheese and, in turn, to the lettuce. This works with pasta sauce too—toss the cheese with the pasta before adding the sauce.

Carla Saluppo
Brecksville, OH

Berry Barrier

Fresh berries used to make the bottom crust of my pie soggy. Not anymore! Now I brush the unbaked bottom crust with well beaten egg whites before filling. This creates a barrier between the fruit and the crust, preventing juices from leaking through.

Amy Cassell
Milwaukee, WI

Cooking Corn

Why wait for a pot of water to boil? Simply refrigerate husked sweet corn in resealable plastic bags, then microwave it. Add water to the bag (1 T. per ear) and microwave the corn for a few minutes—ovens vary in power, but I've found that 2 minutes on full power works well. Leave the bag open slightly so steam can vent.

Nancy Gandy
Corpus Christi, TX

Pizza Wheel Cutter

In a hurry one day, I grabbed a pizza wheel instead of a knife to slice sandwiches. It worked great! I've also used the pizza wheel to cut through lasagna, quesadillas, and brownies with good results.

Debbie Spencer
Tallahassee, FL

Buttered Bread Crumbs

Here's an easy method for making buttered bread crumbs to top gratins and casseroles. Butter one side of a slice of white or wheat sandwich bread. Tear it into pieces, place it in a food processor, and grind for several seconds. One slice of bread yields about $1/2$ cup of crumbs.

Barbara Reese
Kiawah Island, SC

share your **tips** with *Cuisine at home*
and techniques

If you have a unique way of solving a cooking problem, we'd like to hear from you, and we'll consider publishing your tip in one or more of our works. Just write down your cooking tip and mail it to *Cuisine at home*, Tips Editor, 2200 Grand Ave., Des Moines, IA 50312, or contact us through our email address shown below. Please include your name, address, and daytime phone number in case we have questions. We'll pay you $25 if we publish your tip.

Email: CuisineAtHome@CuisineAtHome.com
Web address: CuisineAtHome.com

grilling Salmon

Burgers and hot dogs are grilling favorites. But this summer, add sizzling salmon to the line-up.

In terms of grilling fish, a lot can be said for salmon. Its bold flavor and firm texture make it ideal for standing up to the rigors of the grill. Plus, its high fat content helps prevent two pitfalls associated with grilled fish—sticking and dryness.

Choosing: You have choices to make when choosing salmon: farm-raised or wild, and fresh or frozen.

Most of the salmon sold in grocery stores is farm-raised Atlantic salmon. Overall, it's a decent product—fairly flavorful and uniform in

l Cut filets from a larger portion of salmon. Aim for filets 2–3" wide, or 6–7 ounces each.

size with a consistent fat content. But wild salmon (king, sockeye, coho) is a whole different ball game, far superior in flavor and texture to farm-raised salmon. Unfortunately, wild salmon is not cheap, nor is it always available (the season runs from late spring through early fall). However, if you can get it, *buy it*. The quality is truly superb.

In general, fresh salmon (wild or farm-raised) is better than frozen. However, if the fresh salmon at your market isn't of very good quality, frozen filets make an okay option.

Buying: Freshness is paramount when buying salmon (or any kind of fish). Plan to cook the fish the day you buy it, and purchase it from a fish market or store with rapid turnover. Be aware of the store's storage practices as well. Ideally, they display the fish on crushed ice, not precut filets packed in styrofoam and plastic wrap. Note its color—bypass any with a grayish hue. And don't be afraid to ask to smell it. There shouldn't be any "off" odor.

Buy a large piece of salmon and have the skin removed. Then just cut filets at home, *see Figure 1*—they will most likely be fresher than precut salmon filets.

Grilling: To help prevent sticking, preheat the grill well in advance, then clean and *lightly* oil the grates (as well as the salmon). But don't go overboard. Too much oil just drips onto the coals and flares up, leaving the fish "sooty."

2 Grill oiled, seasoned filets over medium-high heat. For good marks, place them at a 45° angle to grates.

3 Cover and cook filets 3 minutes. Carefully give them a quarter-turn (45°), then cover and grill 2 minutes.

4 Turn filets over, cover, and grill until fish is just cooked through, about 3 or 4 minutes more.

Grill the filets skinned side up (searing the crosshatch marks in Figures 2 & 3 is optional), then flip them and finish, *Figure 4*. If they stick a bit, continue cooking a minute or so until they release.

To check for doneness, insert a knife into the thickest part of the filet and separate the flakes. It should be barely opaque in the center—residual heat will continue cooking it to perfection.

Cured salmon
WITH CHIPOTLE-CHERRY GLAZE

Tinkering with perfectly grilled salmon may seem like sacrilege. Try this recipe to make a great thing better!

Most of the time, "dressing up" foods with fancy preparations and sauces just masks flavors. But curing fresh salmon with sugar and salt, then grilling it in a spicy-sweet glaze really enhances an already great-tasting fish.

Curing is a step typically used before smoking ham and fish to flavor and preserve them. Here, though, the cure's purpose is to deeply flavor the salmon, much like a brine does for poultry or pork. The fish absorbs the cure's sugar and salt flavors—a great contrast to the BBQ sauce-like glaze. The chipotle chile glaze has some kick, but the cherry preserves in it helps tone down the "fire." And it doesn't stop there! Cilantro-Lime Butter finishes the dish easily—and with style.

cuisineclass

Curing the salmon

Before grilling, the salmon is marinated in sugar, salt, and pepper. This mixture, a "dry cure," is purely to flavor the fish. As it cures, the salmon absorbs some of the dissolved sugar and salt into the filet.

What you get is fish that's seasoned on the inside *and* the outside. The curing effect is subtle—the taste of salt and sugar won't knock you over the head. But the difference between cured and uncured salmon is noticeable. And, the longer the fish is cured, the stronger it tastes.

Four hours imparts just the right amount of salt and sugar flavor without overwhelming the fish. The curing time may be cut to two hours, but its flavor won't be nearly as evident.

Fish Tales

Wild salmon, *left*, tends to be more vibrant than farm-raised. Their diet of shrimp and krill gives the flesh its coral color. To get similar coloring, farmed salmon, *right*, are fed pellets containing coloring agents.

GRILLED SALMON WITH CHIPOTLE-CHERRY GLAZE

MAKES FOUR 6-OZ. FILETS; TOTAL TIME: ABOUT 4½ HOURS

FOR THE CURE—
COMBINE:
½ cup brown sugar
¼ cup kosher salt
1 T. coarse black pepper

RUB CURE OVER:
4 filets (6 oz. each) fresh salmon

FOR THE GLAZE—
PUREE:
½ cup cherry preserves
½ cup ketchup
¼ cup chipotle chiles in adobo
1 t. minced fresh thyme
½ t. ground cumin
Juice of 1 lime
Salt to taste

DRIZZLE IN:
3 T. olive oil

FOR THE SALMON—
MARINATE IN; GRILL:
1 cup Chipotle-Cherry Glaze

SERVE WITH:
Jalapeño-Lime Butter, *Page 9*
Reserved glaze
Grilled corn, potatoes, and scallions

Rub the entire filet generously with cure mixture. Cover and chill for four hours. ▶

Combine brown sugar, salt, and pepper for the cure.

Rub cure generously over salmon filets and place on a baking sheet. Cover and chill for 4 hours.

Puree preserves, ketchup, chiles, seasonings, and lime juice for the glaze in a food processor or blender until smooth.

Drizzle in oil while machine is running. Process until slightly thickened and set aside.

After 4 hours, remove the salmon from the cure and pat the filets dry with paper towels.

Marinate filets in about ⅔ cup of glaze for 15 minutes (reserve the remaining glaze for serving). Preheat grill to medium-high; clean the grates and oil them lightly when hot. Grill filets as on Page 7.

Serve the salmon with Jalapeño-Lime Butter, reserved glaze, and grilled vegetables.

◀During curing, the sugar turns to liquid— it's normal. Pat the filets dry with paper towels.

Glazing, grilling, finishing

While the salmon cures, make the Chipotle-Cherry Glaze. This simple, no-cook sauce gets a ton of flavor from fairly everyday ingredients.

The glaze's kick is from canned chipotle chiles packed in adobo—smoked and dried jalapeños in a vinegar-based sauce. Latin markets carry them in abundance, but many grocery stores have them too. Chipotles are *spicy,* so if you're heat sensitive, cut back on them. And if you don't like cherries, use apricot jam or pineapple preserves instead. The recipe makes more than enough glaze for the fish, but it keeps well for a week in the fridge. Brush it on grilled pork, chicken, or brats.

Grill the fish as shown on Page 7. Again, clean, preheated, and oiled grill grates are *really* important here—the sugar in the cure and glaze are notorious for sticking. But don't panic if that does occur. Just brush more glaze over the filet before serving. No one will see the imperfection!

The final finish to the salmon is a pat of Jalapeño-Lime Butter, *right.* It adds just the right touch of fresh, bright flavor to the spicy grilled filets. You can easily tweak these ingredients to suit you—lemon or orange zest, rosemary or thyme, and garlic or ginger make terrific flavored butters.

JALAPEÑO-LIME BUTTER
Salted butter adds just the right seasoning. If you only have unsalted butter, add salt to taste.

MAKES ¹/₂ CUP
TOTAL TIME: 15 MINUTES + CHILLING

COMBINE:
- 1   stick (¹/₂ cup) salted butter, room temperature
- 1   T. minced fresh cilantro
- 1   T. jalapeño, seeded, minced Juice of ¹/₂ lime

Combine all ingredients in a small bowl using a rubber spatula or spoon. Initially, it won't blend easily, but it will over time.

Place butter on the bottom edge of a sheet of plastic wrap. Lift the bottom edge up and over the butter, rolling into a log. Twist ends of the plastic wrap to seal, then chill or freeze until firm.

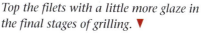

Top the filets with a little more glaze in the final stages of grilling. ▼

▲ *Spoon some of the chipotle glaze over both sides of the cured salmon.*

Divide salmon and vegetables among serving plates. Finish the fish with a pat of softened Jalapeño-Lime Butter. ▶

▲ *Roll flavored butter in plastic wrap, then chill or freeze. Thaw for 15–30 minutes before serving.*

40

online extra
Want more flavored butter recipes? Go to www.CuisineAtHome.com

CITRUS MARINATED
Salmon
with summer greens

One look at this dish and you know exactly how it tastes—light, refreshing, and totally summer.

Sure, it may be too hot to cook, but that's no reason to skip dinner. Grilled salmon with greens is summer eating at its best.

No stovetop work is involved. Simply fire up the grill and cook the citrus marinated salmon as on Page 7 (the marinade doubles as a vinaigrette for the salad). Fresh pineapple and macadamia nuts give flavor and texture to the greens, and grilled red onions make a gorgeous garnish.

The orzo side dish, *right*, is another option—but you'll have to turn on the stove to make it!

Vinaigrette tips

The vinaigrette plays a big role here, flavoring both the salmon and the greens. Citrus zest gives the vinaigrette intensity, but lime zest can be bitter so it's left out.

Marinate the fish in about half of the vinaigrette (the rest goes on the greens), then discard the marinade after using it.

If making the orzo side dish, *below*, toss the hot pasta with the vinaigrette for the best flavor.

▼ *For the vinaigrette, whisk olive oil into citrus juices and seasonings.*

▲ *Grill salmon and slices of onion. The onions will separate into rings a bit—it's okay, just try not to lose them through the grates.*

CITRUS MARINATED SALMON WITH SUMMER GREENS

MAKES FOUR 6-OZ. FILETS
TOTAL TIME: ABOUT 1 HOUR

FOR THE CITRUS VINAIGRETTE—
COMBINE:

Juice and minced zest of
1 orange *and* 1 lemon
Juice of 1 lime
1   T. sugar
    Salt, black pepper, and
    crushed red pepper flakes
    to taste

WHISK IN:

$1/4$ cup extra-virgin olive oil

FOR THE SALMON AND GREENS—
MARINATE:

4   filets (6 oz. each) fresh
    salmon

BRUSH WITH VINAIGRETTE; SEASON:

2   $1/2$"-thick rings red onion

PREPARE:

5   cups mixed spring greens
1   cup fresh pineapple, diced
$1/2$ cup macadamia nuts, coarsely
    chopped

▲ *Plate salmon and onions with greens, then drizzle with more vinaigrette.*

Combine juices and zests of citrus, sugar, and seasonings for the vinaigrette in a small bowl. **Whisk in** olive oil a little at a time until slightly thickened. **Marinate** salmon in $1/3$ cup vinaigrette for 15–30 minutes (no longer or fish will become mushy). **Brush** both sides of onion with some of the vinaigrette and season with salt and pepper.

Preheat grill to medium-high; clean and lightly oil grill grates. **Prepare** greens, pineapple, and nuts; chill until ready to serve.

Remove fish from marinade (discard marinade), season lightly with salt and pepper, and grill as on Page 7. Grill onions while salmon cooks, keeping the rings connected as best you can.

Toss greens, pineapple, and nuts with some of the remaining vinaigrette. Divide greens among four serving plates, place a filet of salmon alongside them, then top the fish with rings of grilled onions. Drizzle fish with additional vinaigrette and serve.

side option

ORZO WITH ARUGULA

MAKES ABOUT 2 CUPS
TOTAL TIME: ABOUT 15 MINUTES

PREPARE:

1   cup dry orzo pasta

STIR IN:

1   cup fresh arugula or
    spinach, stemmed, torn
$1/4$ cup Citrus Vinaigrette,
    above

SEASON WITH:

    Salt and pepper

Prepare orzo according to package directions; drain but do not rinse. **Stir in** the arugula and vinaigrette while pasta is still hot. **Season** and serve with salmon.

Fish Tales

A few "pinbones" may be in the salmon filets. Find them by running your fingertips over the flesh. To remove a bone, use needle-nose pliers to grab it and gently pull it out, taking care not to tear the flesh.

pizza from the grill

Grilled pizza has everything going for it—crispy crust, delicious smoky flavor, and the chance to be outside.

Some of the best pizza comes from coal-fired ovens. Temperatures in them can hit a whopping 900°, cooking a pizza in minutes. Those hot ovens deliver a dynamite crust that's crisp, smoky, and a little charred. To me, it's the perfect pizza.

In the endless quest for pizza perfection at home, I knew I needed hot temperatures along with the ability to produce a little char and smoke. The natural solution was right outside on the deck—the grill.

It doesn't matter whether you own a gas or charcoal grill, the technique is the same and the results are excellent. One side of the grill is hot—this is where the crust gets crispy and charred. The other side, on low heat, is where you slide the crust over and add the toppings.

All this results in an unbelievable pizza that rivals those baked in coal-fired ovens. But there is one more secret to an excellent pizza— underdress it. With this great crust, the last thing you want to do is overload it with too much sauce, cheese, or toppings. Keep it simple.

Making the dough

For grilled pizza, the dough must deliver good flavor as well as the ability to be rolled thinly. This is absolutely necessary so it doesn't burn before it cooks through.

A blend of all-purpose and cake flours makes the dough very elastic (from the all-purpose flour), yet tender (from the cake flour). That, along with proofing, kneading, and rising creates the Italian-style crust you want.

Proofing: Yeast is a living organism that, when activated, causes dough to rise. To trigger its rising powers, proof the yeast in warm water and a little sugar prior to mixing it with the flour. You can tell it's working when the mixture becomes foamy.

Kneading: Kneading is the process of developing gluten which allows dough to stretch. A stand mixer makes it easy, but you can knead by hand too. Stop when the dough is smooth and springs back when poked.

Rising: Pizza dough develops flavor and texture during two rises. The important thing here is to let the dough rise at room temperature (75°)—not in a heated oven or near an air conditioner vent! Hot temperatures will cook the dough, and cold temperatures will slow the yeast down.

◄ *Dissolve yeast and sugar in warm water. The yeast feeds on the sugar and activates quickly.*

Mix flours and salt in stand mixer. Add yeast mixture and knead on low speed 10 minutes. Dough will climb up the hook when ready. ►

Pizza Dough

Makes Enough for Four 12" Pizzas
Total Time: 15 Minutes + 3 Hours Rising

Combine:
- 1   cup warm water (105–115°)
- 1   T. sugar
- 1   pkg. (¼ oz.) active dry yeast (2¼ t.)

Mix:
- 2¼ cups all-purpose flour
- 1   cup cake flour
- 1   T. kosher salt

Add:
- 2   T. olive oil

Combine water, sugar, and yeast. Proof until foamy, about 5 minutes.
Mix flours and salt in the bowl of a stand mixer fitted with a dough hook.
Add oil to yeast mixture once it has proofed, then pour into flour mixture. Knead on low speed 10 minutes (if kneading by hand, knead same amount of time).

Place dough in a lightly oiled bowl, turning to coat. Cover with plastic wrap and let rise in a warm place until doubled, about 2 hours.

Punch dough down and divide into four balls, pinching the bottoms closed. Cover with plastic wrap, and let rise in a warm place another hour.

▲ *After two hours, the dough will have doubled in size. Punch it down.*

▲ *Divide dough into four balls. Pinch bottoms to keep air out. Let rise 1 hour.*

Topping grilled pizza

The sky's the limit with pizza toppings, but these three ideas may help guide you. Remember these things: Layer the toppings in the order in which they're listed, and *don't overload the crust.* Add fresh herbs at the last minute—the residual heat will release their flavor.

Grilled pizzas cook quickly so have all the toppings ready, and set up an area near the grill for them.

▲ Pepperoni Pizza: *Brush dough with olive oil, then top with fresh mozzarella, sliced pepperoni, and some Oven-Roasted Tomato Sauce. Sprinkle with thinly sliced fresh spinach, grated Parmesan cheese, coarse sea salt, and red pepper flakes.*

◄ Mediterranean Pizza: *Brush dough with olive oil, then top with cubed fontina, slices of salami, quartered marinated artichoke hearts, and slivered kalamata olives. Sprinkle with diced fresh tomatoes and grated Parmesan cheese. Add torn fresh basil leaves when the pizza is off the grill.*

▲ Sausage Pizza: *Brush dough with olive oil, then top with grated white Cheddar, cooked and sliced link Italian sausage, and some Oven-Roasted Tomato Sauce. Sprinkle with thinly sliced red onion, grated Parmesan cheese, coarse sea salt, and crushed red pepper flakes. Add torn fresh basil before serving.*

OVEN-ROASTED TOMATO SAUCE

This recipe make more sauce than you'll need for pizzas. Use leftovers as a light pasta sauce.
MAKES 5 CUPS; TOTAL TIME: 50 MINUTES

COMBINE:
8	cups (4 lb.) Roma tomatoes, quartered
1	cup yellow onion, chopped
4	cloves garlic, whole
2	t. kosher salt
1	t. red pepper flakes
1	t. sugar

TOSS WITH:
1/2	cup olive oil

STIR IN:
1/2	cup fresh basil, chiffonade

Preheat oven to 450°.
Combine tomatoes, onion, garlic cloves, salt, pepper, and sugar in a large casserole dish.
Toss with olive oil and roast 35–40 minutes until tomatoes have softened. Remove from oven and mash with a potato masher, keeping tomatoes a bit chunky.
Stir in basil.

Grilling pizza

With the toppings ready to go, you're literally minutes away from pizza nirvana.

Shaping: Roll out the dough on a dry work surface dusted with flour. Shape it into a 10–12" circle or rectangle—don't worry if it's not perfect. An irregular shape makes it look rustic.

On the grill: To transfer the dough to the grill, use your fingertips to lift it by the edges and drape directly onto the hottest part of the grill. The high, direct heat from the fire will penetrate the crust and firm it up. Use tongs to move the crust around if the grill has hot spots.

Toppings: Before adding toppings, move the crust to the cool side of the grill. (If you don't have a double burner, move the crust to a baking sheet to top.) Then return the pizza to the hot side for final cooking—check it frequently for burning. Use a pizza wheel to slice, and listen for the great crunch!

▲ *Roll dough out from the center to the edge on a lightly floured work area.*

1 Preheat grill with one side set to medium-high, the other side to low. Place dough over hot side, close lid, and cook 2–3 minutes. The crust will bubble and grill marks will appear underneath.

2 Use tongs to flip crust over and move to the cool side of grill. Brush with olive oil—it adds flavor and contributes to the crispy texture.

3 Add toppings (see Page 14 for order). Keep quantities light so they cook quickly. Return pizza to hot side of grill for 4–5 minutes.

4 Pizza is done when cheese is melted. Remove from grill using a pizza peel or the back of a baking sheet.

stuffing a
chicken breast

Chicken breasts get a summer makeover in this simple, outdoor dish. Great for parties, but easy enough for weeknights.

Here's a great technique for stuffing a chicken breast (beef and pork may be stuffed this way too). No messing with needles and twine—this method is quick, easy, and best of all, delicious. Ideal for summer, when you want kitchen time kept short.

Stuffed with ripe tomatoes from the garden, this is the perfect summer meal. But there are a few things you should know before getting started.

Selecting: To form a good-sized pocket, select boneless, skinless chicken breast halves that weigh about six ounces and are at least 1/2" thick.

You *could* use breasts with the skin still on, but since the filling helps keep the chicken moist, there's really no need. Plus, the

skin is more prone to shrivel up, stick to the grill, and cause grease flare-ups. If you ask me, it's much less trouble to just use skinless.

Preparing: Before stuffing, prepare the chicken by rinsing it under cold water, patting it dry, and then trimming away any excess fat.

Washing the chicken won't remove harmful bacteria (cooking them does that). But it will make the chicken less slippery so the pockets are easier to cut.

Stuffing a chicken breast

A deep pocket within the chicken breast it the key to keeping the filling in place. Here's how to do it.

Pocket: Forming a perfect pocket starts in the thickest part of the chicken, *see Figure 1*. This way, you'll have room to create a hole for filling without poking through a side.

Use the palm of your non-slicing hand as a guide and place it on top of the thickest part of the breast. Insert the knife into the breast, *see Figure 2*, feeling to make sure that the knife stays parallel with the cutting board. A thin-bladed knife, such as a boning knife, works best.

Now slowly "saw" in and out, moving the knife as in *Figures A–C*. The incision should take up no

1 To make a large pocket for the filling, start in the thickest part of the breast.

2 Use your hand as a guide to make sure you cut parallel to the board.

more than 1/2–3/4 the length of the breast. A small "tail" will remain uncut at the thin, narrow part of the breast.

As you remove the knife, slice the opening of the pocket just a tad wider. There should be enough room to fit either a spoon or a few fingers, whatever you prefer to stuff with. And finally, use your index finger to feel the inside of the pocket. Break apart any layers of meat the knife may have missed, making sure the pocket is large enough to hold 1/4 cup of filling.

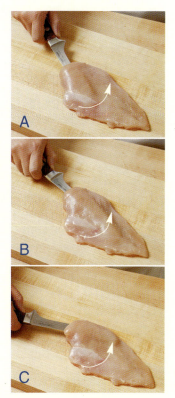

A

B

C

Stuffing: When preparing the filling, keep the size of the ingredients small—you don't want them poking through the chicken. And be sure the filling is cold before stuffing the breasts to help prevent bacterial growth.

Hold the pocket open with one had and stuff it with the other, *see Figure 3*. Fill the breast until mounded, then lightly press on it to evenly distribute the filling and insure that the entire pocket is stuffed.

SUMMER STUFFED CHICKEN BREASTS
MAKES 4 CHICKEN BREASTS; TOTAL TIME: 40 MINUTES

PREPARE:
4 boneless, skinless chicken breast halves, *above*

COMBINE:
1 cup feta cheese, crumbled
3/4 cup Roma tomatoes, seeded, chopped
1/4 cup chopped fresh parsley
1/4 cup fresh lemon juice
3 T. olive oil
1 T. lemon zest, minced
1 T. garlic, minced
Salt and pepper to taste

COAT WITH; GRILL:
Olive oil, salt, and pepper

SERVE WITH:
Lemon Herb Beurre Blanc

Preheat grill to medium-high.
Prepare breasts for stuffing, cutting pocket as illustrated above.
Combine feta, tomatoes, parsley, lemon juice, olive oil, zest, garlic, salt, and pepper in a bowl. Stuff each breast with 1/4 cup filling.
Coat both sides of breasts with oil, salt, and pepper.

Oil grill grates, then grill chicken, covered, 10–12 minutes per side, *Page 18*.
Serve with Lemon Herb Beurre Blanc, *Page 19*.

3 Make sure the pocket is thoroughly stuffed. Aside from its great flavor, the filling looks terrific when the chicken is sliced.

cuisinetechnique

Grilling

Once the chicken breasts have been stuffed, follow these simple techniques for hassle-free grilling. (If grilling isn't an option, roast the chicken, uncovered, at 350° for 45 minutes.)

Preparing to grill: Preheat the grill to medium-high and season both sides of the stuffed breasts with olive oil, salt, and pepper. Be sure to add the oil *before* the seasonings since it helps them cling to the chicken.

And to keep the chicken from sticking to the grill, oil the grates right before grilling, *see Figure 4*. Otherwise the oil will burn off.

Grilling: Grill the chicken breasts towards the back and center of the grill—where the heat is usually the hottest. Place the top side of the chicken down first, *see Figure 5*. This serves two purposes. One, it cooks the filling quickly. And two, it makes for prettier chicken. If the top of the breasts starts to brown too quickly, flip them over and continue cooking on the side that's hidden when presented, *see Figure 6*.

Doneness: Every grill acts a little differently, so time alone can't always determine doneness—but a thermometer can.

The chicken breasts are done once they've reached an internal reading of 160°. This verifies that both the filling and chicken are thoroughly cooked.

Resting: This step is just as important as grilling, so don't skip it! As the final stage of the cooking process, resting allows the chicken to finish cooking on its own heat—inside out.

Remove the breasts from the grill and let rest, whole and uncut, for 5–10 minutes.

4 Too much oil can cause flare-ups. So, use a paper towel dipped in oil to grease the grill grates.

5 Begin by placing the breasts on the grill so the flat side of the chicken is facing you.

6 Cover and grill the chicken 10–12 min. Flip, then grill 10–12 more minutes. (To make the cool-looking grill marks, see Page 7.)

7 Remove chicken breasts from grill and let rest. Then, slice and serve.

beurre blanc Sauce

Literally meaning "white butter," a beurre blanc [burr BLAHN] is a traditional French sauce that's great with eggs, vegetables, seafood, and of course, stuffed chicken breast.

A beurre blanc is also very versatile. You can easily complement specific dishes just by whisking in a few extra seasonings. This Lemon Herb Beurre Blanc, for example, goes great with the Summer Stuffed Chicken on Page 17. And the Curry Beurre Blanc on Page 21 is perfect with the Indian-Style Chicken.

Although cream is not usually part of the recipe, it is included here. Since a beurre blanc can break (separate) easily, the cream is used to help stabilize the sauce.

The key techniques to making a good beurre blanc are to use very cold butter and whisk continuously. Both help the butter emulsify, or combine, with the liquids.

BASIC BEURRE BLANC
MAKES ³/₄ CUP; TOTAL TIME: 15 MINUTES

REDUCE:
- ¹/₄ cup dry white wine
- 2 T. white wine vinegar
- 2 T. shallots, minced

ADD; REDUCE:
- 1 T. heavy cream

OFF HEAT, WHISK IN:
- 1 cup cold unsalted butter, cut into tablespoons

FOR THE LEMON HERB BEURRE BLANC—
STIR INTO BASIC BEURRE BLANC:
- 1 T. fresh lemon juice
- 2 t. minced fresh thyme
- 2 t. minced fresh chives
- 2 t. minced fresh parsley
- Salt and pepper to taste

Reduce wine and vinegar with shallots over medium-high heat until liquid is reduced by half, 2–4 minutes.

Add cream; simmer until reduced by half, about 1 minute.

Off heat, whisk in butter, 2 T. at a time, until melted.

Warm water bath
To hold the sauce for serving, place it in a bowl, then set it into a larger bowl of warm water. This will prevent the sauce from solidifying. Be sure the water isn't too hot, or the sauce will likely separate.

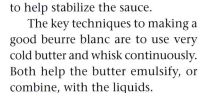

▲ *Reduce wine and vinegar by half, then add 1 T. cream.*

▲ *Add cold butter, whisking continuously until completely melted.*

▲ *Finish the sauce, flavoring it with additional seasonings, such as Lemon Herb or Curry.*

stuffed chicken breast
Indian-style

Quick, easy, and patio-perfect, this dish is packed with all the good things of summer— sunshine colors, bright flavors, and warm spices.

Indian food in the summer? Absolutely! Many Indian meals are cooked in a tandoori (clay) oven whose signature mark is bright red food that's perfectly charred. What better way to replicate this method than with your own backyard grill— red food coloring optional.

This recipe is the perfect introduction to Indian cuisine. It only calls for common ingredients that can easily be found at any grocery store. Yogurt, spinach, garlic, and paprika—most are probably in your kitchen already. To make the stuffed chicken even more authentic, serve it over basmati rice and garnish with cilantro, tomatoes, and cashews.

The Curry Beurre Blanc is a must-have addition to the dish. But I'll warn you now, it's so good you might need to make a double batch!

Tandoori-style

Aside from tasting great, tandoori chicken just looks cool. For this backyard BBQ version, the marinade helps achieve that tandoori style. It adds bright color, an intense curry flavor, and leaves parts of the chicken dark and charred. To get a dish that looks even closer to the real tandoori deal, just add a few drops of red food coloring to the marinade!

Ricotta cheese is included in the filling. No, it's not Indian, but it is somewhat similar to paneer, a fresh Indian cheese. In Indian households, paneer is often made every day—ricotta is much easier to come by.

INDIAN-STYLE STUFFED CHICKEN BREASTS

MAKES 4 CHICKEN BREASTS
TOTAL TIME: 45 MINUTES + MARINATING

FOR THE CHICKEN—
PREPARE:
- 4 boneless, skinless chicken breast halves, *Page 17*

FOR THE MARINADE—
MIX:
- 1 cup plain yogurt
- 1/2 cup fresh lemon juice
- 2 T. fresh ginger, minced
- 1 T. garlic, smashed
- 1 T. paprika
- 2 t. curry powder
- 1 t. cayenne
- 1 t. ground cumin
- 1 t. ground coriander
- 1 t. kosher salt

FOR THE FILLING—
COMBINE:
- 1 pkg. (10 oz.) frozen spinach, thawed, squeezed dry
- 3/4 cup ricotta cheese
- 2 T. plain yogurt
- 1 shallot, minced
  Salt and pepper to taste

SERVE WITH:
- Curry Beurre Blanc, *right*
- Basmati rice
- Toasted cashews
- Diced Roma tomatoes
- Chopped cilantro

Prepare chicken for stuffing.
Mix ingredients for marinade in large bowl.
Combine ingredients for filling in a second bowl. Stuff chicken with about 1/4 cup filling per breast, *Page 17*. Marinate stuffed breasts for 15 minutes.

Preheat grill to medium-high. Oil grill grates, then grill the chicken, covered, for 10–12 minutes per side, *Page 18*.
Serve with Curry Beurre Blanc over basmati rice and garnish with cashews, tomatoes, and cilantro.

CURRY BEURRE BLANC

MAKES 3/4 CUP
TOTAL TIME: 15 MINUTES

PREPARE:
  Basic Beurre Blanc, *Page 19*
STIR IN AT THE END:
- 1/4 cup coconut milk
- 2 T. fresh cilantro, chopped
- 1 T. curry powder
- 1 t. sugar
- 1 t. crushed red pepper flakes
  Salt to taste

Prepare Basic Beurre Blanc.
Stir in coconut milk, cilantro, curry powder, sugar, crushed red pepper flakes, and salt at the end.

◄ *Squeeze the spinach completely dry or the filling will be too runny.*

▲ *Before grilling, marinate stuffed chicken breasts for 15 minutes.*

▼ *The marinade helps the grill marks become even more apparent. (See Page 7 for instructions on how to make them.)*

Vanilla

For a true taste of the tropics, forget packing suitcases or finding misplaced passports. The exotic flavor and aroma of vanilla beans will take you there.

I thought I knew plenty about vanilla extracts and beans. But it wasn't until I linked up with William and Ruth Penzey, owners of Spice Work in Wisconsin, that I realized I still had plenty to learn. Now you, too, can benefit from their infinite knowledge.

Why so expensive?

Vanilla is one of the three most expensive spices, sandwiched between saffron and cardamom. It is the product of *Vanilla planifolia*, the only orchid to produce edible fruit (called pods), and is the world's most labor-intensive agricultural crop. This is mainly due to its unique pollination technique and time-consuming harvesting and curing processes.

The varieties

Although grown all over the tropics, the most highly regarded vanillas come from Mexico, Madagascar, and Tahiti.

Mexican and Madagascar (or "Bourbon," not having anything to do with the whiskey) vanillas are argued to be the best. Experts claim that Mexican vanilla has a natural note of spice, so pair it with spices like cloves, allspice, and cinnamon to enhance their flavors. Madagascar has a creamy and smooth flavor, and makes a high-quality all-purpose vanilla. But in reality, both taste types fairly similar and you can easily replace one for the other.

Tahitian vanilla has a more untraditional flavor, characterized as fruity, floral, and sweeter than Mexican and Madagascar vanilla. It's the product of the plant *Vanilla tahitensis* and is rather difficult to come by (Spice Work does carry it). If you come across this variety, try it in fruit pies, tarts, even smoothies!

Bean vs. extract

In recipes, vanilla beans and vanilla extract are often interchangeable (half of one bean is roughly equivalent to 1–2 teaspoons extract). Purists prefer to use a bean over extract since it provides a true vanilla flavor. It's also what to use if you want those infamous black speckles decorating your dish. Extract, on the other hand, is easier to come by, more efficient to use, and much more cost-effective.

Purchasing vanilla

When purchasing vanilla beans and extract, look for labels that specify their country of origin. It's the best guarantee of quality.

Be extra discriminating with Mexican vanilla extract, though. Due to Mexico's labeling policy, tonka beans are often added to stretch the flavor of the costlier vanilla bean. Tonka beans contain coumarin, a potentially toxic substance banned by the FDA. Buy from a reputable source and there's nothing to worry about.

Great places to start are **Spice Island** (available in most grocery stores) and **Nielsen-Massey** (available at gourmet food shops and health food stores). For reliable mail order, call **Penzeys** at **(800) 741-7787**, or **Spice Work** at **(414) 258-7727**.

◄ *To use a bean, slice down the middle and scrape out the seeds with the back of a knife.*

vanilla **varieties**

While expensive, vanilla beans and high-quality extracts provide the purest, most intense flavor. Their shelf life is long, and a little goes a long way, so it's money well spent. Less expensive extracts lack the same intensity, but they may be used in a pinch. Avoid imitation vanilla at all costs!

▲ *Make sure the label reads "pure vanilla extract" and specifies using beans from Madagascar, Mexico, or Tahiti.*

Imitation & White Vanilla

Imitation vanilla synthetically reproduces vanillin, which is only *one* of vanilla's hundreds of natural compounds. The result is an incredibly fake taste that lacks both the depth and complexity that pure vanilla extract boasts.

White vanilla is one more imitation product that is sometimes necessary in recipes when an all white color is desired, like wedding cakes.

Vanilla Extracts

Extract is made by soaking vanilla beans in alcohol to *extract* their flavor. Higher quality beans provide the richest tasting extracts.

Vanilla extracts must contain at least 35% alcohol by volume— an FDA regulation. Anything less is no longer considered an extract but a "flavoring."

Selecting: As a general rule, more expensive extracts provide the best vanilla flavor. Select those made with Madagascar, Mexican, or Tahitian beans. They are best.

Storing: Keep extracts in a cool, dry area away from direct sunlight. Stored properly, they will last indefinitely.

Using: In most recipes calling for vanilla extract (cookies, brownies, cakes), the extract's quality becomes less apparent— its flavor lessens when exposed to prolonged heat. But in recipes that do not require extensive cooking, like some ice creams, the use of high-quality vanilla extract is essential. Use it whenever you want a truly rich taste.

Vanilla Beans

Selecting: Select vanilla beans from Madagascar, Mexico, or Tahiti. They should be moist, plump, and aromatic, between 5–7" long. Dried out beans are difficult to work with and less likely to have an abundant seed mass, which is where most of the vanilla flavor comes from.

Storing: Keep beans in a cool, dry area out of direct sunlight. The beans can start to dry out after a year, but storing them in an airtight container helps.

As the bean ages, white crystals may form on the outside of the pod. These crystals are vanillin, the major flavoring unit in vanilla. Their appearance is the result of the curing process and the sign of a good bean.

Using: To get the most flavor out of a bean, use it in liquid-based recipes, like custards. Slice the bean open, scrape out its seeds, then steep them both in a liquid ingredient (like milk or cream) before cooking.

Double Strength Extract

Double strength (or double fold) extract uses twice the number of vanilla beans in the same amount of alcohol as single strength vanilla extract.

Using: Use half the amount a recipe calls for. Or, match it teaspoon for teaspoon for an even deeper vanilla flavor.

summer's
grilled vegetables

Take advantage of summer's finest with these two easy-to-make dishes. Serve them as an appetizer or a light meal.

Sometimes the recipe trail isn't always clearly marked. There are some foods that look really appealing uncooked, yet appear less than appetizing when cooked. This is especially true for large portobello mushrooms and deep purple eggplant—they just don't live up to their uncooked natural good looks. But these recipes can change that.

Part of a portobello's appeal is size—big and thick. This makes it a "no-brainer" for stuffing with colorful vegetables. Grilling it really enhances its meaty flavor.

Cooked eggplant can turn mushy and brown in a heartbeat. You can avoid this by leaving a little skin on the eggplant and grilling it quickly. Don't like goat cheese? Try fresh mozzarella.

GRILLED STUFFED PORTOBELLO MUSHROOMS

MAKES 6 MUSHROOMS
TOTAL TIME: ABOUT 30 MINUTES

FOR THE STUFFING—
SAUTE IN 1 T. OLIVE OIL:
1   cup yellow onion, diced
1   cup yellow bell pepper, diced
ADD AND SAUTE:
4   cups fresh arugula or spinach
1   cup tomatoes, chopped
2   t. garlic, minced
1   t. crushed red pepper flakes
    Salt to taste
OFF HEAT, ADD:
1½ cups mozzarella (*not* fresh mozzarella), cubed
½ lb. Italian sausage, cooked, minced
FOR THE MUSHROOMS—
FILL; SPRINKLE WITH:
6   portobello mushroom caps, (4" diameter) stemmed and gills removed, see *Page 28*
    Grated Parmesan cheese

Preheat grill to medium.
Saute onion and bell pepper in oil until soft, about 5 minutes.
Add arugula, tomatoes, garlic, pepper flakes, and salt; saute 1 min.
Off heat, add mozzarella and cooked, minced sausage.
Fill caps with stuffing; sprinkle with Parmesan. Grill until cheese melts and mushrooms cook through, 5 minutes.

Mince the sausage after cooking so it doesn't overpower the other stuffing ingredients. ▼

▲ *Fill each portobello cap with ½ cup of stuffing, then grill over medium heat.*

GRILLED EGGPLANT "SANDWICHES"

MAKES 4 SANDWICHES
TOTAL TIME: ABOUT 30 MINUTES

FOR THE TOMATO SALSA—
COMBINE:
1 1/2 cups tomatoes, seeded, diced
2 T. fresh basil, sliced
2 T. olive oil
1 T. balsamic vinegar
   Salt to taste
FOR THE SANDWICHES—
STIR TOGETHER:
1/2 cup olive oil
1 t. paprika
   Black pepper to taste
ASSEMBLE; GRILL:
1 eggplant, peeled, sliced 1"
   thick (with pocket)
4 oz. goat cheese, sliced into
   1/2"-thick rounds
4 slices baguette, 1/2" thick,
   brushed with olive oil
TOP WITH:
   Tomato Salsa and basil sprigs

Preheat grill to medium.
Combine tomatoes, basil, 2 T. oil, vinegar, and salt for the salsa.
Stir together olive oil, paprika, and pepper for the sandwiches.
Assemble sandwiches, inserting goat cheese rounds into each eggplant pocket. Spoon seasoned oil on both sides of eggplant, then grill until golden brown, about 3 minutes per side. Toast both sides of baguette slices on grill, transfer to a platter, then arrange eggplant on top.
Top with salsa and basil.

For pockets, alternate slicing the eggplant all the way through with slicing it three-quarters of the way through. ▼

▲ *Fill each pocket with goat cheese; coat with paprika oil.*

Grill until eggplant is golden and goat cheese softens. ▼

faster**with**fewer

Cucumbers

Overwhelmed by the garden's onslaught of cucumbers? These four recipes give you plenty of options to put them to good use.

MEXICAN CUCUMBER-MANGO SALAD

This salad is an offshoot of a popular snack in Mexico. Serve it as a refreshing side dish or salsa for fish and chicken.

MAKES ABOUT 3 CUPS
TOTAL TIME: 30 MINUTES

1	cup cucumber, diced
1	cup mango, diced, see *Basic Cuisine, Page 28*
1	cup jicama, peeled, diced
1/4	cup red onion, minced
1/4	t. chili powder
	Juice of 1 lime
	Pinch salt and sugar
	Cilantro leaves

Combine all ingredients in a mixing bowl; let stand at least 5 minutes. If waiting longer than that, add the cilantro just before serving.

▲ *Jicama [HEE-kah-mah] is a crunchy vegetable popular in Latin America. You can find it in many grocery stores. Use a peeler to remove its skin.*

GREEK CUCUMBER SALAD

Stuffed into pita pockets with leaf lettuce, grilled chicken, and feta cheese, this salad can make a simple sandwich too.

MAKES ABOUT 3 CUPS
TOTAL TIME: 30 MINUTES

1	cup cucumber, diced
1	cup tomatoes, chopped
1/2	cup canned chickpeas, drained, rinsed
1/4	cup kalamata olives, pitted, sliced
1/4	cup scallions, sliced
1/4	cup coarsely chopped parsley
	Juice of 1 lemon
1	t. garlic, minced (1 clove)
1	t. sugar
	Salt and pepper to taste
2–3	T. extra-virgin olive oil
3	T. chopped fresh mint
	Toasted pita bread, torn, *optional*

Combine the cucumbers, tomatoes, chickpeas, olives, scallions, and parsley in a large bowl.

Whisk together lemon juice, garlic, sugar, salt, and pepper for the vinaigrette in a bowl.

Drizzle olive oil into lemon juice mixture in a steady stream. Stir in mint and adjust seasonings to taste.

Toss salad with vinaigrette and toasted pita bread pieces (if using) just before serving. Serve at room temperature.

Toast one lightly oiled pita in a 400° oven until crisp. Tear it into large pieces and add them to the salad just before tossing with the vinaigrette. ▶

CUCUMBERS IN DILLED SOUR CREAM

Salting the cucumbers draws out excess moisture and helps keep the salad from getting overly watery. This is perfect with fried chicken and outstanding on grilled hot dogs!

MAKES ABOUT 2 CUPS
TOTAL TIME: ABOUT 30 MINUTES

1	large cucumber, halved lengthwise, seeded, sliced into 1/4"-thick half-moons
1	t. kosher salt
3	T. mayonnaise
3	T. sour cream
3	T. red onion, minced
2	T. white wine vinegar
1	T. sugar
1	T. chopped fresh dill

▲ *Scoop seeds from halved cucumbers with a spoon.*

Place cucumber slices in a colander; sprinkle with salt, tossing to coat. Let stand for 15 minutes, then rinse and pat dry with paper towels.

Combine mayonnaise, sour cream, onion, vinegar, sugar, and dill in a mixing bowl. Add cucumber slices and toss to coat. Let salad stand for at least 5 minutes before serving, or chill for up to one day.

▲ *Salt cucumber slices to draw out moisture. Rinse and dry before tossing with dressing.*

OPEN-FACED TOASTED CHEESE SANDWICHES WITH PICKLED CUCUMBERS

Here's a quick and simple lunch that's terrific with tomato soup. The cucumbers are also great on ham or roast beef sandwiches.

MAKES 4 SANDWICHES
TOTAL TIME: 30 MINUTES

1	large cucumber, thinly sliced
1	t. kosher salt
1/4	cup white wine vinegar
2	T. sugar
2	t. chopped fresh dill
1	t. Dijon mustard
1/2	t. prepared horseradish
4	slices rye bread, halved
4	oz. white Cheddar cheese, thinly sliced
	Butter and Dijon mustard

Spread one side of each slice of bread with butter and the other side with Dijon. Heat a large nonstick skillet or griddle over medium heat. Add bread, buttered side down; top each slice with a single layer of cheese. Toast until cheese is melted and the bread is golden brown and crisp on the bottom.

Divide sandwiches among four serving plates, top with cucumbers, and serve immediately.

Place cucumber slices in a colander; sprinkle with salt, tossing to coat. Let stand for 15 minutes, then rinse and pat dry with paper towels.

Combine vinegar, sugar, dill, 1 teaspoon mustard, and horseradish in a mixing bowl. Add cucumber slices and toss to coat. Let cucumbers stand at least 5 minutes, or chill for up to one day.

▲ *Top bread with cheese. Toast until cheese is melted and bottom of bread is crisp.*

basiccuisine

peeling peaches

▲ *Before boiling, cut an "x" in the bottom of the peaches to help the skin peel off easily.*

If you're making the Summer Peach Pie on Page 38, it's best to peel the peaches. To do that, bring a large pot of water to a boil and have a bowl of ice water ready. Cut a small "x" in the bottom of each peach, then drop the fruit into the boiling water for about 10 seconds. Remove the peaches with a slotted spoon and immediately transfer them to ice water to stop the cooking. When cool, gently pinch the cut on the bottom of the peach—the peel should slip right off. If it doesn't, boil the peach for a few more seconds, then transfer to ice water again. Trim off any stubborn peel with a knife.

gilling portobellos

The gills on the underside of mushroom caps are completely edible and harmless—in fact, most recipes don't require their removal. But portobello mushrooms have especially dark gills which can cause any dish they're in to turn black and unappealing.

To remove their gills, first trim out the stem with a paring knife. Scrape off the gills using the edge of a teaspoon—but don't scrape too deeply into the flesh. A dark tint will remain on the portobello, but it's fine.

If stuffing smaller crimini or button mushrooms, use the same technique with a smaller utensil, like a melon baller or espresso spoon.

◄ *Remove the mushroom stem by trimming it from the base with a paring knife.*

seeding **tomatoes**

Seeding tomatoes not only removes seeds but eliminates some of their watery quality. The first step is to cut the tomato across its equator, *right,* to expose the seed chambers. In the bottom photo, you can see the chambers clearly. The half on the left is cut correctly so you can reach each chamber. The one on the right, cut top to bottom, exposes only two.

To remove the seeds, gently squeeze each tomato half. You can also scrape out the seeds using your finger, a small spoon, or chopstick.

dicing **mangoes**

When dicing a mango, it's helpful to start with a brief anatomy lesson. In the center of the fruit is a large flat pit. On both sides of the pit are two fleshy sections. Cut off these portions to form two "lobes." Don't slice too close to the pit as the flesh nearest the pit is firmly attached and tends to be very stringy.

To dice, make crosshatch cuts in the flesh, taking care not to go through the peel. Turn the mango "inside out," then cut the cubes off the peel.

Score the flesh, then bend back lobe to expose the diced mango. ▶

▲ *Slice off lobes from both sides of the mango.*

fresh Corn Soups

There's nothing better than soup made with fresh sweet corn. It is the essence of summer.

Sweet corn is a great vehicle for soup making. It goes well with so many ingredients and yet never loses its distinct flavor—even with chiles and peppers.

Using poblanos in the corn chowder adds a spicy richness unique to the chile. If you can't find poblanos at your grocery store, check out a local Mexican market or farmers market.

The base for the bisque is made with sweet red bell peppers. Sauteed and pureed, they create a brightly flavored and brilliantly colored soup—perfect against summer's yellow corn.

POBLANO CORN CHOWDER

MAKES ABOUT 7 CUPS
TOTAL TIME: 45 MINUTES

CUT KERNELS FROM:
8   ears sweet corn (4 cups)
PUREE:
2   cups corn kernels
1   cup whole or 2% milk
SAUTE IN 2 T. VEGETABLE OIL:
2   poblano chiles, seeded, diced
1 1/2 cups white onion, diced
1   t. garlic, minced
ADD:
2   cups chicken broth
2   cups corn kernels
1   t. sugar
1   t. kosher salt
1/2 t. cayenne
STIR IN:
     Pureed corn
1 1/2 cups tomato, diced
1/4 cup feta cheese, crumbled
GARNISH WITH:
     Chopped fresh cilantro
     Diced avocado
     Lime slices

▲ *To cut kernels from ears of corn, stand cob upright, then carefully slice straight down.*

Cut kernels from ears of corn.
Puree 2 cups corn kernels and milk in a blender.
Saute chiles, onion, and garlic in oil in soup pot over medium heat. Cook 4–5 minutes.
Add broth, remaining corn, and seasonings. Simmer 5 minutes.
Stir in pureed corn, tomato, and cheese. Simmer to heat through and melt cheese, about 3 minutes.
Garnish servings of soup with cilantro, avocado, and lime.

Puree corn with milk—it will be very thick and have a rough texture. ▶

▲ *Add pureed corn to the soup. Simmer to heat through and melt cheese.*

CORN AND RED PEPPER BISQUE

Makes 8 Cups; Total Time: 45 Minutes

Sweat in 3 T. Olive Oil; Puree:

- 2 lb. red bell peppers, chopped (6 peppers)
- 2 cups yellow onion, chopped
- 1 cup carrot, diced
- 1 T. garlic, roughly chopped

Add:

- 4 cups fresh corn kernels
- 3 cups low-sodium chicken broth
- 2 T. fresh lemon juice
- 2 t. kosher salt
- 1 t. sugar
- 1/4 t. cayenne

Stir in:

- 1/2 cup half and half

Garnish with:

- Basil Crema, *right*
- Fresh basil sprigs

Sweat peppers, onion, carrot, and garlic in a large pot over medium-low heat for 15 minutes. Puree in blender until smooth. Return to soup pot.

Add corn, broth, lemon juice, and seasonings. Bring to a boil, reduce heat, and simmer 5 min.

Stir in half and half. Simmer a few minutes to heat through.

Garnish servings of soup with Basil Crema and basil sprigs.

To core bell peppers, slice down all sides of peppers from top to bottom. ▶

◀ *Sweat vegetables to soften, then puree. Return to same pot.*

▲ *Add corn, broth, lemon juice, and seasonings to soup. Simmer 5 min.*

basil crema

To make Basil Crema, blanch and drain 1 cup basil leaves. Puree basil in a blender with 1/2 cup half and half. Add 1 cup sour cream; mix until smooth.

▲ *Blanch basil in boiling water a few seconds. Transfer to ice water to stop cooking; drain.*

Puree basil and half and half. Add sour cream and blend.▼

wares
ice cream makers

Homemade ice cream used to be reserved for special occasions. But automatic makers have changed all that!

Let's face it—the ice, rock salt, and cranking required to create old-fashioned homemade ice cream makes it a major production. It's pretty fun on the 4th of July, but that's about it.

Automatic models have transformed the entire homemade ice cream experience! They produce the same great taste and soft-serve texture, minus all the time, mess, and trouble. Homemade ice cream isn't just for holidays anymore.

Testing: The ultimate test of an ice cream maker is the quality of ice cream it produces. So with "really good ice cream" as the guiding criteria, we tested (and double-tested) eight automatic ice cream makers using four cups of 40° vanilla ice cream base. Each maker generated different results and volume in various amounts of time.

The secondary set of criteria focused on practical concerns, like how easily it assembles, operates, and stores. Here is what we learned about automatic ice cream makers along the way.

Motors: There are two types of motors available: top- and bottom-mount. Top-mount motors churn ice cream by turning a *paddle* in the canister and don't require high wattage. But motors located on the bottom actually turn the *canister* while the paddle stays stationary. They require higher wattage to spin the heavy canister. So which design is better? Each has advantages, but both motors work equally well.

Storage: Finding storage space for bulky appliances is always an issue. Top-mount models have a clear advantage with only a small motor, paddle, and shield to store. The canister should be kept in the freezer so it's ready to make ice cream when you are.

Freezing material: Ice cream freezes due to continued contact with the walls of the frozen canister. The walls are filled with a liquid refrigerant that must be frozen solid before use, taking up to 24 hours.

Getting air: The hidden ingredient in ice cream is the air that's incorporated during the mixing and freezing process. Premium ice cream keeps air to a minimum—too much yields fluffy ice cream with little taste. We gauged added air by the volume of ice cream produced.

The bottom line: Four models churned their way to the top, creating good ice cream with a variety of methods and designs. All fall into the $50 range, take about 30 minutes to freeze the ice cream, and have warranties that cover everything but abuse. While it comes down to the best combination of features for *you,* you won't go wrong with any of these machines.

Cuisine Test Kitchen Recommendations:
These four models cranked out good ice cream time after time.

Cuisinart — $49.99

On the market for six years, the artfully designed Cuisinart ICE-20 goes together and operates with clear simplicity. With 50 watts to power smooth quiet rotations of the 1½-quart double-insulated canister, it delivered 4½ cups of good, but slightly grainy, ice cream. An automatic shut-off feature prevents overheating, but during one test it stopped the motor at 28 minutes—just a little early. Additional canisters are sold separately so you can churn one batch after another! Three-year warranty. Available at kitchen and department stores, or go to **cuisinart.com** for an ordering source.

Krups La Glacière — $59.95

Double insulated walls help keep the canister cold so the Krups can turn out thick, super-creamy ice cream in record time (an average of 4½ cups in just 20 minutes). At first, its top-mount motor can be a little tricky and awkward to get into place, but practice makes perfect—and it requires minimal storage space. The 15-watt motor is more than adequate to power the paddle on this 1½-quart model. One-year warranty. Order online at **cooking.com**, or call **(800) 663-8810**, item #102689.

Girmi — $49.95

The Italian-made Girmi (meaning "to turn and to mix") operates with the quietest motor tested. Its 50 watts turned the canister effortlessly, producing 5 cups of very smooth ice cream in 34 minutes. Easy assembly, clear-cut operation, and great results have kept this model in production for over 10 years with no major design changes. The 1-quart capacity listed on the packaging is a misnomer, referring to *liquid* capacity only. The canister actually holds 1½ quarts of finished ice cream. Three-year warranty. Order online at **tabletools.com** or call **(888) 211-6603**, item #92004.

Salton Big Chill — $39.95

This multi-piece model features a unique compact freezing "disk" that sits in the bottom of a plastic canister, *see inset*. Although the motor is off to the side, it operates as a bottom-mount unit, turning the canister and freezing the ice cream as it rotates directly over the frozen disk. Creamy, *incredibly* smooth ice cream is the reward for an unorthodox method, noisy churning, and cumbersome storage. With a 1½-quart finished ice cream capacity, it yielded 5¼ cups in 30 minutes. One-year warranty. Order online at **tabletools.com** or call **(888) 211-6603**, item #55009.

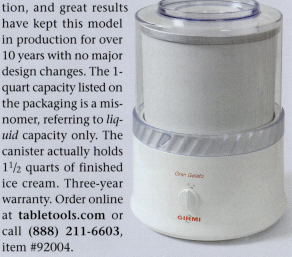

Super
flavored
Ice creams

Ben & Jerry's teaches us how to make premium ice cream at home—with the kind of over-the-top combinations and additions that make them legendary!

The world of ice cream hasn't been the same since Ben & Jerry's put their stamp on it. Their guiding principles of abundance and fun ushered in a new era of ice cream—where too much isn't *quite* enough, and only the ingredients are sacred.

That is just the kind of ice cream mixologist Eric Fredette creates at Ben & Jerry's. As one of the "Flavor Gurus," Eric dreams up flavors that lure you and me to the store late at night! And he did the same for us, developing three recipes tailored to making ice cream at home. Eric starts with rich, creamy vanilla and progresses to an incredible fruit variation. Then he tops it off with an abundant *Cuisine at home* signature ice cream you won't want to miss.

BEN & JERRY'S

It all started in 1978 when Ben Cohen & Jerry Greenfield began making ice cream in an old renovated gas station in Burlington, Vermont. They soon became popular for their innovative flavors, and the rest, as they say, is history.

Acquired by Unilever in April, 2000, Ben & Jerry's operates as an independent subsidiary, continuing to adhere to the product, economic, and social mission statements the company was built on. And the 600 employees still go home with three pints of ice cream every day!

Made with Vermont dairy products and all-natural ingredients, Ben & Jerry's is sold in stores nationwide and at 260 Ben & Jerry's Scoop Shops. For information on flavors, locations, and all things Ben & Jerry, go to **benandjerrys.com**.

Base rules

Each of these ice creams is built on a sweet cream base made of eggs, sugar, cream, and milk. Different flavors are created by adding ingredients to that base. The vanilla and raspberry versions use the same base, while the measurements and procedure for the chocolate version are slightly altered for good balance.

The eggs in the base add richness, provide creamy texture, and help the ice cream hold up in the freezer. If you're uncomfortable using raw eggs, look for *pasteurized* eggs in the shell—they're available at some supermarkets.

Incorporating too much air into the base results in fluffy ice cream that lacks depth. So use a whisk and whip by hand—an electric mixer froths in extra air.

VANILLA ICE CREAM

MAKES ABOUT 5 CUPS
TOTAL TIME: 10 MINUTES +
CHILLING AND FREEZING

FOR THE BASE—
WHISK:
2 eggs
2 egg yolks
WHISK IN:
1 1/3 cup sugar
ADD:
1 1/3 cup heavy cream
1 1/3 cup whole milk

FOR VANILLA ICE CREAM—
STIR IN; CHILL:
2 t. vanilla extract

Whisk eggs and yolks until light and fluffy, about 1 minute.
Whisk in sugar a little at a time. Continue whisking until completely blended, about 1 minute more.
Add cream and milk.
Stir in vanilla. Chill to 40°, 2 hours or overnight. Freeze in ice cream maker as directed by the manufacturer.

Whisk sugar into eggs until thick and the color lightens. ▼

Pour mixture into electric ice cream maker while it's running so the paddle doesn't freeze and lock. ►

Ice cream is finished when it reaches the soft-serve stage. For firmer ice cream, transfer to an airtight container and freeze for a day or two. ►

chefathome: *Ben and Jerry's Ice Cream*

RASPBERRY CRUNCH ICE CREAM

The foundation for this crunchy raspberry version is the base for Vanilla Ice Cream on Page 35.

MAKES 7 CUPS

TOTAL TIME: 15 MINUTES + CHILLING AND FREEZING

PREPARE:
   Ice Cream Base, *Page 35*

TOSS TOGETHER:
2   cups fresh or frozen raspberries
$^1/_2$ cup sugar
2   T. fresh lemon juice

ADD TO BASE, RESERVING $^1/_2$ CUP:
   Berry mixture

LAYER WITH:
   Reserved berry mixture
$1^1/_4$ cups granola

Prepare ice cream base; chill to 40°.
Toss raspberries, sugar, and lemon juice together. Cover and refrigerate 2 hours, stirring and mashing berries into large chunks after 1 hour.
Add berry mix to chilled base, reserving $^1/_2$ cup berries to layer in ice cream. Freeze in ice cream maker as directed by the manufacturer.
Layer ice cream, reserved berries, and granola in a plastic container, working quickly; freeze until firm.

Building fruit flavor

For this ice cream, maximum flavor is coaxed out of the raspberries (either fresh or frozen) by soaking them in sugar and lemon juice for a couple of hours. The sugar extracts the fruit's natural juices and enhances the flavor, while the acidity in the lemon juice keeps the color bright.

The fruit flavor is expanded by using the raspberry mixture in two stages. First, the majority is mixed into the base before freezing. The rest is then added between ice cream layers to create dark swirls of raspberry pieces. Chunky granola is sprinkled in, too, providing crunch. It stays surprisingly firm in the ice cream!

Expect the churning process to take up to twice as long as other ice creams—the added sugar in the fruit slows it down.

▲ *Stir raspberry mixture into chilled base just before freezing ice cream.*

◄ *Layer ice cream, reserved berry mixture, and granola three times (parfait-style) in an airtight storage container.*

Signature ice cream

What a kick! Ben & Jerry's actually created an original ice cream for *Cuisine at home*—with a name that's as fun as the ice cream! It packs a double chocolate punch with both unsweetened chocolate and cocoa powder in the base. Then it follows up with brownies, pecans, and caramel for the final knock-out.

Ben & Jerry's has a reputation for innovative ice cream "add-ins." Here are their guidelines for add-in success at home: Use quality, ready-made ingredients for convenience. Keep items big enough to identify—and don't be stingy with them. Freeze the chunks of add-ins briefly so they stay intact when folded into the ice cream. And, finally, since add-ins require sturdy, solid ice cream, freeze it a day or two before serving so it can harden.

"WHEN TURTLES GO BROWNIE" ICE CREAM

Go ahead and use purchased brownies and caramel sauce—when combined with the ice cream, you won't know they're not homemade.

MAKES 7 CUPS; TOTAL TIME: 30 MINUTES + CHILLING AND FREEZING

MELT:
2   oz. unsweetened chocolate

WHISK IN:
1½ cups whole milk
⅓   cup unsweetened cocoa powder

FOR THE BASE—

WHISK:
2   eggs

WHISK IN:
1   cup sugar

ADD; COMBINE WITH CHOCOLATE:
1   cup heavy cream
1   t. vanilla extract

FOLD IN:
1½ cups brownie chunks (½" cubes), frozen
¾   cup pecan halves, toasted in butter and salt, chilled

LAYER WITH:
½   cup caramel sauce, room temperature

Melt chocolate in a bowl set over simmering water.

Whisk in milk, followed by the cocoa, until incorporated and *very* smooth. Remove from heat and cool.

Whisk eggs for the base until light and fluffy, about 1 minute.

Whisk in sugar a little at a time until completely blended, about 1 minute more.

Add cream and vanilla. Combine cooled chocolate and ice cream base. Chill to 40°, 3 hours or overnight. Freeze in ice cream maker as directed by the manufacturer; remove paddle.

Fold in brownies and pecans.

Layer ice cream with caramel sauce in plastic container, working quickly to minimize melting. Freeze until firm.

▲ *Thoroughly whisk cocoa into the chocolate and milk mixture.*

Fold brownies and nuts in by hand so they stay intact.▼

Drizzle each ice cream layer with caramel sauce, then freeze until very firm. ▶

Pie tips

❖ Use cold butter to make pie dough. This will enhance the crust's flakiness by preventing the butter from melting into the dough during mixing.

❖ Chill the dough at least 1 hour before rolling out (overnight is best). It will be easier to handle and, thus, less likely to be overworked. The dough can also be frozen—thaw it in the refrigerator before rolling it out.

❖ Glass pie plates are great for a brown bottom crust. Use one if you can.

❖ When rolling the dough, use a fair amount of flour. Flip the dough over often, especially early on in rolling, to help keep it from sticking.

❖ Bake the pie on a baking sheet lined with parchment to catch any dripping juices.

summer
peach pie

There's only one reason to fire up the oven this summer—to make a fresh peach pie!

When was the last time you had pie made with fresh peaches? For most people, peach pies are not homemade, they're purchased—and that's a crying shame. Assembly-line pies with heavy crusts and meager amounts of canned fruit filling are sad sights, indeed.

It's time to raise the bar on peach pie, and this recipe does it. Full of fresh fruit flavored with vanilla, in a crust that's easy *and* to die for—what's not to like?

Obviously, ripe peaches are key, so choose fruit with a strong peach scent

and no green tinge (that means it's not ripe). Do not squeeze the fruit to determine whether or not it's ripe—that just bruises it. Buy $3^1/_2$ pounds of peaches to yield the required three pounds of peeled, pitted fruit, *see Basics, Page 28*.

Dried peaches also play a role in this pie. For one, they soak up some of the liquid from the peaches so the filling doesn't get too runny. And second, they really punch up the pie's peach flavor.

Pie making is inherently scary because of the dough, but don't let that stop you. Mix the dough gently, then chill it before rolling, and you'll be fine. You could use a plain top crust, but do try weaving the lattice—you'll look like a pie-baking pro!

Making pie dough

The trick to great pie dough is all in how it's handled. A delicate touch is required, otherwise you will have crust like shoe leather. Here are things to watch for.

As you cut the fats into the flour, make sure bits of butter (about the size of peas) are still visible. They create a flaky crust.

Stir in just enough ice water that the dough starts to clump. Amounts will vary, so start with the small measurement and add more as needed. If the dough is crumbly when pinched, it needs water, but not so much it's sticky.

Pinch a portion of dough to determine if more water is needed. ▼

FLAKY PIE DOUGH

MAKES ONE 9" LATTICE-TOP PIE
TOTAL TIME: 15 MINUTES + CHILLING

BLEND:
2½ cups all-purpose flour
2 T. sugar
¼ t. table salt
CUT IN:
½ cup shortening
½ cup cold unsalted butter, cubed
STIR IN:
4–7 T. ice water

Blend flour, sugar, and salt in a large bowl until well mixed.

Cut in shortening and butter with a pastry blender until mixture resembles coarse cornmeal. Some pea-size pieces of butter should still be visible.

Stir in 4T. ice water with a fork, adding more water 1 teaspoon at a time if dough seems dry when pinched. Divide dough in half, press each half into a disk, and wrap in plastic. Chill dough for at least 1 hour before rolling out.

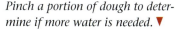

▲*Cut the fats into the dry ingredients. Small bits of butter are fine.*

◄*Wrap the dough in plastic and chill for at least 1 hour— chilling overnight is even better.*

Filling facts

For the filling, slice the peaches 1" thick so they keep their shape during baking. Then macerate (soak) them in sugar and lime juice—the resulting syrup is then used to soften the dried peaches.

Instant tapioca makes a terrific pie thickener—it gels very clear and is lighter tasting than flour or cornstarch. Be sure to finely grind the tapioca first, then mix with sugar so it blends throughout the filling.

Macerate the peach slices in sugar and lime juice, then drain, reserving the syrup. Simmer the dried peach pieces and vanilla bean in the syrup until peaches are soft. ▼

◄ *Finely grind tapioca in a coffee grinder.*

▲ *Gently combine fresh peaches with the simmered dried fruit and ground tapioca.*

SUMMER PEACH PIE

The pie tastes best the day it's made. Store any leftovers at room temperature—great for breakfast!

MAKES ONE 9" PIE
TOTAL TIME: ABOUT 2½ HOURS + COOLING

PREPARE:
1 recipe Flaky Pie Dough, *Page 39*

TOSS TOGETHER:
3½ lb. peaches, peeled, pitted, sliced, *see Basics Page 28*
1 cup sugar
Juice of 1 lime

SIMMER; STIR INTO FRUIT:
1½ cups syrup drained from peaches
6 oz. dried peaches, snipped
1 vanilla bean, split, scraped

COMBINE; ADD:
¼ cup sugar
3 T. instant tapioca, ground

SPRINKLE OVER:
1 cup fresh raspberries, *optional*

BRUSH WITH:
Half and half
Coarse or granulated sugar

SERVE WITH:
Vanilla ice cream

▲ *Roll out one portion of chilled dough to about 14" in diameter. Fold the round carefully into quarters, then transfer to a pie plate and unfold.*

Prepare pie dough and chill.

Toss peaches with sugar and lime juice, and macerate for at least 30 minutes. Drain fruit, reserving the syrup—you should have about 1½ cups. If you have more than that, pour off the excess; less, add water to make 1½ cups.

Simmer the peach syrup, dried peaches, and vanilla pod and seeds in a saucepan over medium heat. Cook until peaches are soft, 15–20 minutes. Remove the vanilla pod, then stir the dried peach mixture with the fresh peaches.

Combine ¼ cup sugar and ground tapioca in a small bowl, then sprinkle over the peach mixture; stir gently to combine. Let stand for 15 minutes while you roll the dough. Preheat oven to 425° with rack in lower third.

Roll one of the chilled dough disks on a lightly floured work surface until about ¼" thick and 14" in diameter. Transfer dough to a 9" pie plate, then fill with the prepared peach mixture.

Sprinkle optional raspberries randomly over the peaches. Do not stir them into the filling or they will get crushed.

Roll the second pie disk like the first, then cut into strips with a pastry wheel or knife. Weave a lattice top, trim edges, and crimp.

Brush top and edges of pie with half and half and sprinkle with sugar. Place pie on a parchment-lined baking sheet and bake in the lower third of the oven for 30 minutes. Reduce temperature to 350° and continue baking 50–60 minutes more. Cool pie for at least 3 hours before serving.

Serve with vanilla ice cream.

Weaving and baking

Weaving the lattice top is easier than you think. As you go along, keep an eye on the photos below—they'll help you get your bearings.

First, roll out the dough, trim the sides, then cut it into seven wide strips. Lay three strips horizontally across the pie, then fold back the center strip halfway. Now, at the point where the strip folds over, lay a fourth strip vertically. Unfold the center strip, then fold back the other two horizontal strips. Vertically place a fifth strip where these two strips fold over, then unfold.

Half the pie should now be covered with lattice. Good job! Now simply weave the last two strips on the other half of the pie, just like you did the on the first half.

Trim the excess dough from the edge, leaving an inch of overhang. Patch any "thin" spots with some excess dough trimmings. To crimp the edge, just pinch the dough between your thumb and forefinger as shown in the inset photo below. Crimp the edges well so the filling doesn't bubble over too much.

Brush the top with half and half, then sprinkle with sugar for sparkle (coarse sugar, such as *Sugar in the Raw* is nice, but regular sugar is just fine). Place the pie on a parchment-lined baking sheet (spray the paper with nonstick spray) and bake—the initial high temperature helps set the crust. Cool the pie a few hours before slicing so the filling thickens—it's a long wait, but *so* worth it.

Roll out the second portion of dough to 12–14" in diameter. Trim the edges to even out the sides, then cut into seven 1½"-wide strips. ▶

◀ Lay three strips horizontally across pie. Fold back the center strip halfway.

Place a strip vertically to the first three; unfold the center strip. Now fold back the other two horizontal strips. Add another vertical strip; unfold. ▶

▲ Repeat the same weaving technique on the other half of the pie using the remaining two strips.

Trim edge, leaving 1" of overhang. Fold the edge under, then crimp, pinching as in the inset photo. Brush the top with half and half, sprinkle with sugar, and bake. ▶

◀ Bake until the top and bottom crusts are golden, and the filling is bubbly and thick. Remove the pie from baking sheet while warm (or it'll stick) and cool before slicing.

from **our** readers

Q&A

questions & answers

SIFTED FLOUR

What is the purpose of sifted flour? Should it be measured before or after sifting?

*Evan Rusch
Cleveland, MN*

Aside from breaking up lumps, sifting helps aerate, or add oxygen to, flour. This makes the flour better able to combine with liquid ingredients and allows for a much fluffier batter.

As for *when* to measure the flour, the recipe should indicate. In Dorie Greenspan's book *Baking with Julia*, it clarifies that in recipes calling for "1 cup sifted flour," sift flour *before* measuring. For "1 cup flour, sifted," measure *after* sifting.

Not sifting flour as required prevents dough from rising as well as it should. So be sure to follow the recipe exactly.

DELI-STYLE OLIVES

What is the correct way to store olives sold in bulk?

*Barbara Davis
Minneapolis, MN*

Deli-style olives are a great way to sample a variety of different olives, but storing them does require a bit of extra care.

To prevent bulk olives from drying out, they are often sold soaking in brine—scoop some of that brine into your container with the olives. Chilled, they'll be fine for a couple of months.

Without brine, olives last only a couple of weeks. To keep them longer, make a brine with $1/2$ teaspoon salt per 1 cup water.

ROSE WATER

I have a recipe with rose water. What is it and how is it used?
*Magali Rutschman
Las Vegas, NM*

Rose water is a flavoring traditionally used in Indian and Middle Eastern dishes. It's also used in baking, sometimes as a substitute for vanilla extract.

Rose water is a diluted version of the more potent rose *essence*, which is made from a distillation of rose petals. Rose water has an intensely floral, perfumey fragrance that's a lot like walking into a florist! Surprisingly, most of that strong scent (and the flavor associated with it), disappears with cooking. This was evident in a scone recipe we tried that called for two teaspoons rose water—in the end, the rose flavor was so faint it was hardly noticeable.

If you want to use rose water in a recipe, you can usually find it at your local health food store or international grocer. Or, shop online at **ethnicgrocer.com**.

EXTRA EGGS

How long can I store extra egg whites or yolks?

*Maria Isabel Valdes
Guatemala City, Guatemala*

The American Egg Board recommends either refrigerating or freezing extra egg yolks and whites. If you plan on using the leftovers within a couple of days, refrigeration is best. Stored in an airtight container, egg whites will last up to four days. Egg yolks, however, should be kept in water to prevent them from drying out. Just place the yolks in a small container and fill with water until covered. They will keep for one to two days.

If you have an abundance of whites or yolks that you won't get to soon, freeze them. Egg whites can be frozen as is, just store them in a covered container fit for freezing. Egg yolks, on the other hand, are a bit trickier. When frozen, yolks tend to become gelatinous. To prevent this, add salt (for savory items) or sugar (for sweets) before freezing. A simple ratio to follow is $1/8$ teaspoon salt, or $1 1/2$ teaspoon sugar or corn syrup, for every four yolks ($1/4$ cup).

Make sure to thaw egg products safely by either running cold water over the container, or placing it in the fridge overnight.

GOING EGGLESS

Why do some cake recipes omit eggs? Aren't they necessary?

Antonia Ellis
New York, NY

Eggs perform multiple roles in cakes. They add air to the batter and help blend together ingredients that don't usually like to mix—oil and water, for example.

Nevertheless, some cake recipes don't call for them. During World War II, rationing became commonplace and many of the cakes that were once laden with eggs (some recipes called for over 20!) went eggless. To make up for their loss and the purpose they served, recipes substituted additional oil and baking powder, or a combination of baking powder and baking soda.

SWEATING

What does the cooking term "sweat" mean?

Melissa Mobley
Des Moines, IA

Sweating is a cooking method in between sauteing and steaming. The technique allows ingredients to cook in their own juices (unlike steaming) and without browning (unlike sauteing). It's useful when you want to avoid the caramelized flavor and color that often characterize sauteing.

To sweat onions, for instance, place them in a pan with a little bit of butter or oil and cook, covered, over low heat until tender.

MAKING BASIL LAST

What is the best method for storing fresh basil?

Norah Leary Jones
Chicago, IL

Lee Jones at The Chef's Garden, Inc., says that to make fresh basil last you need to avoid extreme temperatures. Basil keeps best at temperatures between 50–54°. Most refrigerators are set too low, so find a cool, dark area instead.

Store basil in a vase with water or in an *unsealed* plastic bag with a damp paper towel (it gets too hot in a sealed bag). Kept in either of these ways, basil can last for up to one week.

MICRO-GREENS

What are micro-greens?

Jesse Gazzuolo
San Francisco, CA

Micro-greens are the sprouts of common greens that are harvested at a height of 1–2 inches. The greens themselves can be anything, just as long as they're small—cress, broccoli, clover, and arugula are common examples.

Try using micro-greens in stir-fries, salads, or as a garnish. Find them at gourmet food shops, or order some through Diamond Organics at **888-ORGANIC (674-2642), diamondorganics.com**.

But it's more fun, not to mention cheaper, to grow your own micro-greens. Kits are available online at **sproutpeople.com**, or by calling **(877) 777-6887.**

tell**me** *more*

Fresh Mozzarella

This is not your everyday pizza cheese—it's better! Originating in Italy, *mozzarella di bufala* is traditionally made from the milk of water buffalo. It has a soft texture and deliciously rich flavor, but can be hard to find in America. For a more readily available alternative, opt for fresh mozzarella made from cow's milk. With a similar texture and milder flavor, it offers a great introduction to the cheese.

A classic way to try fresh mozzarella is in a Caprese [kah-PREH-seh] salad. Alternate slices of ripe red tomatoes, fresh mozzarella, and whole basil leaves on a platter. Drizzle with olive oil, then sprinkle with coarse sea salt and freshly cracked pepper.

Balls of fresh mozzarella are usually sold soaking in water (which is sometimes salted)—this keeps the cheese cool and adds moisture. If you can't find fresh mozzarella in your area, order some from the **Mozzarella Company** at **(800) 798-2954** or **mozzco.com.**

grandfinale

WATERMELON SIPPER

Seedless watermelon really saves time here—if you can find one, buy it!

MAKES FOUR 16-OZ. DRINKS
TOTAL TIME: 10 MINUTES + FREEZING

PUREE; FREEZE:
6   cups watermelon, seeded,
       cut into chunks
$^1/_3$ cup fresh lime juice
$^1/_3$ cup sugar

POUR OVER CUBES:
6–8 oz. ginger beer, *see below*

GARNISH WITH:
    Fresh mint sprigs

Puree watermelon, lime juice, and sugar in a blender or food processor. Pour into two ice cube trays and freeze solid. Place 3 or 4 watermelon cubes into each serving glass.
Pour ginger beer over the cubes.
Garnish each drink with a sprig of fresh mint.

watermelon
sipper

▲ *Puree watermelon, lime juice, and sugar in a blender. Freeze watermelon mixture in ice cube trays until solid.*

What is ginger beer?
Jamaican in origin, ginger beer is a carbonated, usually non-alcoholic beverage similar to ginger ale, but with more "bite." Its spiciness is due to a substantial amount of ginger. Find ginger beer alongside other drink mixers (such as club soda) at specialty food stores and some grocery stores.

Cuisine at home®

taste rules!
pan-roasted
Pork Chops

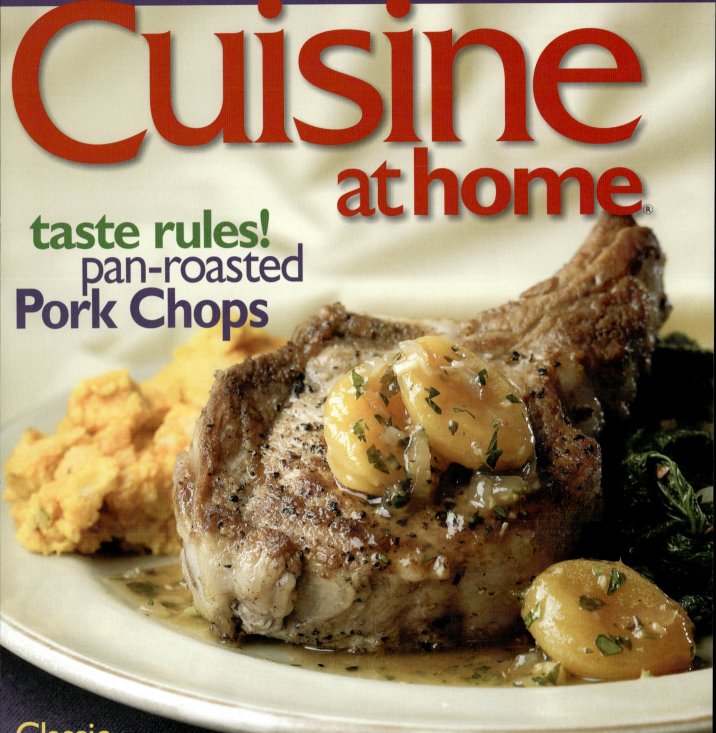

Classic
Roast Beef
tender, tasty, and foolproof

Bumped-up Breakfast
2 wonderful weekend recipes

Issue No. 41 October 2003
A publication of August Home Publishing

Cuisine at home®

Publisher
Donald B. Peschke

Editor
John F. Meyer

Senior Editor
Susan Hoss

Associate Editor
Sarah Marx Feldner

Assistant Editor
Sara Ostransky

Test Kitchen Director
Kim Samuelson

Art Director
Cinda Shambaugh

Assistant Art Director
Holly Wiederin

Senior Graphic Designer
April Walker Janning

Image Specialist
Troy Clark

Photographer
Dean Tanner

AUGUST HOME
PUBLISHING COMPANY

Corporate:

Corporate Vice Presidents: Mary R. Scheve, Douglas L. Hicks • *Creative Director:* Ted Kralicek • *Professional Development Director:* Michal Sigel *New Media Manager:* Gordon C. Gaippe • *Senior Photographer:* Crayola England *Multi Media Art Director:* Eugene Pedersen • *Web Server Administrator:* Carol Schoeppler • *Web Content Manager:* David Briggs • *Web Designer:* Kara Blessing *Controller:* Robin Hutchinson • *Senior Accountant:* Laura Thomas • *Accounts Payable:* Mary Schultz • *Accounts Receivable:* Margo Petrus • *Research Coordinator:* Nick Jaeger • *Production Director:* George Chmielarz • *Pre-Press Image Specialist:* Minniette Johnson • *Electronic Publishing Director:* Douglas M. Lidster • *Systems Administrator:* Cris Schwanebeck PC • *Maintenance Technician:* Robert D. Cook *H.R. Assistant:* Kirsten Koele • *Receptionist/Administrative Assistant:* Jeanne Johnson • *Mail Room Clerk:* Lou Webber • *Office Manager:* Natalie Lonsdale *Facilities Manager:* Kurt Johnson

Customer Service & Fulfillment:

Operations Director: Bob Baker • *Customer Service Manager:* Jennie Enos *Customer Service Representatives:* Anna Cox, Kim Harlan, Cheryl Jordan, April Revell, Deborah Rich, Valerie Jo Riley, Tammy Truckenbrod • *Buyer:* Linda Jones *Administrative Assistant:* Nancy Downey • *Warehouse Supervisor:* Nancy Johnson *Fulfillment:* Sylvia Carey

Circulation:

Circulation Operations Director: Sandy Baum • *Circulation Marketing Director:* Wayde J. Klingbeil • *Circulation Marketing Analyst:* Patrick A. Walsh • *Renewal Manager:* Paige Rogers • *Strategic Business Analysts:* Kris Schlemmer, Paula M. DeMatteis • *Circulation Fulfillment Manager:* Steph Forinash • *Art Director:* Doug Flint *Senior Graphic Designers:* Mark Hayes, Robin Friend

www.CuisineAtHome.com

talk to Cuisine at home
Questions about Subscriptions and Address Changes? Write or call:

Customer Service
2200 Grand Avenue,
Des Moines, IA 50312
800-311-3995,
8 a.m. to 5 p.m., Central Time.

Online Subscriber Services:
www.CuisineAtHome.com
Access your account • Check a subscription payment • Tell us if you've missed an issue • Change your mailing or email address • Renew your subscription • Pay your bill

Cuisine at home® (ISSN 1537-8225) is published bi-monthly (Jan., Mar., May, July, Sept., Nov.) by August Home Publishing Co., 2200 Grand Ave., Des Moines, IA 50312. *Cuisine at home®* is a trademark of August Home Publishing Co. ©Copyright 2003 August Home Publishing. All rights reserved. Subscriptions: Single copy: $4.99. One year subscription (6 issues), $24.00. (Canada/Foreign add $10 per year, U.S. funds.)

Periodicals postage paid at Des Moines, IA and at additional mailing offices. "USPS/Perry-Judd's Heartland Division automatable poly". Postmaster: Send change of address to *Cuisine at home®*, P.O. Box 37100 Boone, IA 50037-2100. *Cuisine at home®* does not accept and is not responsible for unsolicited manuscripts. PRINTED IN CHINA

editor's letter

We've got to talk. We'll start with food and then move on to solicitation (no, not for money, just your opinion). First food. At *Cuisine*, we always try to give you plenty of tips and techniques as well as solid, straight forward recipes that not only taste good, but also really work. I don't expect you to remember everything (I can't), but try not to forget three simple rules I follow: salt is okay, butter makes everything better, and always use fresh herbs.

I've talked about using salt and butter before, and unless you have dietary restrictions, don't be afraid to use either, judiciously of course. But fresh herbs are a different story. Excess won't hurt and I strongly encourage you to use them often. For those of you who haven't experimented with fresh herbs, do it. They make a world of difference with their bright, clean fragrance, and their flavors can breathe new life to even your oldest recipes. Fortunately, most grocery stores now carry fresh herbs year-round, and while they're a touch pricey, I definitely think they're worth it. Give them a try and see if you agree that fresh herbs dramatically improve your cooking.

Now for the solicitation. I need your help by seeking your opinion on American food. Next year we're running an article on 25 foods that have most influenced American cooking and how we eat. Foods like Campbell's Soup, White Castle Hamburgers, German dachshund sausage (hot dogs), Swanson TV Dinners, and Cool Whip have all played a role in our culinary culture.

Here's what I'd like you to do. Send me up to three of your nominations and a brief explanation of why you think your choices have been the most influential. We'll compile the votes over the next month and then start working on the article. You can send your nominations by mail to:

Cuisine at home
American Foods
2200 Grand Avenue
Des Moines, IA 50312

Or send your opinions by email to sfeldner@augusthome.com. Thanks for helping. I look forward to seeing your ideas, and be sure to try fresh herbs in your next recipe.

table of contents

from **our** readers

tips
and techniques

Squash Seeding
The seeds inside winter squash, such as acorn and butternut, can be tough to remove. After cutting the squash in half, scrape out the seeds with an ice cream scoop.

Phyllis Larsen
San Francisco, CA

Recycle and Reuse
I use empty herb and spice bottles to hold my special blends of spice and rub mixes. I also buy large bulk containers of spices (they're cheaper), and then place a portion of that spice into a smaller bottle to save space in a cabinet.

Shreath Miller
Powder Springs, GA

Safer Water Bath
When baking individual flans or custards in a water bath, use your gravy separator to add the hot water to the pan. Put the ramekins in place and pour. No more danger of water accidentally dripping into the ramekins or the oven.

V. Gail Zilai
Big Spring, TX

Slick Utensils
When making pancakes or egg dishes, use cooking spray on both sides of the spatula for easy flipping and cleanup.

Mary Jane Hershatter
Clinton, CT

Better Scallion Chopping
Slicing a scallion in half lengthwise before chopping will give you smaller pieces. Split the scallion from the top to the root end and chop.

Tom Polder
Atlanta, GA

Binder Clips
My husband does a lot of paperwork at the kitchen table, and leaves a lot of heavy-duty binder clips behind. I started to amass quite a collection, and used one to close a powdered sugar bag. Great discovery!

The clips come in various sizes that are perfect for clamping small bags of nuts or big bags of potato chips. Binder clips are sturdy, easy to store, outperform their plastic counterparts, and the price is sure right.

Mary Lieb
Durango, CO

Quicker Pie Crust

Most recipes call for wrapping pie dough in plastic wrap, then refrigerating it for 30 minutes or more before using. But if you add *frozen* butter pieces to the dough, it will be cold enough to roll without chilling first.

Elaine Sweet
Dallas, TX

Juicing in Reverse

Rather than squeezing a lemon into a bowl with the cut side down, hold the cut side up as you squeeze. This way, the juice will spill over the edges of the lemon while the seeds stay inside the shell—no more fishing out seeds.

Christine Thomas
Paso Robles, CA

Shake it Smooth

For a well chilled, smooth, perfectly blended vinaigrette, shake it with an ice cube. Combine all ingredients for the vinaigrette in a container with a secure top. Add an ice cube and shake, then discard the ice before using.

Sandra Brown
Portland, OR

Peeling Garlic Cloves

My hands become sticky trying to remove the papery outer skin of garlic cloves. But not anymore with this method.

First, separate the bulb into individual cloves by pushing the whole head with the palm of your hand. Chop off the root end of each clove, then smash each clove to break the peel using the flat side of a chef's knife. Place the cloves in a bowl filled with cold water and start peeling—most skins will fall off immediately and your hands won't become sticky!

Hope Borsato
Norland, WA

More Counter Space

When I need more work space in my small kitchen, I put a baking sheet or cutting board over the second sink to add counter space.

Joyce Hill
Dallas, TX

Coconut Milk Cubes

Canned coconut milk spoils quickly, so pour whatever you don't use into ice cube trays and freeze. Once frozen, pop them out and store in a freezer bag. Add the cubes to the blender when making fruit smoothies, or to flavor a pot of hot soup or stew. The cubes may also be thawed overnight in the refrigerator. Just stir them to blend, then use in a favorite recipe!

Rachel Matesz
Phoenix, AZ

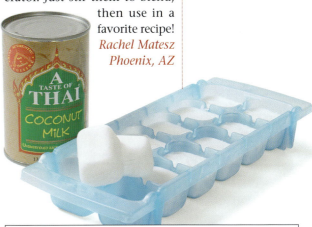

"Sugared" Cookies

Use confectioner's sugar for rolling out sugar cookie dough instead of using flour. It adds more sweetness, works better than flour, and you're not adding more flour than needed to the dough.

Ann Sutherland
Troy, NY

share your **tips** with *Cuisine at home*
and techniques

If you have a unique way of solving a cooking problem, we'd like to hear from you, and we'll consider publishing your tip in one or more of our works. Just write down your cooking tip and mail it to *Cuisine at home*, Tips Editor, 2200 Grand Ave., Des Moines, IA 50312, or contact us through our email address shown below. Please include your name, address, and daytime phone number in case we have questions. We'll pay you $25 if we publish your tip.

Email: CuisineAtHome@CuisineAtHome.com
Web address: CuisineAtHome.com

Classic roast beef

We all grew up with roast beef, potatoes, and gravy. So why isn't it on today's dinner tables more often? Now there's no excuse to pass it by.

A few decades ago, roast beef was almost a weekly menu item in many households. But today's lifestyles demand economical, healthful meals that can be made without much fuss. As a result, roast beef has taken a back seat to chicken.

But believe it or not, this classic roast beef meal actually meets those criteria. Save swank prime rib and tenderloin cuts for the holidays—this is all about the often overlooked eye round roast. True, it isn't a serious contender in the category

of super-flavorful, fork-tender beef cuts (it comes from a steer's back thigh). But of all the roasts tested, the eye round came out on top in terms of availability, ease of roasting and carving, flavor, and texture. The $4 a pound price tag isn't bad either— so reasonable that I cook two roasts just to have leftovers (see Pages 10–11)!

Of course, potatoes and gravy are here too, and *must* be included in the meal. Since they're both made right in the roasting pan, there's no reason to skip them.

GREMOLATA RUBBED ROAST BEEF AND ROASTED POTATOES

Makes Two 2–3-lb. Roasts; Total Time: About 2 Hours

FOR THE POTATOES—
PARBOIL:
1½ lb. russet potatoes, peeled and cut into large chunks

FOR THE GREMOLATA—
COMBINE:
¾ cup chopped fresh parsley
¼ cup fresh thyme leaves
1 whole head garlic
3 T. olive oil
1 T. kosher salt
   Zest of one lemon, chopped

FOR THE BEEF—
SEAR IN 2 T. OLIVE OIL; TOP WITH GREMOLATA AND ROAST:
2 eye round roasts (2–3 lb. each), seasoned with salt

Preheat oven to 400° with rack on the bottom.

Parboil potatoes in salted water for 15–20 minutes. Drain, reserving the water for gravy.

Combine all gremolata ingredients in a large resealable plastic bag. With the flat side of a meat mallet, crush the garlic cloves with the herbs.

Sear seasoned roasts in oil in a large roasting pan until brown.

Remove roasts; top with gremolata.

Arrange potatoes in the pan and place the meat on the other side.

Roast meat and potatoes for 45 minutes. Cook until the meat reaches desired doneness, 130–135° for medium (see Page 8 for a detailed explanation of doneness).

Scrape gremolata from the roasts into the roasting pan. Remove meat and potatoes; allow roasts to rest for 15 minutes before carving.

Prepare gravy as on Page 9.

Before roasting

There are a few steps that need to be taken before the roasting can begin. Here's how to get started.

Potatoes: First, parboil the potatoes so the outside is cooked while the center is still a bit hard. It may seem like a frivolous step, but this makes a big difference. The roasted potatoes are fluffy inside, like mashed potatoes, and crisp outside.

Roasts: Next, sear the roasts in a heavy roasting pan on top of the stove, *Figure 1*. This colors and flavors the outside of the meat and establishes a base for the gravy.

An herb and garlic gremolata [greh-moh-LAH-tah] is rubbed on the seared roasts, *Figure 2*. It gives

1 Sear roasts in oil over med.-high heat, adding a bit more oil if meat starts to scorch. Parboil potatoes.

good flavor to the meat, but where it really shines is in the gravy. After the beef has roasted, the gremolata is scraped off and simmered in the gravy to enhance its flavor.

I'm not kidding when I say this gremolata is *coarse*. Roughly chop the parsley, thyme, and lemon zest, then smash it all together with a whole head of *unpeeled* garlic. Don't worry—it'll be strained out later.

2 Divide gremolata between roasts. It won't stick well, so just pat it on top of each roast.

cuisineclass

Roasting and finishing

Before the roasts go in the oven, add a couple more tablespoons of oil to the empty roasting pan, then the drained potatoes, *Figure 3*. Save at least two cups of the potato water for gravy, and be sure most of the water drips off the potatoes so oil doesn't spatter. They may break apart a bit as they're stirred in the oil, but that's okay—that rough surface on the outside is what creates their crisp crust. Arrange the potatoes on one side of the pan, then put the roasts in opposite them.

3 Add oil and potatoes to the pan. Arrange in a single layer to one side. Return the meat to the pan and roast.

Cook the meat and potatoes for 45 minutes on the lower oven rack. When time is up, check their progress using an instant read thermometer, *Figure 4*. They probably won't be done, but this reading will give you an idea of how long they should continue roasting. Check their temperature every 10 or 15 minutes until you reach the desired doneness—for medium, go for 130–135°; medium-rare, 125° or so. The roasts' internal temperature will rise 5–10° as they rest, so if it's higher than 135° out of the oven, the meat could wind up overcooked.

After the roasts are done, scrape the gremolata from them into the roasting pan, *Figure 5*, and allow the meat to rest. To take advantage of the brown residue coating the bottom of the pan, make the gravy on the stove—right in the roaster! After sauteing the onions, deglaze with wine, scraping bits off the bottom, *Figure 6*. This will give the gravy deep color and rich flavor.

4 After 45 minutes, take a temperature reading and turn potatoes. Roast to 130–135°.

5 Remove the potatoes, then scrape the gremolata from the meat. Transfer meat to plate to rest.

6 Saute onion and seasonings 3–4 minutes. Deglaze with wine, scraping bits from the pan. Simmer until wine evaporates.

online **extra**

Want more info? Visit www.CuisineAtHome.com for a guide on different cuts of beef for roasting.

41

CLASSIC BEEF GRAVY

This may seem like a lot of gravy, but you'll be glad to have it when serving the leftover roast beef the next day!
MAKES ABOUT 3 CUPS
TOTAL TIME: ABOUT 20 MINUTES

SAUTE:
1   cup yellow onion, diced
1   T. tomato paste
2   bay leaves
DEGLAZE WITH:
1/4 cup dry red wine
SPRINKLE IN:
3   T. all-purpose flour
GRADUALLY WHISK IN; SIMMER:
2   cups reserved potato water
1   can (14 oz.) low-sodium
     beef broth
FINISH WITH; STRAIN:
2   T. unsalted butter
1   T. balsamic vinegar
     Salt and pepper to taste
     Meat juices from the roasts

Saute onion, tomato paste, and bay leaves over medium heat with the gremolata from the beef in the roasting pan (you may need to be on two burners). Cook until onion softens.
Deglaze with wine, scraping the pan. Simmer to evaporate liquid.
Sprinkle flour over the onion mixture—it will be pasty.
Gradually whisk in reserved potato water and beef broth. Whisk constantly to prevent lumps. Simmer until slightly thick, about 5 minutes.
Finish gravy with butter, vinegar, seasonings, and any juices that have accumulated as the roasts have rested. Strain, then serve with sliced beef and roasted potatoes.

Flour is the primary thickener for this gravy, *Figure 7*, but the starch in the reserved potato cooking water will also help to thicken. To reduce lumps, whisk in the broth and potato water a little at a time. (If you forget to save the water, add another can of beef broth.)

Simmer the gravy for a few minutes to thicken it and eliminate any starchy taste from the flour. If the roasts have leeched juice while resting, add it along with the butter and vinegar, *Figure 8*, then strain. Finally, slice the roast crosswise and against the grain, as thinly as you can.

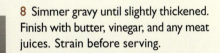

8 Simmer gravy until slightly thickened. Finish with butter, vinegar, and any meat juices. Strain before serving.

7 Sprinkle in flour, stirring to coat. Then whisk in water and broth.

Roast Beef Encores

It may surprise you but Buffalo, New York has given us two of America's finest—Buffalo wings and a roast beef sandwich known as the kummelweck.

A "weck" is a hot French dip sandwich served with horseradish and au jus. The real kicker, though, is the roll—a German kaiser laced with caraway seed (kummel) and coarse salt. The rolls are hard to find outside of Buffalo, so make your own using regular kaiser buns. They're *almost* as good as the real deal!

kummelweck **sandwich**

KUMMELWECK SANDWICH
MAKES 6 SANDWICHES
TOTAL TIME: 30 MINUTES

FOR THE ROLLS—
BRUSH WITH TWO BEATEN EGGS:
6   kaiser rolls, split
COMBINE; SPRINKLE ON TOPS:
2   T. caraway seeds
2   T. coarse salt
FOR THE JUS—
SAUTE IN 1 T. OLIVE OIL AND
1 T. UNSALTED BUTTER:
1   cup yellow onion, chopped
ADD, REDUCE, AND STRAIN:
4   cups low-sodium beef broth
1/2 cup dry white wine
2   T. garlic, chopped
1   T. tomato paste
2   t. minced fresh thyme
FOR THE SANDWICH—
WARM IN JUS:
1 1/2 lb. leftover roast beef,
     thinly sliced
SERVE WITH:
     Prepared horseradish and jus

Preheat oven to 375°.
Brush kaiser roll tops with egg.
Combine caraway and salt; sprinkle generously on rolls. Bake 5 min.
Saute onion for the jus in oil and butter until golden brown.

Add remaining jus ingredients and simmer over medium-high heat until reduced by half, about 15 minutes. Strain; return jus to pan.
Warm sliced beef in the jus—dip, don't simmer them in the jus. Arrange slices on the bottom half of a weck roll. Dip the underside of the roll tops into the jus and place on top of the beef.
Serve with horseradish and a side of hot jus.

◄ *Brush tops of rolls with egg wash. Coat with caraway-salt mixture and bake.*

Dip beef slices in hot jus to warm through. The meat should stay pink. ►

A hand-held salad? Why not! The spicy, sweet, tangy flavors of Thai beef salad are a great way to showcase leftover roast beef.

The most unusual ingredient here is the noodles. Find *mai fun* in many grocery stores or Asian markets. Tear the bundle apart into smaller, more manageable bundles before frying.

THAI BEEF SALAD WRAPS

MAKES ABOUT 10 WRAPS
TOTAL TIME: ABOUT 1 HOUR

FOR THE DRESSING—
SIMMER; REDUCE:

1	cup water
1/2	cup fresh lime juice
1/2	cup brown sugar
3	T. garlic, minced
1	t. chili garlic paste (or 1/2 t. crushed red pepper flakes)

FOR THE WRAPS—
FRY IN 3 CUPS VEGETABLE OIL:

1/2	bundle (about 3 oz.) rice stick noodles (mai fun)

PREPARE:

2	cups leftover roast beef, thinly sliced, julienned
1	cup bean sprouts
1/2	cup fresh mint leaves
1/2	cup fresh cilantro leaves
1	cucumber, seeded, bias sliced
1	yellow or red bell pepper, julienned
10	large leaves red leaf lettuce

Simmer water, lime juice, sugar, garlic, and chili garlic paste in a small saucepan over medium heat. Reduce until dressing thickens slightly, about 20 minutes.

Fry noodles in small batches in oil heated to 375°. Remove and drain on a paper towel-lined plate.

Prepare remaining ingredients and arrange on a large platter. To serve, have each diner assemble their own wrap: Start with a lettuce leaf, then follow with some of the roast beef, fried noodles, and vegetables. Drizzle with some dressing before eating.

▲ Mai fun *are thread-like Chinese rice noodles that are fried until crisp. Half of a 7-oz. package is all you need here.*

▲ *Heat oil in a saucepan to 375°. Drop small bundle of noodles in oil—they'll puff instantly (see inset).*

Thinly slice leftover roast beef, then cut into julienne strips. ▶

thai beef salad wraps

Cornmeal griddle cakes

Try these cornmeal griddle cakes this weekend for a terrific change of pace in the morning. Sour cream infuses them with richness while cornmeal supplies the texture and flavor.

Cornmeal cakes

Pancakes out of a box are fine for fast-paced weekday mornings, but are just a tad boring for weekends. So when you want something different, give these cornmeal griddle cakes a shot. You probably have all the ingredients on hand, and whipping them up takes just about as long as mixing their boxed buddies.

You can use either yellow or white cornmeal, but I like yellow for the deep color it gives the cakes. Also, be sure to mix the dry ingredients with the wet just before cooking. This keeps the batter from rising too much and turning foamy.

GRIDDLE CAKE TIPS

❖ The griddle should be around 350°. You can tell if it's hot enough by sprinkling a few water droplets on the surface. When the droplets "dance," it's good to go.

❖ Using a measuring cup will result in uniform cakes. For a 4–5" cake, use $^1/_3$ cup.

❖ A "test" griddle cake is a good idea—the first one usually fails. Adjust the heat if necessary.

❖ The cakes must be golden before turning. Aside from making them look good, it also gives the inside time to cook. If the cakes get too dark, turn the heat down.

❖ To keep cooked cakes warm, preheat the oven to 275°. Place cakes in a single layer on a parchment-lined baking sheet and hold in the oven. Serve within 15 minutes or the cakes will get soggy.

CORNMEAL GRIDDLE CAKES

MAKES 12 GRIDDLE CAKES; TOTAL TIME: 20 MINUTES

FOR THE DRY INGREDIENTS—
COMBINE:
$^3/_4$ cup all-purpose flour
$^3/_4$ cup yellow cornmeal
2   T. sugar
1   t. baking powder
$^1/_2$ t. baking soda
$^1/_2$ t. kosher salt

FOR THE WET INGREDIENTS—
BEAT:
3   eggs
WHISK IN:
$^3/_4$ cup sour cream
$^3/_4$ cup whole milk
$^1/_4$ cup unsalted butter ($^1/_2$ stick), melted

Preheat griddle to 350°.
Combine dry ingredients and mix thoroughly.
Beat the eggs in a separate bowl just until blended.
Whisk the sour cream, milk, and melted butter into the eggs. Pour the wet ingredients into the dry and whisk to blend. Do not overmix—a few lumps are okay.

Lightly grease the surface of the griddle with vegetable oil before making each batch of cakes (this will help the cakes turn golden). Use $^1/_3$ cup measure to pour batter onto the oiled griddle.

The griddle cakes are ready to turn when they look dry around the edges and bubbles break to form holes that don't close.

add ons

Apple Cornmeal Cakes: Fold 1 diced apple into batter.

Corn Cakes: Add 1 cup fresh or frozen corn kernels to batter.

Apple Butter Syrup: Blend 3 T. apple butter into $^1/_2$ cup maple syrup; warm gently.

cinnamon toast
bread pudding

A breakfast standard gets extra special treatment in this make-ahead breakfast dish. What a great way to wake up!

There's one big problem with breakfast—it's too early in the morning. Until the coffee kicks in, cereal or toast is about all that's doable. But this dish changes that since all the work is done the night before. The pudding soaks overnight in the fridge, to be baked in the morning. Even without caffeine it's easy.

Bread pudding is seen primarily on dessert menus, and this recipe is sweet enough that it could easily follow dinner. But don't underestimate its impact as a day opener. Breakfast is written all over it—fruit, bread, eggs. Go on, treat yourself!

Broiled cinnamon Texas toast (the thick-sliced stuff) is the pudding's base. Broil *both* sides of the bread for flavor, and cool on a rack (not on the baking sheet) so it stays crisp for better custard saturation. And make an extra piece of toast— it's an awesome bedtime snack!

CINNAMON TOAST BREAD PUDDING WITH PINEAPPLE AND CARAMEL

MAKES 6–8 SERVINGS; TOTAL TIME: 1¹/₂ HOURS + CHILLING OVERNIGHT

FOR THE TOAST—
SPREAD WITH BUTTER:
10   slices Texas toast-style bread
COMBINE; SPRINKLE ON BREAD AND BROIL:
¹/₂   cup sugar
1   t. ground cinnamon

FOR THE CARAMEL AND PINEAPPLE—
BOIL:
1   cup brown sugar
6   T. heavy cream
ADD AND SIMMER:
6   rings fresh pineapple (¹/₂"
      thick), cut into half-moons

FOR THE CUSTARD—
WHISK:
1   cup whole milk
³/₄   cup heavy cream
4   eggs
¹/₃   cup sugar
1   t. vanilla extract
      Pinch salt

FOR THE MAPLE WHIPPED CREAM—
WHIP TO SOFT PEAKS:
1   cup heavy cream
¹/₄   cup pure maple syrup

SERVE PUDDING WITH:
      Maple Whipped Cream
      Toasted chopped pecans

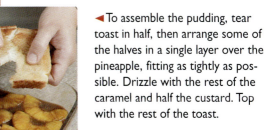

Preheat broiler to high with rack two notches down from the broiler element.

Spread both sides of bread with soft butter for the toast.
Combine cinnamon and sugar. Sprinkle both sides of bread with cinnamon sugar and arrange on a baking sheet. Watching carefully, broil until brown on one side. Flip and broil the second side until browned. Cool toast on a rack.

Boil brown sugar and cream for the caramel in a skillet over med.-high heat .
Add pineapple and simmer 2–3 minutes, spooning caramel over the fruit. Arrange pineapple in an ungreased 11 x 7" baking dish and drizzle with half the caramel.
Whisk together all ingredients for the custard in a large pitcher.

◄ To assemble the pudding, tear toast in half, then arrange some of the halves in a single layer over the pineapple, fitting as tightly as possible. Drizzle with the rest of the caramel and half the custard. Top with the rest of the toast.

◄ Drizzle remaining custard over the bread, then lightly press bread down to saturate. Cover pudding with plastic wrap and chill overnight.

In the morning, bake pudding at 325° until puffed and a knife inserted in the center comes out clean, about an hour. Cool 5 min., loosen edges with a knife, then invert onto a platter. ►

Whip cream and syrup together.
Serve warm pudding with Maple Whipped Cream and toasted pecans.

cuisinetechnique

pan-roasting
the perfect chop

Here's to "the other white meat." Taste this chop and you'll see why it merits all the publicity it's been getting.

I like pork, a lot. It's one of my favorite meats. But all too often it's served dry and overdone, then smothered in gravy to try and cover up the mistake.

Well, gone are the days of depending on a restaurant for quality chops. Here's a fool-proof method for getting the job done yourself. And what's even better, with a little extra time, the juices left over from the pork chop can easily be turned into a show-stopping apricot sauce (Page 19).

When cooking chops, roasting alone doesn't give them the deep color they deserve. But frying makes it too easy to overcook them. The best way to prepare the perfect pork chop is to use a combination of the two—quickly searing the outside to give the meat a beautiful golden color, and slowly roasting the inside to maintain its natural juices.

The perfect chop

Here's all you need to know for cooking the perfect chop.

Choosing a chop: Choose bone-in pork chops that are 1–1¼" thick. They should have only a small amount of fat around the edges and, to insure tenderness and flavor, some marbling of fat in the meat.

Boneless chops work too, but since the bone helps keep the meat moist, reduce the cooking time to prevent the meat from drying out.

The pan: Because the chops are cooked both on the stovetop and in the oven, make sure that the pan is ovenproof (no plastic handles) and has a tight-fitting cover.

Seasoning: Although it adds great flavor, salt tends to dry pork out, extracting too much of its moisture. To avoid this, season the chops just before cooking them.

Browning: The purpose of browning is twofold. Quick exposure to high heat gives the chops great color. But even more importantly, it releases the meat's natural flavors into the pan, and that's what will provide the base for the delicious sauce.

Once positioned in the pan, don't fidget with the chops. They'll get much better color if left alone. The pork chops are ready to flip when they no longer stick to the pan. That's how you know when they've completely browned, *Figure 1*.

Roasting: Since browning is more aesthetic than practical, getting the meat cooked on the inside is still required. Roasting allows the meat to cook slowly in its own juices, without drying out, *Figure 2*.

The finished chop: The pork chops are done at 140°. Both browning and roasting help achieve this temperature, but resting them is like icing on the cake, allowing carryover heat to finish the job, *Figure 3*.

When you cut the chop, the meat should have a slightly pinkish hue. Don't worry, it's safe to eat! The pinkness just means that there's still juice (and flavor) in the chop.

PERFECT PORK CHOPS
MAKES 4 PORK CHOPS
TOTAL TIME: 15 MINUTES

SEASON WITH SALT AND PEPPER:
4 6-oz. bone-in pork chops,
 1–1¼" thick
BROWN IN 2T. VEGETABLE OIL. COVER, ROAST, THEN REST.

Preheat oven to 375°.
Season both sides of pork.
Brown chops over medium-high heat. Cover pan, transfer to oven, and roast for 7 min. Rest chops before serving.

1 Brown chops in an oven-proof pan, about 3 minutes per side.

2 Roasting the chops in a covered pan helps concentrate the heat around them.

3 Place roasted chops on a platter and cover tightly with foil. Let rest for 15 minutes, or while you make the sauce.

▲ *Don't wash that pork chop pan! It's full of great flavor. Use the leftover juices as the base for the Apricot Sauce.*

autumn dinner

The shift from summer to autumn brings comfort back to the table. This fall dinner starts the season off right.

Even I am a little reluctant to pair fruit with meat, but apricots and pork just seem to naturally go together. The next time you're in need of an impressive meal, look no further than this beautiful autumn dinner.

On the preceding pages you learned how to cook the best pork chop. Now round out the dinner with a good pan sauce and an interesting side dish. The sauce is easy—it's a simple reduction flavored (and thickened) with a little apricot jam.

And for a flawless complement to this autumnal meal, make the Squash Spoon Bread on Page 20. Winter squash always tastes great with something a little sweet. The apple juice and jam in the sauce round out the taste of the spoon bread perfectly.

Making the sauce

The leftover pan juices make a super-flavorful base for this apricot pan sauce. Here's what to do.

Caramelize: Caramelizing onions makes them sweeter than they would be if simply sauteed. To caramelize, cook them slowly until they turn golden brown, releasing their natural sugars.

The spices: Coriander and cumin are two spices whose powerful aromas are intensified when heated. Adding them early on in the cooking process allows their flavors to bloom into the sauce.

Deglaze: Deglazing is commonly done with wine. In this recipe, I use vinegar instead, since it's a great flavor enhancer.

Jam: Pectin is the natural thickener in jam. It also helps thicken this sauce, giving it body, as well as sheen that makes it look really nice on the chop.

◀ *Caramelize the onion and spices in the juices left over from the chops.*

Add the dried apricots once the liquid has reduced and the jam is incorporated. ▶

◀ *Be sure to turn off the heat before adding the herbs. It helps prolong their bright green color.*

Coriander and cilantro
are from the same plant but taste vastly different. Coriander is the seed of the plant, and comes either ground or whole. Cilantro (also called "fresh coriander" or "Chinese parsley") is the leafy green.

APRICOT SAUCE

This sauce takes time to make. Keep the chops tightly covered until ready to serve so they stay warm.

MAKES 1 CUP
TOTAL TIME: 45 MINUTES

CARAMELIZE:
1   cup yellow onion, diced
2   t. ground coriander
1   t. ground cumin

ADD AND SAUTE:
1   T. garlic, minced
2   t. fresh ginger, minced

DEGLAZE WITH:
2   T. apple cider vinegar

ADD AND REDUCE:
2   cups apple juice
1   cup low-sodium chicken broth

WHISK IN:
1/3 cup apricot jam

STIR IN:
1   cup dried apricots
2   t. lemon zest, minced

FINISH WITH:
2   T. unsalted butter
1   T. minced fresh parsley
1   T. minced fresh thyme
     Salt to taste

Caramelize onions with spices, about 10 minutes.
Add garlic and ginger; saute 1 min.
Deglaze pan with vinegar.
Add juice and broth. Simmer until reduced by half, about 15 minutes.
Whisk in jam until combined.
Stir in dried apricots and lemon zest; simmer until thickened, 10–15 minutes. Remove pan from heat.
Finish with butter, herbs, and salt.

option

Don't Like Apricots?

No problem! This sauce is delicious with dried plums too. Just substitute equal amounts of both apple jelly for the apricot jam, and dried plums for the apricots. Omit the lemon zest as well.

Making spoon bread

Spoon bread is a traditional southern side dish named for its soft, pudding-like consistency. Get it in the oven before making the pork and sauce so that everything hits the table at once.

Vegetables: For this recipe, there's no one preferred method for cooking the squash (boil, microwave, etc.), but roasting intensifies its flavor. To roast, slice the squash lengthwise and scoop out the seeds. Place it cut side down on a lightly oiled baking sheet, and roast at 400° for 45 minutes, or until it can be easily pierced with a skewer. Let cool, scrape out the flesh, and puree.

The carrots add some color and sweetness to the squash. To cook them, roast along with the squash for about 30 minutes.

Baking: Bake until the spoon bread is just set. To test for doneness, shake it gently. The center should wiggle, but only slightly. Do not overbake or it'll be dry.

SQUASH SPOON BREAD
MAKES 6 CUPS; TOTAL TIME: 2 HOURS

PUREE:
2½ cups cooked butternut squash
½ cup cooked carrots

SAUTE IN 1 T. BUTTER:
½ cup yellow onion, chopped

ADD; BRING TO A BOIL:
1 cup water
½ cup whole milk
2 t. minced fresh rosemary

WHISK IN:
¾ cup yellow cornmeal

COMBINE:
Cornmeal mixture
Squash/Carrot puree
½ cup heavy cream
3 egg yolks
2 T. unsalted butter, softened
2 t. kosher salt
¼ t. cayenne

BEAT; FOLD IN:
3 egg whites

Preheat oven to 375° with rack in the middle.
Puree cooked vegetables.
Saute onions until translucent.
Add water, milk, and rosemary to onions; bring to a boil.
Whisk in cornmeal and cook, stirring constantly, for 1 minute. Remove from heat.
Combine cornmeal mixture, vegetable puree, cream, egg yolks, butter, salt, and cayenne in a large bowl.
Beat egg whites until stiff peaks form, then fold into batter.

Place in a greased 2-quart casserole dish and bake 45 minutes to 1 hour, or until set.

Ready-to-use squash and carrots

Even if you're short on time, this recipe can still be made—just use frozen vegetables instead.

Two 12 oz. packages of pre-cooked squash and one small bag of carrots is all you need. Reheat them according to the instructions on the package, measure, and then puree (if needed).

◄ *Puree the carrots and squash in a food processor or blender until smooth.*

◄ *To eliminate its gritty texture, cook the cornmeal in the rosemary-flavored milk mixture.*

add-in

CHEDDAR BACON SPOON BREAD

The easiest way to make a great thing better? Add bacon and sharp Cheddar cheese!

MAKES 6 CUPS
TOTAL TIME: 2 HOURS

ADD TO BATTER:

2   cups sharp Cheddar cheese, shredded
1   cup bacon, diced, sauteed until crisp, and drained

Add cheese and bacon to batter when you combine the cornmeal and squash mixtures. Proceed as on Page 20.

41

online **extra**

Want a recipe for sauteed greens? Visit www.CuisineAtHome.com

▲ *Beat the egg whites until stiff peaks form. (See Basics on Page 22 for instructions on beating egg whites.)*

▼ *Gently, fold the egg whites into the cornmeal mixture. (See Basics on Page 23 for instructions on folding.)*

▲ *Place batter into a greased 2-quart casserole dish and bake until set.*

beating **egg whites**

Recipes calling for egg whites often require that they're beaten to a certain stiffness. *Soft peaks* are when the whites gently droop, *right*; *stiff peaks* are able to stand upright, *above*. Overbeaten whites look curdled, *bottom*.

For best results, use room temperature whites. Cold ones still whip but take longer. Also, make sure both the bowl and beaters are clean. Traces of fat (oil, butter, egg yolks) prevent the whites from reaching their full potential. And finally, to help increase the white's stability, add cream of tartar or vinegar ($1/8$ tsp. per egg white) before whipping.

roasting **peppers**

When it comes to pepper preparation, don't confuse roasting with blistering or charring. Roasting peppers is a slower process that's done at moderate heat in an oven or low grill. It not only separates the skin from the flesh but also concentrates the natural sugars in the pepper.

Place peppers on a baking sheet and roast at 400° for 25–30 minutes or until the flesh is quite soft, turning them twice. Place them in a bowl or bag and seal. After 10 minutes, peel off the skins with your hands. Do not rinse the peppers!

Blistering is done over or under direct flame to char the skin. The flavor is more bitter, and blistering also discolors the flesh.

▲ *After roasting, seal the peppers in a bowl to steam so peeling is easy.*

what is **zesting?**

If you're looking for turbo citrus flavor in a dish, zest is the
answer. Zest is the perfumey
outer skin of citrus fruit such
as lemons, oranges, and
limes. This outermost skin
contains highly concentrated
and flavorful aromatic oils.

To zest, use a zesting
tool, a paring knife, or what
I've found to work best, a
plain old peeler. Peel only the
colored part of the skin away
from the fruit—do not dig
into the white, bitter pith. If
you cut too deep, scalp away
the pith with a paring knife.
Julienne strips or mince finely.

how to **fold**

Folding is a technique used
to gently blend a light, airy
mixture with a denser one.
The intent is to maintain as
much air as possible as both
are incorporated together.

First, blend $1/4$ of the light
mixture into the heavier one
to bring it to similar consis-
tencies. Then place the
remaining light mixture on
top. Using a spatula, cut
through the middle of the

▲ *For best results, blend some
of the light mixture into the
heavier one before folding.*

mixture, going to the bottom of the bowl. Twist the spatula so
it's parallel to the side of the bowl, bring up some of the mixture from the bottom, and deposit it on top. As you fold with
the spatula in one hand, turn the bowl with the other hand.
Repeat folding until fully incorporated, working quickly.

cuisinereview

wares
hand mixers

Forget the bells, whistles, and wattage. A hand mixer needs solid functions, design, and performance.

Mixers are a lot like cars—any brand will get you to your destination. But there's definitely a difference in the ride, handling, and meaningful options on each model. They determine how pleasant the drive will be.

At first it seemed overwhelming—the plethora of mixers with dizzying amounts of features, speeds, and attachments. But side-by-side testing of 10 different brands made it clear what's important—not just getting the job done, but making every aspect of operation smooth and easy.

Speeds: Mixer speeds generally range from 3 to 9, but some go as high as 16. While multiple speeds do not necessarily provide more power, they do give you *control* of the power, with more settings in between low, medium, and high.

Each brand has a different range of speeds. If high is too fast on a particular mixer, you can always choose a lower setting. But there's nowhere to go if the lowest speed is too fast.

Wattage: Don't judge a mixer on wattage alone. High wattages will not always mix faster or better. It's the efficiency of the motor that counts—and that can't be measured in wattage. Mixer performance is a truer test.

Balance: Both motor placement and design affect the balance of a mixer whether it's mixing or just standing. Good weight distribution makes it more comfortable to operate and able to stand firm on the counter.

The design of the base, mixer tilt, and cord placement also help determine how solid it sits. And stability is a very practical concern. It's aggravating to have a cord that constantly gets in the way, or a mixer that keeps tipping over.

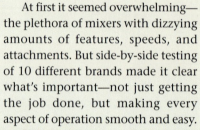

Wide center-post beaters are clunky and rough to operate compared to wire beaters, which are much easier to maneuver in a bowl. The thin wires also make cleaning less of a problem.

Extras: Some mixers come with whisks, dough hooks, sifters, bowls, spatula attachments, cookie cutters—you name it. These extras are only an added value if you need or plan to use them. A lot of unnecessary accessories cannot make up for an inadequate mixer. Do you want your dollars to go into accessories or into the motor and smart design? Wire whisks are the only attachment we found worthwhile, whipping cream fast and easily.

Mixer reviews: Performance is the bottom line. While all the mixers tested handled the tasks, and many have their good points, just a few excelled and covered all the bases. We clearly found KitchenAid to be the best all-around mixer, driving like a luxury model. But there are two other mixers that offer good reasons to buy—speed and price. There's something for everyone, so choose the model with features that mean the most to you.

For a listing of online hand mixer purchasing sources, go to:
CuisineAtHome.com.

Cuisine Test Kitchen Recommendations

KitchenAid $37.89–79.95

KitchenAid didn't miss a detail when designing their hand mixers. With the highest scores for balance, solid design, noise level, and overall handling, the straightforward KitchenAid is unbeatable. Ideal cord design and placement means it never gets in the way of setting the mixer down. Add perfect weight distribution and the result is unequaled balance when mixing or standing.

KitchenAid hand mixers have DC (Direct Current) motors that are measured in rpm's instead of watts. While all four models have the same motor, they're programmed differently to provide for varying degrees of speed. Because they share the same winning design features that make them handle so well, we're recommending all of them! The 3- and 5-speed models are the basic mixers—good, solid performers. And the 7-speed model comes in colors (seven of them). But when pressed to choose, the 9-speed is our favorite for the extra-slow low speed and fastest high speed of the four. They all have round cords for easy cleaning, smooth beater ejection, and a 1-year full warranty. Available at kitchenware and department stores.

The 3- and 5-speed models have mechanical controls and the same low, medium, and high speeds. The digital 7-speed adds a lower setting, while the 9-speed has still lower and higher settings, along with a whisk attachment, see inset.

Cuisinart SmartPower 5-Speed $39.95

For getting the job done fast, the 220-watt Cuisinart beats the competition. This *very* fast (and *very* noisy) model makes quick work of most any mixing task. The low speed is quite fast, kicking up dry ingredients, and the high setting races. It has extra large beater heads, a blue pull lever that ejects beaters with unmatched ease, and a round cord that swivels—a plus for left-hand users. Cuisinart also makes three other models: A similar 3-speed version, and 7- and 9-speed models with digital controls, lower beginning speeds, and a Smooth Start feature that begins slowly and works up to the speed (to reduce splatters). The 9-speed also has a clever "count-up" feature that displays how long you've been mixing, and a wire whisk attachment. All have an impressive 3-year warranty. Available at department and kitchenware stores.

Black & Decker PowerPro MX85 5-Speed $19.99

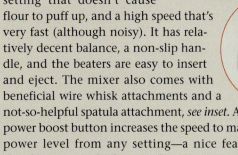

An economy model that's a worthy contender, this Black & Decker 200-watt mixer has a mechanical control setting that moves from left to right. The 5 speeds include a low setting that doesn't cause flour to puff up, and a high speed that's very fast (although noisy). It has relatively decent balance, a non-slip handle, and the beaters are easy to insert and eject. The mixer also comes with beneficial wire whisk attachments and a not-so-helpful spatula attachment, *see inset*. A power boost button increases the speed to maximum power level from any setting—a nice feature for chunky spots or thick areas. Carries a 1-year warranty. Look for it in department or hardware stores.

Food authority Lynne Rossetto Kasper hosts Minnesota Public Radio's weekly show **The Splendid Table**® heard nationally since 1996.

An award-winning author, broadcaster, and cooking teacher, Lynne is also one of America's leading Italian food experts and cultural historians. Her first cookbook, **The Splendid Table**, is based on Lynne's explorations of the northern Italian region of Emilia-Romagna. Her second book, **The Italian Country Table**, includes 200 recipes personally collected from farmhouse cooks throughout Italy.

To listen to her show, check out Lynne's comprehensive food website **splendidtable.org** for station listings and times.

the basics of
risotto

Don't let anyone tell you that risotto is tricky or tough to make. All it requires is a little attention, stirring, and a great teacher!

When she talks about risotto, Lynne Rossetto Kasper's rich voice radiates with the same excitement and awe we hear on her radio show. She marvels that such a simple dish can shine with flavors that absolutely sing!

Risotto [ree-ZAW-toh] is a creamy rice dish from northern Italy known for its unique cooking method: Stock is added to rice in increments, allowing it to simmer and absorb before the next addition. As it's stirred, the rice slowly releases a sticky starch that combines with the stock, creating a velvety sauce. Lynne instructs us in the necessary ingredients and then shows us just what to do and watch for when making risotto.

The Classic White Risotto stands on its own as either a first course or main dish. But just like pasta, risotto can also be a vehicle for other flavors. Just about anything (even leftovers) can be added to risotto. Lynne encourages, "Take what you have and use your imagination!"

Getting ready for risotto

Blending a few subtle but distinctive ingredients creates Classic White Risotto. The great flavor and texture depend on good stock, Arborio rice, and Parmigiano-Reggiano cheese.

Ingredients: Stock is important here because the rice absorbs and takes on its flavor. Use canned broth alone *only* if you're really in a pinch for time. And never, ever use bouillon cubes. The salty, chemical aftertaste throws off the delicate balance of the risotto.

Have the ingredients ready before beginning to make risotto. Mince the onion, measure the wine, and grate the cheese so you can stay close to the stove to stir and add stock.

Process: Making risotto is more a matter of look and taste than time and measurements. But don't let that intimidate you. You just need to know when to add stock and determine when the rice is done. Lynne's step-by-step instructions on Page 28 give you all the necessary details.

Have Ready:

Quick Stock, *see recipe below*

unsalted butter

minced onion

imported Arborio rice

dry white wine

grated Parmigiano-Reggiano cheese

Quick Stock

A good stock can be built on canned chicken broth. Lynne likes to use either the College Inn or Manischewitz brands for good chicken flavor.
Makes 7–8 Cups; Total Time: 40 Minutes

5 cans (14 oz. each) low-sodium chicken broth, chilled, with fat skimmed off
3 medium onions, unpeeled, coarsely chopped
1 large stalk celery with leaves, coarsely chopped
½ large carrot, coarsely chopped
2 sprigs flat-leaf parsley
1 large clove garlic, crushed
¼ t. dried basil

Making this stock doesn't take a lot of time or attention, but it yields big flavor results. And it can even be made ahead—refrigerate up to four days or freeze up to three months.

Bring all ingredients to a boil in a large saucepan. Lower heat so the broth bubbles slowly; cover tightly and cook 30 minutes.
Strain the stock.

Italian Rice

Only imported Italian rice should be used for risotto—like Carnaroli, Arborio, Vialone Nano, or Baldo. The grains release a starch during the cooking process that results in the special creamy consistency that distinguishes risotto. Although often referred to as short-grain, Italian rice is technically medium-grain. Don't substitute other rices. Long grain rices have a starch that produces fluffy, separate grains—great for pilaf, but not risotto.

Lynne likes to use Carnaroli but advises that Arborio is also good and probably the easiest to find. It's available at most supermarkets and any Italian market.

Parmigiano-Reggiano

Produced in only a handful of provinces in northern Italy, Parmigiano-Reggiano is *the* one and only Parmesan cheese. Anything else is an imitation. It has full flavor and is speckled with white flecks that crackle pleasingly on the tongue.

When Parmesan is first folded into risotto, nothing happens for a few moments. Then, as the cheese warms, its wonderful fragrance fills the room and permeates the rice.

Look for vertical stenciling on the rind repeating the words "Parmigiano-Reggiano." Buy it in chunks and then grate up to the hard ½" rind. (Save the rind to cook in soups for great flavor.) *Please* don't use the powdered stuff in the green tube—the flavor will ruin the risotto.

CLASSIC WHITE RISOTTO

MAKES ABOUT 6 CUPS
TOTAL TIME: 30 MINUTES

HEAT:
6–7 cups Quick Stock, *Page 27*

MELT, THEN ADD:
2   T. unsalted butter
1   cup onion, minced

STIR IN:
2   cups imported Arborio rice

ADD:
1/3   cup dry white wine

STIR IN STOCK.

OFF HEAT, FINISH WITH:
1   T. unsalted butter
1   cup Parmigiano-Reggiano
      cheese, grated
      Salt and pepper

Heat stock to a gentle simmer.

Melt butter in a heavy **5–6 quart**
pan over medium heat. Add onion;
cook until clear but not brown.

Stir in rice and saute until rice
edges become transparent, about
3 minutes.

Add wine, stirring until absorbed,
less than 1 minute.

Stir in the heated stock 1 cup at a
time. Each cup must be absorbed
before the next is added.

Off heat, finish with butter
and cheese. Season with salt and
pepper to taste.

Risotto is creamy—never
soupy or dry. It should
have flow and movement,
yet enough substance to
mound on a spoon. ►

◄ Saute onion, then add rice, stirring so it doesn't stick or brown.
Sauteing the rice prepares it to
absorb the stock. Cook 3 minutes
or until the rice edges become
transparent, leaving a white dot
in the center of each grain. The
white core is what gives the rice
its unique texture.

◄ Add wine, then stir stock
into rice one cup at a time,
allowing stock to simmer gently as the rice absorbs it.
Stirring does not have to be
constant, but should be fre-
quent. A wooden spatula
works better than a spoon,
making wide sweeps that protect the rice from sticking.

◄ It's time to add more stock
when a spatula pulled through
leaves a fairly clean trail behind.
Excess liquid should be absorbed,
but don't wait until it's dry. After
using 5 cups of stock, add it in
1/2 cup increments, tasting rice
for doneness. The outside should
be tender while the center has a
pleasant resistance to the bite.

◄ Remove from heat when
the rice is ready, just before
the stock is completely absorbed. Stir in the butter and
cheese. Once blended, let the
risotto rest for a minute. The
rice will swell a little as it
absorbs the final flavorings.

cuisinerecipe

Farmwomen in Italy say risotto welcomes just about anything from the pantry or garden.

Lynne's Classic White Risotto is the perfect canvas for any number of flavorful additions. This Cuisine add-on uses salami, peas, and tomatoes to make a complete meal.

RISOTTO CONFETTI

MAKES 8 CUPS, TOTAL TIME: 35 MINUTES

SAUTE IN 1 T. UNSALTED BUTTER:
4   oz. hard salami, cut into
     ¹/₄"-wide strips

PREPARE RISOTTO, ADDING:
10   oz. frozen peas

OFF HEAT, STIR IN:
1   T. unsalted butter
1   cup Parmigiano-Reggiano
     cheese, grated
     Salt and crushed red pepper
     flakes to taste
     Sauteed salami
1   cup cherry tomatoes, quartered
2   T. minced flat-leaf parsley

Saute salami in butter in a heavy 5–6 quart pan. Transfer to a plate, reserving drippings in the pan.
Prepare Classic White Risotto as on Page 28, using the pan the salami was sauteed in. Add just 1 T. butter to saute the onion. Add frozen peas with final ¹/₂ cup of stock.
Off heat, stir in butter, cheese, and seasonings. Then add the salami, tomatoes, and parsley, stirring gently.

Frozen peas cook quickly in the heated stock and rice. ▶

▲*Saute salami strips until the edges are lightly browned.*

Chicken Pozole *chili*

What a wonderful autumn soup! Flavorful, filling, different, and with just enough kick to warm up any fall day.

First, let's clear up some confusing food terminology. *Chili* refers to the stew while *chile* is a pepper. Most chilies have chiles as an ingredient.

And here's another word to add to your vocabulary: *pozole*. Pozole [poh-SOH-leh] is a traditional Mexican stew (and also the Spanish word for *hominy*). Pozole includes hominy—dried corn that's been soaked in slaked lime until its skin comes off, causing the kernels to swell. Hominy is excellent in stews, and is sold in cans at your grocer.

Pozole is typically made with a flavorful chile sauce. Commercial brands tend to be full of preservatives and salt, so make your own using dried chiles. But don't get freaked out—the chiles are easy to find and the sauce is quick to prepare. Make it ahead and chill it until you're ready to make the pozole. It's also great on enchiladas.

This chili, like most, is better the second day. If you're planning to make it ahead, put off adding the lettuce until right before serving.

CHICKEN POZOLE CHILI

MAKES ABOUT 8 CUPS
TOTAL TIME: 1–1¼ HOURS

Which chile to use?

Moderately spiced dried chiles are the ticket here. You're looking more for flavor than heat. Generally, the rounder the tip of a pepper, the milder the heat. Cascabel [KAS-kuh-behl], also called chile bola, work well, as do ancho, pasilla, and guajillo chiles.

To use in the pozole, crush the chile with your hand and remove the stem, core, and seeds. Since the dried chiles will simmer in broth, there is no need to rehydrate.

FOR THE CHILE SAUCE—
COMBINE AND SAUTE:

3	cups tomatoes, chopped
2	cups yellow onion, chopped
8	cascabel chiles, crushed, stems and seeds removed
6	cloves garlic, smashed
¼	cup olive oil
2	T. chopped fresh oregano
½	t. kosher salt

ADD AND SIMMER; PUREE:

2	6" corn tortillas, chopped
2	cups low-sodium chicken broth

FOR THE CHILI—
SAUTE IN 2 T. OLIVE OIL:

2	cups yellow onion, sliced

STIR IN:

1	T. garlic, minced
1	T. chili powder
2	t. ground cumin
1	t. ground coriander
1	t. kosher salt
¼	t. cayenne

ADD AND SIMMER:

3	cups low-sodium chicken broth
2	cups cooked chicken breast, shredded
2	cups romaine lettuce, chiffonade
1	can (15.5 oz.) yellow hominy, drained, rinsed
	Chile Sauce

FOR THE AVOCADO SALAD—
COMBINE:

1	ripe avocado, peeled, pitted, diced
¼	cup scallions, minced
2	T. chopped fresh cilantro
½	t. kosher salt
	Juice of ½ a lime

GARNISH CHILI WITH:

Avocado Salad
Crumbled feta cheese

Combine ingredients for the chile sauce in a large bowl. Stir in the olive oil to coat. ▼

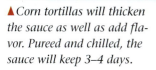

▲*Corn tortillas will thicken the sauce as well as add flavor. Pureed and chilled, the sauce will keep 3–4 days.*

▲*Drain and rinse the hominy—it's canned with lots of salt. Stir into chili. Prepare Avocado Salad while chili simmers.*

Combine tomatoes, onion, chiles, garlic, oil, and seasonings for the sauce. Saute over med.-high heat for 10 minutes.

Add tortillas and broth; simmer 20 minutes. Puree in blender.

Saute onion for the chili in olive oil in large pot over medium heat until softened, about 5 minutes.

Stir in garlic and seasonings. Cook for 2 minutes.

Add broth, shredded chicken, lettuce, hominy, and chile sauce. Simmer 10 minutes.

Combine all of the ingredients for the salad.

Garnish servings of chili with Avocado Salad and feta cheese.

pork chili verde

Chili Verde has been enjoying a popularity explosion. Taste what all the fuss is about.

Chili Verde, or green chili, is a magical balance of caramelized pork, roasted chiles, and plenty of tomatillos. Here's how to max out these flavors.

First, start by *searing* the pork to caramelize (brown). To sear, cook the meat in small batches over high heat. This creates a crust on the meat as well as on the bottom of the pot.

Second, loosen this flavorful crust by *deglazing* the pot with liquid. Tequila works well since it complements the other ingredients. If tequila isn't an option, substitute chicken broth or water.

Third, thicken with *masa harina* (Spanish for "dough flour"). This is the flour used to make corn tortillas. Find it in the baking aisle of the supermarket.

Finally, use fresh tomatillos [tohm-ah-TEE-oh]. Found in the produce section, they look like small green tomatoes and have an unusual sour lemon-herb flavor that mellows as they cook.

Anaheim chiles
Also known as the California green chile, this mild pepper is one variety of the New Mexico chiles. It's green in color with a long, slender shape measuring 6–8". Anaheims are used to make the "mild green chiles" found in cans in the Mexican section of the supermarket. And they are often the chile of choice when make chiles rellenos.

PORK CHILI VERDE

MAKES 6–7 CUPS; TOTAL TIME: 1–1¼ HOURS

After roasting, allow the chiles to steam in a covered bowl. This makes it easier to peel off the skin. ▼

▲ *Sear pork in 2 batches to evenly brown, not steam, the meat. It will take about 5 minutes per batch.*

FOR THE CHILES—
ROAST IN OVEN; PEEL AND CHOP:
8   whole Anaheim chiles

FOR THE CHILI—
SEAR IN 2 T. VEGETABLE OIL:
1½   lb. pork loin, trimmed, cut into ½" cubes, seasoned with salt

DEGLAZE WITH:
2   T. tequila

ADD AND SWEAT:
3   cups yellow onion, diced
2   cups tomatillos, diced
3   T. garlic, chopped
     Roasted chiles
     Seared pork loin

STIR IN:
¼   cup masa harina
1   T. ground cumin
2   t. dried leaf oregano
1   t. ground coriander
1   t. kosher salt

ADD:
3   cups low-sodium chicken broth

FINISH WITH:
1   T. fresh lime juice

SERVE AND GARNISH WITH:
     Cooked white rice
     Sour cream
     Chopped fresh cilantro

Roast chiles in oven at 400°, see *Basics, Page 22*. Place in a bowl, cover with plastic, and steam 10 minutes. Peel, remove stems and seeds, and chop to make 2 cups.

Sear pork on all sides in a large pot over high heat. Do it in two batches, using 1 T. oil per batch.

Deglaze with tequila.

Add onion, tomatillos, garlic, roasted chiles, and seared pork. Sweat over medium heat until onion softens, about 10 minutes.

Stir in masa harina and seasonings to coat all ingredients.

Add broth and bring to a boil. Reduce heat to low and simmer for 30 minutes.

Finish with lime juice right before serving.

Serve with rice and garnish with sour cream and cilantro.

◄ *Deglaze the pot with tequila, scraping up all the bits (and flavor) on the bottom.*

---

make it a
menu

Smoked Gouda quesadillas

Sliced fresh tomatoes

Mango sorbet

Add masa harina and stir well to coat. The masa thickens the chili and adds flavor. ►

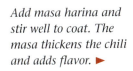

allabout

*p*ure
maple syrup

As a kid, pancakes were just a vehicle for syrup—super-sweet without a trace of real maple. But your grown-up tastes demand something better.

With such a significant price difference between imitation and real maple syrup, the cheaper option can be quite convincing. But make no mistake, those few extra dollars you pay for the real stuff are worth every penny.

The tree
As long as you have a maple tree of adequate size (at least 12 inches in diameter so that the tree can be tapped safely), you can make maple syrup. Any of the over 100 varieties will get the job done. Serious maple producers, though, choose to use sugar, black, or red maple trees, with sugar being the most traditional. These varieties produce the sweetest and highest yield of sap.

Maple trees commonly grow in the eastern provinces of Canada and in the United States—from Maine to Minnesota and as far south as Virginia.

Quebec is the world's largest producer of maple syrup, providing 75% of the supply. Vermont is the largest U.S. producer.

Tapping for sap
Sap is what naturally flows from maple trees. *Syrup* is what the sap is turned into. In order for sap to be efficiently removed, taps are drilled into the tree to help navigate where the sap drains.

Tapping season occurs in early spring and lasts 4–6 weeks. Its success is dependent upon Mother Nature—in order for the sap to flow, cold nights and warm days are crucial. As the sap continually freezes and thaws, enough pressure is created within the trees to force the sap out. Without these significant changes in weather, the sap won't run.

The season ends when the trees begin to bud. Once the trees "break bud," a chemical change takes place in the sap that turns the syrup bitter.

Making syrup
Maple syrup is made by reducing the sap into a sweeter, more condensed form. The sap is boiled down until most of the water has evaporated and the sugars are concentrated. On average, it takes 40 gallons of maple sap to produce 1 gallon of syrup! No wonder pure maple syrup wears such a hefty price tag.

Grading maple syrup

Some states (namely Maine, Vermont, New Hampshire, New York, and Massachusetts) grade their maple syrup. Although the requirement to do so is determined from state to state, the practice is seen as an advantage since it assures consistency in the grade of syrup packaged.

Now, ever since the first day of school, we've been taught that a grade of "A" is better than a "B." But this isn't the case for maple syrup—its grades are determined by color and flavor. Grade A comes in three shades and flavor intensities, *see right,* all of which are lighter in flavor than B. Each type has its strong suits, but let your personal preference guide you when buying. (For a maple grading sampler pack, call **Morse Farm at (800) 242-2740,** or go online to **morsefarm.com**)

Incidentally, the same maple tree can produce different grades of syrup, and the type of grade tapped can change from day to day. (This is mainly due to unpredictable changes within the sap.) But as a general rule, lighter grades are from sap that was tapped at the start of the season. As the days warm up, the sap can get darker.

Grade A Light Amber

Very light color
Mild maple taste

Good for maple candy, maple cream, cake icing, ice cream, and delicate sweets.

Grade A Medium Amber

Medium color
Traditional maple taste

Great all-purpose syrup. Most popular table syrup.

Grade A Dark Amber

Dark color
Strong maple taste

Powerful flavor holds up well in baking. Common table and all-purpose syrup.

Grade B

Darkest color
Strongest flavor

Sometimes called "cooking syrup." This grade can be used as a table syrup, but its intense flavor makes it best for cooking.

What to look for

The label: Make sure the label reads "pure maple syrup" (see bottom right). That way, you're guaranteed to get nothing more than the real deal.

The ingredients: Keep it simple. Pure maple syrup should contain nothing more than itself. Anything else, and you know you've got an imposter (see bottom left).

The container: Buy maple syrup sold in glass or plastic containers. The decorative tins are tempting, but after about three months, the syrup tends to take on its metallic flavor.

Changes: If crystals form at the bottom of the container, it's no big deal. But if a thin layer of mold forms on the top of the syrup, it's best to just pitch it.

How to store
Store unopened maple syrup in a cool, dry area out of direct sunlight—it will keep for 1–2 years. Opened maple syrup should be stored in the refrigerator and used within 6 months. In the freezer, maple syrup will last indefinitely.

Artificially Flavored Maple Syrup
Made with 2% Real Maple Syrup

INGREDIENTS:
PURE MAPLE SYRUP GRADE A DARK AMBER.
Product of Canada.

Easy dips

Got chips? You'll want plenty because these simple-to-do dips put dairy case versions to shame. A party has never tasted better!

SUN-DRIED TOMATO DIP

Cut calories by using reduced fat cream cheese and yogurt. This also makes a great spread on a chicken sandwich!
MAKES ABOUT 2½ CUPS; TOTAL TIME: 15 MINUTES

8	oz. cream cheese, softened
1	cup plain lowfat yogurt
¾	cup oil-packed sun-dried tomatoes, drained
⅓	cup shallots, coarsely chopped (about 3 shallots)
1	T. fresh lemon juice
½	t. lemon zest, minced
½	t. kosher salt
⅓	cup chopped fresh parsley
1	T. minced fresh tarragon
	Bagel chips

Blend cream cheese, yogurt, tomatoes, shallots, lemon juice, zest, and salt in a food processor until smooth.
Fold in parsley and tarragon, then chill for at least 1 hour.
Serve with bagel chips.

Fold the herbs into the dip, then chill before serving. ▶

RED PEPPER CHEDDAR DIP

*There's not much that **doesn't** taste good with this dip smeared on it—potato chips, cucumbers, breadsticks, they're all terrific. It does wonders for a roast beef sandwich too.*
MAKES ABOUT 2 CUPS; TOTAL TIME: 15 MINUTES

¾	cup sharp white Cheddar cheese, shredded
4	oz. cream cheese, softened
¼	cup plain yogurt or sour cream
¼	cup mayonnaise
¼	cup bottled roasted red peppers, diced
2	t. Tabasco
	Salt to taste
2	pieces thick-sliced bacon, diced
3	scallions, sliced (½ cup)
	Flavored breadsticks

Blend all ingredients except bacon and scallions in a food processor until fairly smooth.
Saute bacon until crisp; drain. Reserve some bacon bits and scallions for garnish, then fold the remainder into the cheese mixture. Chill at least 1 hour.
Garnish dip with reserved bacon and scallions.
Serve with breadsticks, sliced cucumbers, or rounds of sliced toasted baguette.

◀ *Fold bacon and scallions into the dip (save some for garnish). Chill before serving to blend flavors.*

CURRIED AVOCADO DIP

This lightly spicy dip is perfect on chilled poached shrimp, cucumber spears, or lime-flavored tortilla chips.
Serve it within an hour of making or it will darken a bit.
Makes About 2¹/₂ Cups; Total Time: About 15 Minutes

¹/₂	cup cilantro leaves and stems, packed
¹/₄	cup plain lowfat yogurt
3	T. shredded sweetened coconut
2	T. fresh lime juice
1	T. fresh ginger, chopped
¹/₂	t. curry powder
1	serrano or jalapeño, seeded and sliced
1	shallot, peeled, chopped
	Salt to taste
2	ripe avocados, peeled, pitted, and chopped
	Chilled poached shrimp, peeled and deveined

Blend all ingredients except the avocado and shrimp in a food processor until minced. Scrape down the sides of the bowl to insure even blending.
Add chopped avocado and blend until very smooth. Taste for seasoning, then transfer to a serving dish.
Serve with poached shrimp.

Slice around avocado from top to bottom, then twist halves to separate. ▼

▲ *Strike the pit with the knife blade, then twist it out. Peel off the skin and chop.*

FETA PEPPER DIP

My brother, Jerry, makes a feta dip that inspired this version. Our favorite dipping "utensils" for it are BBQ potato chips, but it's also an awesome spread for beef or lamb burgers.
Makes About 2¹/₂ Cups; Total Time: 15 Minutes

8	oz. feta cheese, crumbled
8	oz. cream cheese
¹/₂	cup mayonnaise or plain yogurt
¹/₂	cup pickled peppers (pepperoncini and/or sweet red cherry peppers), sliced
¹/₄	cup scallions, sliced
¹/₂	t. lemon zest, minced
	Black pepper to taste
	Extra-virgin olive oil
	BBQ potato chips

Blend feta, cream cheese, and mayonnaise in a food processor until smooth, scraping down sides of bowl periodically. Transfer to a mixing bowl.
Fold in peppers, scallions, lemon zest, and black pepper. Transfer to a serving dish and chill dip for at least 1 hour.
Drizzle dip with olive oil.
Serve with BBQ potato chips or toasted pita triangles.

Remove the stem of the peppers then slice into rings. It's okay to leave the seeds in—the peppers aren't terribly spicy. ▼

Pickled peppers run the gamut from sweet to a little spicy. The pepperoncini have a bit of heat, so I balance the dip's flavor by using mild, sweet cherry peppers too.

Caramel apple Cake

It's the height of apple season! Combine them with caramel and moist white cake for a spectacular autumn trio.

Homemade cake just may become a thing of the past. It's a shame, but with all sorts of cookbooks touting the magic of mixes, it's no surprise.

But before you forever swear off baking a cake from scratch, give this one a try. Even though it has three components (cake, filling, icing), none are difficult to execute. A single taste just may convince you to ban cake mixes from your kitchen!

Caramel cake is a Southern tradition consisting simply of white cake frosted with a super-sweet caramel icing. This is one cake that's invited to (and shows up at) nearly every party. Where there is food, there is caramel cake—potlucks, picnics, church suppers, everywhere.

The big difference between that traditional cake and this one is a layer of tart, spicy sauteed apples in the middle. It is a departure from tradition, but given how perfectly suited caramel and apples are to each other, it's not a big leap at all.

Baking the cake

This cake is easy, but it does need more attention than a boxed mix. Here is what to look out for.

Creaming: Properly creaming the butter and sugar aerates the batter and gives the cake a finer texture. To do it right, the butter must be room temperature, not hard or squishy, and the creaming time long, 4–5 minutes.

Adding ingredients: Add the egg whites a little at a time so they thoroughly blend into the butter. And by alternately adding dry and wet ingredients, the batter resists curdling (which is bad for the cake's flavor and texture).

Overmixing: Take care not to overmix the batter. It develops gluten (a protein), making the cake tough, and causes tunnel-like holes to form. To prevent it, add the last of the flour by hand.

Baking and cooling: Bake the cakes until a toothpick comes out clean. Cool them in the pans a bit before turning out to cool *completely*—do not assemble the cake with warm layers (they're not sturdy enough to support each other). Cooled, the layers may be frozen for up to a month.

BUTTERMILK CAKE LAYERS

MAKES TWO 9" ROUNDS
TOTAL TIME: ABOUT 1 HOUR

CREAM:
2   cups sugar
³/₄   cup unsalted butter, room temperature (1¹/₂ sticks)

GRADUALLY ADD:
5   egg whites, lightly blended

SIFT TOGETHER:
2³/₄   cups all-purpose flour
¹/₂   t. baking soda
¹/₂   t. table salt

COMBINE; ADD ALTERNATELY WITH DRY INGREDIENTS:
1   cup buttermilk
2   t. vanilla extract

Preheat oven to 350° with rack in the center. Grease two 9" round cake pans with nonstick spray. Line with rounds of parchment paper, spray again, and dust with flour.
Cream sugar and butter in a large mixing bowl until light.
Gradually add egg whites, beating until well blended.
Sift flour, baking soda, and salt.
Combine buttermilk and vanilla. Add ¹/₃ of the flour mixture to the butter mixture; mix just until blended. Add ¹/₂ the buttermilk mixture and blend just to incorporate. Scrape the bowl, add half the remaining flour, and blend. Scrape bowl again, then add the remaining buttermilk. Fold in the last of the flour by hand, making sure no flour is at the bottom.

Divide batter among prepared pans, about 2¹/₂ cups per pan. Bake for 40–45 minutes, or until a toothpick inserted in the center comes out clean. Cool cakes on a rack for 5 minutes, turn out onto a cooling rack, and peel off the parchment. Cool before filling and frosting.

▲ *Cream butter and sugar until they're noticeably lighter in color, about 5 minutes. Gradually beat in the egg whites.*

▲ *Alternate adding dry and wet ingredients to butter mixture. Do not overmix.*

Divide batter between pans and smooth tops with a spatula. ▶

▲ *Bake cakes, cool briefly, then turn out of the pans and peel off parchment. Carefully invert and cool completely before assembling.*

Making the filling and icing

While the cake is in the oven, make the apple filling. The thing to remember here is not to stir the fruit too much during cooking. Prolonged contact with the pan helps caramelize the apples.

The caramel icing, on the other hand, requires a bit more attention. But don't worry—it's nothing overwhelming. First, be sure to use a saucepan with high sides. The icing foams up a lot and can bubble over easily. Next, stir the mixture fairly often as the sugar dissolves and the butter melts. But once it's smooth, stir only occasionally or else the icing could turn grainy.

Begin to time the cooking process when the icing comes to a rolling boil. After 8 minutes or so, it should be caramelized to about the color of peanut butter.

Cool the icing slightly, then beat until it thickens to the point that it's spreadable, yet still can drip down the sides. Assemble the cake immediately.

SPICED APPLE FILLING
MAKES ABOUT 1 CUP
TOTAL TIME: ABOUT 20 MINUTES

SAUTE IN 2 T. UNSALTED BUTTER:
3   Granny Smith apples, peeled, thinly sliced
$1/4$ cup sugar
1   t. ground cinnamon
   Juice of $1/2$ a lemon
   Pinch of salt
DEGLAZE WITH:
3   T. apple juice or water

Saute apples in butter over medium-high heat with sugar, cinnamon, lemon juice, and salt. Cook until fruit begins to caramelize around the edges, about 15 minutes. Stir periodically, but not so much that the apples don't caramelize.
Deglaze with juice, stir, and cook another 2–3 minutes, or until liquid is nearly (but not totally) evaporated. Cool apples before filling cake.

After boiling 3–4 minutes, the icing will look like this. ▼

▲ *The icing will have begun to caramelize after boiling 7–8 minutes.*

CARAMEL ICING
MAKES ABOUT $2^1/2$ CUPS
TOTAL TIME: ABOUT 20 MINUTES

BOIL:
2   cups sugar
1   cup unsalted butter, cubed (2 sticks)
$1/2$ cup buttermilk
1   t. baking soda
1   t. fresh lemon juice
   Pinch of salt
TOP CAKE WITH:
   Chopped dry roasted peanuts

Boil all ingredients (except for the peanuts) in a tall, heavy saucepan over medium heat, stirring until butter melts and mixture starts to boil. Cook, stirring occasionally, until icing caramelizes, about 8 minutes. Remove from heat and cool 5 minutes. It will continue to caramelize off heat.

Beat icing with a hand mixer until lighter in color and thick, about 5 minutes. It should be liquid enough to drip down the sides of the cake. Assemble cake as on Page 41.

Top cake with chopped peanuts.

▲ *Beat slightly cooled icing with a hand mixer until thickened.*

Putting it together

Once the icing is beaten, you have to put the cake together quickly. If you wait, the icing will stiffen and make for problematic spreading. However, if it does thicken a bit, just thin it out with a teaspoon or two of buttermilk or milk. Achieving the ideal consistency is tricky, but the perfect icing will flow from a spoon in a thick stream when poured.

To assemble, start by spreading about one cup of icing over one of the cake layers. Push the icing to the edges but don't force it to drip over, *Figure 1*. It will happen naturally when the apple filling and the second cake layer are positioned on top.

Now, carefully arrange the apple filling on the icing. Get the apples as close to the edge as possible without spilling over. If there's any juice left in the saute pan, drizzle it over the apples—it'll soak into the top cake layer.

Place the second cake layer on the first, *Figure 2*, then pour the remaining icing on top. Working quickly, spread it to the edge and gently push it over so it drips down, *Figure 3*. Finally, press the nuts into the icing on top, *Figure 4*, don't just sprinkle them on. A thin, sugary crust keeps the nuts from sticking unless they're firmly pressed in.

For super-clean slices, use an electric knife to cut the cake. If you don't have one, use a sharp knife and clean the blade after each cut. That way, the icing won't stick so much.

Spread half the icing over the first cake layer, taking it just to the edge. ▼

◄ *Top the iced layer with all of the apple filling. Place the second layer on top of the first.*

Spread remaining icing on the second layer, allowing it to drip down the sides. ▼

Lightly press peanuts into the icing on top, otherwise they won't stick very well. ►

Cutting the cake ▲
For clean looking slices, cut the cake with an electric knife.

from **our** readers

Q&A
questions & answers

Oops!
From Issue 40, the answer to the question on sifting flour should have read: For "1 cup flour, sifted," measure before sifting. For "1 cup sifted flour," measure after sifting.

ALCOHOL SUBSTITUTES
I don't like to cook with alcohol. Can you please recommend good substitutes that I can use?

Julie Brown
Cedar City, UT

The following is a general list of non-alcoholic substitutes that can be used in cooking. Choose the option that best matches the flavor of the dish you are making.

Recipe calls for:	Substitute with:
white wine	white grape juice; chicken or vegetable broth; ginger ale
red wine	grape juice; cranberry juice; chicken, beef, or vegetable broth; flavored vinegar; tomato juice
brandy	white grape juice; apple juice; cherry, peach, or apricot syrup
beer	chicken, beef, or mushroom broth; white grape juice; ginger ale
rum	pineapple juice with almond extract or molasses; vanilla extract
vodka	water; apple cider or white grape juice mixed with lime juice
sherry	vanilla extract; orange or pineapple juice; coffee

BELGIAN WAFFLES
How are Belgian waffles different from others?

Scott Harp
Boston, MA

Hailing from Belgium where they were originally called Brussels waffles, crisp, deep-holed Belgian waffles made their American debut at the 1964 World's Fair in Queens, New York—thanks to Belgian Maurice Vermersch.

Traditionally, Belgian waffles are made with yeast, so the batter needs time to rise. That's what gives the waffles their characteristic lightness and slightly tangy flavor. Today, for the sake of convenience, many Belgian waffle recipes have replaced the yeast with a combination of baking powder and baking soda in an attempt to speed up the process.

The ingredients, not large holes, truly characterize Belgian waffles. So there's no need to buy special equipment to make them. Any waffle iron will work fine.

JAMS, MARMALADES, ETC.
How can you distinguish between jam, jelly, preserves, marmalade, and conserves?

Mikael Kriz
Windsor, Ontario

While jam, jelly, preserves, marmalade, and conserves are all commonly used as spreads, differences remain in their texture and ingredients.

According to the *Food Lover's Companion* by Sharon Tyler Herbst, *jelly* has the thinnest consistency of the bunch—fruits, or sometimes vegetables, are cooked and then strained until smooth and clear. *Jams* are next down the line. Like jelly, the fruit is cooked until soft and almost formless. But instead of being strained, the fruit is pureed. *Preserves* are very similar to jam except the fruit is left in medium to large chunks. *Marmalade* is a type of preserve that contains fruit peels. And *conserves* are a mixture of fruits and nuts that are cooked until thick.

Marmalade

Jelly

Preserves

Conserves

Jam

APPLE JUICE VS. CIDER

Is there a difference between apple juice and apple cider?

Christine Schirmer
New Holstein, WI

There are no FDA labeling requirements that distinguish apple juice from cider. But in general, with regional differences aside (i.e. what the East Coast calls "cider," the West Coast calls "juice"), here's the deal.

Apple cider is commonly associated with unprocessed, freshly pressed juice that's often sold at orchards and farm stands. Bits of apple flesh and skin still remain, and it's the oxidation of these remnants that gives cider the gorgeous brown color for which it's known.

Apple juice is the transparent liquid you find in the juice aisle of the grocery store. It's shelf-stable and filtered, which makes it clear enough to see through.

In other parts of the world, (England and Australia specifically), and slowly gaining back popularity in the States, distinctions are made between "sweet" and "hard" cider. Sweet cider contains 100% juice, while hard cider takes sweet cider one step further, fermenting it into an alcoholic beverage.

apple cider ▼

apple juice ▲

Pancetta

Pancetta [pan-CHEH-tuh] is often referred to as Italian bacon. That is a close comparison, yet not entirely true. Pancetta, made only from pork belly (the Italian word, *pancia*, means "belly"), is salt cured but very rarely smoked. It is sold flat or, more commonly, rolled.

Flat pancetta is usually only lightly seasoned with salt and pepper. Rolled pancetta is often heavily seasoned with such spices as cloves, cinnamon, and juniper berries. In Italy, the fattier cuts of pancetta are considered a delicacy since they have more flavor and are less salty tasting, as the additional fat helps to neutralize the salt flavor.

Pancetta can be used like bacon—eaten alone, added to sauces, or as an additional ingredient to various entrees. Typically fried, pancetta provides a hint of saltiness to a dish without the smoke flavor that bacon otherwise imparts.

Look for pancetta in Italian or gourmet meat markets. If none is available, bacon and prosciutto are adequate substitutes.

SUPERFINE SUGAR

What is superfine sugar and how is it used?

Greg Thorne
Seattle, WA

Superfine sugar (also known as castor or ultrafine sugar) is an incredibly fine grain of sugar, finer than both extrafine and baker's sugars. Its claim to fame is its ability to easily dissolve. Consequently, superfine sugar is often used when making meringue or to sweeten cold liquids—hence its nickname "bar sugar."

Superfine sugar can be substituted teaspoon for teaspoon with granulated sugar. But there's no need to run to the store—it's easy to make your own. Just grind granulated sugar in a coffee grinder, food processor, or blender for about one minute.

Q&A

Do you have a question for *Cuisine at home?*

If you have a question about a cooking term, procedure, or technique, we'd like to hear from you. We'll consider publishing your question in one or more of our works. Just write down your question and mail it to *Cuisine at home*, Q&A Editor, 2200 Grand Ave., Des Moines, IA 50312, or contact us through our email address shown below. Please include your name, address, and daytime phone number in case we have questions.

Email: CuisineAtHome@CuisineAtHome.com
Web address: CuisineAtHome.com

fresh seafood risotto

Build an impressive seafood dinner by adding scallops, shrimp, calamari, and greens to Lynne Rossetto Kasper's wonderful Classic White Risotto on Page 28.

Sear 12 sea scallops in a heated 5–6 quart pan with a little olive oil and butter. For good browning, don't move scallops once they hit the pan. Turn when browned; add shrimp (12 extra large) and 1 cup calamari (^{1}/$_2$" rings). Saute quickly until lightly browned. Remove from pan.

In the same pan, prepare the risotto as on Page 28, scraping the pan as the onions cook. Season with salt and crushed red pepper flakes; finish risotto with butter alone (no cheese). Fold in 3 cups chiffonade spring greens and prepared seafood. Drizzle with a little flavorful balsamic vinegar at the table (optional).

Cuisine at home®

"I can't believe I made this"
Beef Wellington

3 Easy, Elegant Dinners
for the holidays

The Ultimate Dinner:
Lobster Tails
a recipe for celebration

Issue No. 42 December 2003
A publication of August Home Publishing

Cuisine at home®

Publisher
Donald B. Peschke

Editor
John F. Meyer

Senior Editor
Susan Hoss

Associate Editor
Sarah Marx Feldner

Associate Editor
John Kirkpatrick

Assistant Editor
Sara Ostransky

Test Kitchen Director
Kim Samuelson

Art Director
Cinda Shambaugh

Assistant Art Director
Holly Wiederin

Senior Graphic Designer
April Walker Janning

Image Specialist
Troy Clark

Photographer
Dean Tanner

Contributing Food Stylist
Jennifer Peterson

AUGUST HOME
PUBLISHING COMPANY

Corporate:

Corporate Vice Presidents: Mary R. Scheve, Douglas L. Hicks • *Creative Director:* Ted Kralicek • *Professional Development Director:* Michal Sigel *New Media Manager:* Gordon C. Gaippe • *Senior Photographer:* Crayola England *Multi Media Art Director:* Eugene Pedersen • *Web Server Administrator:* Carol Schoeppler • *Web Content Manager:* David Briggs • *Web Designer:* Kara Blessing *Controller:* Robin Hutchinson • *Senior Accountant:* Laura Thomas • *Accounts Payable:* Mary Schultz • *Accounts Receivable:* Margo Petrus • *Research Coordinator:* Nick Jaeger • *Production Director:* George Chmielarz • *Pre-Press Image Specialist:* Minniette Johnson • *Electronic Publishing Director:* Douglas M. Lidster • *Systems Administrator:* Cris Schwanebeck • *PC Maintenance Technician:* Robert D. Cook *H.R. Assistant:* Kirsten Koele • *Receptionist/Administrative Assistant:* Jeanne Johnson • *Mail Room Clerk:* Lou Webber • *Office Manager:* Natalie Lonsdale *Facilities Manager:* Kurt Johnson

Customer Service & Fulfillment:

Operations Director: Bob Baker • *Customer Service Manager:* Jennie Enos *Customer Service Representatives:* Anna Cox, Kim Harlan, Cheryl Jordan, April Revell, Deborah Rich, Valerie Jo Riley, Tammy Truckenbrod • *Buyer:* Linda Jones *Administrative Assistant:* Nancy Downey • *Warehouse Supervisor:* Nancy Johnson *Fulfillment:* Sylvia Carey

Circulation:

Circulation Operations Director: Sandy Baum • *Circulation Marketing Director:* Wayde J. Klingbeil • *Circulation Marketing Analyst:* Patrick A. Walsh • *Renewal Manager:* Paige Rogers • *Strategic Business Analysts:* Kris Schlemmer, Paula M. DeMatteis • *Circulation Fulfillment Manager:* Steph Forinash • *Art Director:* Doug Flint • *Senior Graphic Designers:* Mark Hayes, Robin Friend

www.CuisineAtHome.com

talk to *Cuisine at home*
Questions about Subscriptions and Address Changes? Write or call:

Customer Service
2200 Grand Avenue,
Des Moines, IA 50312
(800) 311-3995,
8 a.m. to 5 p.m., Central Time.

Online Subscriber Services:
www.CuisineAtHome.com
Access your account • Check a subscription payment • Tell us if you've missed an issue • Change your mailing or email address • Renew your subscription • Pay your bill

Cuisine at home® (ISSN 1537-8225) is published bi-monthly (Jan., Mar., May, July, Sept., Nov.) by August Home Publishing Co., 2200 Grand Ave., Des Moines, IA 50312. Cuisine at home® is a trademark of August Home Publishing Co. ©Copyright 2003 August Home Publishing. All rights reserved. Subscriptions: Single copy: $4.99. One year subscription (6 issues), $24.00. (Canada/Foreign add $10 per year, U.S. funds.)

Periodicals postage paid at Des Moines, IA and at additional mailing offices. "USPS/Perry-Judd's Heartland Division automatable poly". Postmaster: Send change of address to Cuisine at home®, P.O. Box 37100 Boone, IA 50037-2100. Cuisine at home® does not accept and is not responsible for unsolicited manuscripts. PRINTED IN CHINA

editor's letter

Growing up, we had a Christmas Eve tradition of being served a simple dinner consisting of oyster stew (a magical combination of cream, butter, and fresh oysters) and a salad—iceberg, of course. At the time it seemed fairly unremarkable, but as memories become more important to me, this simple dinner ranks right up there with the best of classic meals. Who knows why ... perhaps spirits were soaring because the weather man had just tracked Santa on his radar. Maybe it could have been Pop's excitement over a bowl of fresh oysters—his first and last of the year. Or perhaps it was just the general contentment that infiltrated the family as we kids happily slurped down the buttery stew, *sans* oysters, with handfuls of oysterette crackers. Like Pop, we only got to enjoy this butter and cream delicacy once a year too.

It's funny, but when I share this story with others, I'm surprised to learn that many of us had similar holiday traditions. Maybe it wasn't the exact menu, but that once-a-year "oyster stew" made its appearance on Christmas Eve in many of our homes. So I figured there must be something special to the simplicity of the menu and the holidays. With that in mind, I wanted to recreate this "calm-before-the-storm" dinner, but bump it up a bit—actually a lot. So turn to Page 8 and prepare this Lobster Bisque. Compared to most bisques, it's simple to make, but still loaded with flavor. Serve with a simple salad, good artisan bread, and a glass of Chardonnay, and you'll be hard-pressed to find a better dinner on Christmas Eve. It's important to leave kids with things they can remember when the memories of gifts are long forgotten.

But I haven't dropped the ball on "home run" dinners that are coming up. You know, the kind where appearance rates just as high as flavor. Well, these score a perfect 10 on both counts. How about Beef Wellington, Stuffed Lobster, Pork Wellington, Baked Alaska ... a little retro, yet always pleasing. These classics are making a comeback and they're better than ever. What's so nice is that most of these dishes can be made ahead, leaving the last minute details dedicated to presentation rather than preparation.

Have a big holiday and plan to build some good traditions!

table of contents

from **our** readers

tips
and techniques

Test Kitchen Tip
After cooking starches such as mashed potatoes, always wash pans and utensils with cold water. Using hot water will cause residual starch to stick to the pan.

Slick Cuts
To cut dried fruits or other sticky ingredients (like marshmallows), spray your knife or scissors with nonstick cooking spray to prevent sticking.

Judy Higgins
Bronxville, NY

Seasonal Zesting
When citrus is in season we eat a lot of oranges. But before peeling them, we finely zest the orange, then freeze the zest to use through the year in homemade scones, breads, and cakes. The frozen zest is just as tasty as fresh.

Paul Hahn
Brownsburg, VA

Binder Clip Holder
If your thermometer becomes too hot to handle, or it slides into the pan, try this tip. Attach a binder clip to the pan, resting the thermometer in one of the "wings."

Jack Jones
Baltimore, MD

Multi-tasking Container
Living in Hershey, Pennsylvania, we use a lot of Hershey's cocoa in recipes—which leaves us with a lot of empty containers. Instead of throwing them away, we wash the containers and use them for storing BBQ rubs, sauces, even kosher salt. Because of the wide opening, a small measuring cup fits easily inside. For quick identification, change the label as needed.

Bill Ray
Hershey, PA

Chocolate Enhancer
When making a chocolate cake from a boxed mix, I use cooled, prepared coffee in place of the water. It enhances the chocolate flavor, and best of all, the cake tastes like it was from scratch!

Kelly Zdrojewski
Loveland, OH

Taming a Lemon
To obtain quick fresh lemon juice (with no cleanup!), first slice the lemon in half. Place the cut halves into a resealable plastic bag and close. Firmly press the lemons between the heel of your hand and the countertop. Now, snip off a small corner of the bag and pour out the juice. When finished, toss out the bag with the lemons and seeds. No fuss, no muss.

Edward M. Clemenco
San Jose, CA

Roasted Tomatoes

Grape tomatoes are expensive, so if they're a little past their prime (a bit wrinkled), don't throw them away—roast them.

Prick tomatoes with a fork and roast on a parchment-lined baking sheet at 425° for 20 minutes. Reduce oven temperature to 375° and roast an additional 20–30 minutes. Watch carefully to make sure they caramelize, not burn. Roasted tomatoes can be used in sauces, salads, and even sandwiches! They're also delicious with grilled chicken or fish.

Laura Minich
Fort Walton Beach, FL

Keeping Current

I prepare Asian recipes, so it's necessary to have various spices and dried herbs in my pantry. To insure the best quality for my recipes, I write the date on the container when I open it. To keep my supply as fresh as possible, I check all the dates regularly.

Maureen Riley
Laguna Niguel, CA

Anti-Onion

I love onions, but my husband won't touch them. So when a soup or stew calls for them, I wrap and tie the prepared onions in cheesecloth (sauteing first if required). The bundle goes in with the remaining ingredients, then after finishing the dish, I just remove the onion bundle and discard.

Meredith Lepper
Wellesley, MA

Herb Extender

To extend the life of fresh herbs, roll them in a moistened paper towel, then place the roll into a plastic freezer bag. Seal and store in the crisper drawer of the fridge.

Emilie C. Quigley
Glenside, PA

Rolling Along

I found an easy way to roll out cookie dough without adding extra flour—roll the dough between two sheets of waxed paper. Place the rolled dough (still between the waxed paper) onto a cookie sheet and freeze briefly. To cut shapes, simply remove the top sheet of waxed paper. You'll find that cutting and separating the shapes will be much easier too.

Caryl Murchison
Colorado Springs, CO

Uncanny Storage

When opening a can that contains more than what is needed, I remove the label (or enough to identify the product) and wrap it around a plastic storage container. Secure the label with a rubber band, and date the "label" with a marker.

Linda Jawitz
New York, NY

share your **tips** with *Cuisine at home*
and techniques

If you have a unique way of solving a cooking problem, we'd like to hear from you, and we'll consider publishing your tip in one or more of our works. Just write down your cooking tip and mail it to *Cuisine at home*, Tips Editor, 2200 Grand Ave., Des Moines, IA 50312, or contact us through our email address shown below. Please include your name, address, and daytime phone number in case we have questions. We'll pay you $25 if we publish your tip.

Email: CuisineAtHome@CuisineAtHome.com
Web address: CuisineAtHome.com

The Ultimate Dinner: Lobster Tails

Lobster isn't just for those fortunate coastal dwellers. Even the land-locked can enjoy this simple luxury.

▲ *North Australian*

▲ *Caribbean*

▲ *Maine*

▼ *South African*

▼ *New Zealand*

▼ *West Australian*

Without a doubt, lobster is one of the most extravagant meals you can put on the table. You *know* it's a special occasion when lobster is served.

Trouble is, cooking a whole lobster can be scary—especially if you didn't grow up in Maine! Its high price tag and labor-intensive eating ritual pretty much limits a lobster dinner to steak houses and seafood restaurants.

But lobster tails are different. They easily bring out the gourmet cook in everyone—without dealing with live seafood and the mess of cleaning it. The tail contains the bulk of a lobster's meat, so it's a logical place to concentrate your efforts. And, since tails are always sold frozen (never fresh), they're convenient to store. Sorry, but lobster tails still cost a lot. Cook them right, though, and they're worth every cent.

Normally I wouldn't tell you to buy frozen seafood, but with lobster tails, it's the only choice you have—and actually, it's the best choice. Once a lobster is killed, the meat begins to deteriorate. But since most tails are flash-frozen on the boats, the quality of the meat is preserved.

When choosing tails, you may have a few decisions to make depending on how well-stocked your fish market is. Lobsters are caught all over the world, and it's likely that their geographical origin will be printed on the package. While all the tails shown here were great, my favorites were those from Maine and South Africa.

These two have one thing in common—they're from cold water. In fact, the only tails here that are *not* are the Caribbean and North Australian. Cold water tails tend to be sweeter and firmer than those from warm water. Warm water tails are still good, but if given a choice, opt for cold water ones.

Select lobster tails whose shells are free from large cracks and breaks. And avoid those that are encased in a thick layer of ice—since they're priced by weight, you'll wind up paying a pretty penny for an overly icy lobster tail!

Preparing and cooking

I meant it when I said preparing lobster tails was easy! Once thawed (either overnight in the fridge or under cold, running water), only splitting and steaming are left.

Splitting: A split tail better exposes the meat, making it easier to eat. To split, place the tail on a towel, shell-side down. Position the tip of a chef's knife at the point where the fan connects to the tail. Slice between the "swimmerets," down the length of the tail through the meat. Don't "saw" or the meat will shred. To crack through the shell, you'll need to lean on top of the knife—it will take some muscle.

Steaming: Because lobster meat is high in protein and extremely low in fat, a moist-heat method of cooking is best to keep it from drying out. With steaming, you get pure lobster flavor that's not diluted since it absorbs less water than boiling.

Use salted water for steaming. The saltiness it imparts is minimal, but not insignificant—this water provides a delicious base for the Lobster Bisque on Page 9. And an inexpensive vegetable steaming basket is perfect for holding the split tails.

Lobster is cooked when the meat is firm and opaque. A split 8-oz. tail (4 oz. each) steams in just 5–7 minutes.

Broiling or grilling: Even though I don't show them here, they *are* options. (See the Back Cover for broiling.) Both are dry-heat methods so moisture evaporates, intensifying flavors. But they also makes it easy to overcook the tails.

▲ *Perfection in its simplicity— steamed lobster drizzled with citrus juice and dipped in melted butter.*

▲ *To split, start at the fan and slice the knife down and through the meat. A towel keeps it steady.*

Devein the split tail. Look for the vein along the edge of the shell, between the shell and the meat. ▼

I like how the tails curl naturally when cooked. But to keep them straight, read Basics, Page 24 before steaming. ▼

▲ *Steam tails shell-side down; the shell protects the meat from the intense heat of the steam. Cover and cook 5–7 min.*

holiday eve
Lobster Bisque

Rich and robust, the holidays deserve this very special bisque.

Lobster bisque is a treat, but a restaurant isn't the only place to find it. Making it at home is easy, and with this recipe, you'll probably get more lobster in your bowl than a restaurant would ever serve—*half a tail* per person! (For appetizer servings, "garnish" the soup with lobster.) Bisques are often rich, but this has just enough cream to smooth it out.

Making bisque

Can't imagine making bisque at home? You can! Here's how.

Stock: It may seem odd to saute lobster shells and reuse steaming water, but doing both adds deep flavor to the stock.

Bisque: A classic bisque is thickened with a little white rice. Just be sure the rice is *totally* cooked before pureeing so the soup is smooth.

Pureeing hot liquids is dangerous—steam causes pressure to build inside the blender. That's why it's crucial to blend in batches and work from a low to a higher speed.

Lobster: Since the lobster is steamed already, it only needs brief sauteing to warm it through before serving—keep the meat whole so there's less chance of overcooking it. Slice before adding it to the soup.

◄ *Use a fork to pull out the steamed tail meat in one piece.*

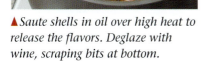

▲ *Saute shells in oil over high heat to release the flavors. Deglaze with wine, scraping bits at bottom.*

Puree bisque in batches, starting on the lowest setting then gradually increasing to high. ►

LOBSTER BISQUE
MAKES 6–7 CUPS; TOTAL TIME: ABOUT 2 HOURS

FOR THE LOBSTER STOCK—
STEAM:
- 2   lobster tails (8–10 oz. each), split in half, *Page 7*
- 4   cups water
- 1   T. sea or kosher salt

SAUTE IN 2 T. OLIVE OIL:
-     Lobster shells, meat removed

DEGLAZE WITH; ADD AND SIMMER:
- 2   cups dry white wine
- 3   cups low-sodium chicken broth
-     Reserved lobster water

FOR THE BISQUE—
SAUTE IN ¹⁄₄ CUP UNSALTED BUTTER:
- 1   cup fennel, chopped
- ¹⁄₂   cup shallot, chopped

STIR IN AND SIMMER; PUREE:
-     Lobster Stock
- 1   cup fresh tomato, peeled, seeded, diced
- 2   T. brandy
- 2   T. raw white rice
- 1   T. tomato paste
- 1   t. paprika
- ¹⁄₄   t. cayenne
- 1   bay leaf
- 1   thyme sprig

ADD:
- ¹⁄₂   cup heavy cream
- 1   t. fresh lemon juice

SAUTE IN 1 T. UNSALTED BUTTER:
-     Reserved lobster meat

Steam lobster tails in salted water for 5–7 minutes. Remove tails and reserve steaming water for stock. When cool enough to handle, remove the tail meat. Chill until ready to use.

Saute lobster shells in oil in a stock pot over medium-high heat for 5 minutes. Stir occasionally.

Deglaze with wine. Add broth and reserved lobster steaming water. Simmer until reduced to 6 cups, about 45 minutes; strain.

Saute fennel and shallots for the bisque in butter, about 5 minutes.

Stir in stock, tomato, brandy, rice, tomato paste, herbs, and seasonings; simmer 40–45 minutes. Remove bay leaf and thyme sprig, then puree liquid in two batches. Return soup to the pot.

Add cream and lemon juice.

Saute lobster meat in butter over medium-high heat just until warmed through. Slice tails into ¹⁄₂" pieces and arrange on bisque. Serve immediately.

▲ *Before serving, reheat lobster meat in butter. Slice tails into chunks, then add to servings of bisque.*

seafood-stuffed
Lobster Tails

There's nothing wrong with lobster, melted butter, and lemon. But this definitely puts that classic to the test!

As delicious as steamed lobster is, this stuffed tail makes it almost too good for words—lobster tail combined with crabmeat and cream sauce for a rich, elegant, and satisfying meal. Stuffed into lobster shells, this is one dinner that receives high marks for visual impact, and that's *always* important during the holidays.

To "stretch" the lobster and keep the grocery bill down, pasteurized crab is used too. Find it where you buy fish, sold in cans and refrigerated. If unavailable, have the fishmonger order it.

This tail is just fine on its own, but the rosemary mashed potatoes on Page 27 make an ideal accompaniment.

Stuffing tails

This recipe starts with two pre-cooked lobster tails. See Page 7 for instructions on how to split and steam them. But don't toss out those shells! They make a great vehicle for stuffing.

Cracking: After steaming, remove the tail meat, then crack the shells—they'll hold plenty of filling this way. Bend back until you hear the swimmerets crack.

Tempering: The important technique in this recipe is tempering. If you've made custard or pastry cream before, you know what I'm talking about.

To "temper" is to bring eggs or egg yolks to a higher temperature without scrambling them. If added directly to the hot cream, they'd curdle. Temper by blending the yolks with a few spoonfuls of the warm cream. Then add the tempered yolks to the remaining cream, whisking constantly over low heat.

Stuffing and baking: Stuff the filling among the four split tails—pour any extra sauce onto the filling as well. It'll help keep the lobster moist while baking.

Bake until the sauce bubbles and the crumbs brown. The yolks in the sauce will set, holding the filling together.

◄ Crack the shell to flatten its natural V-shape. This way, it holds more filling.

▲ To temper egg yolks, blend them with a small amount of the warm cream sauce.

◄ Turn off heat, then slowly pour the tempered egg yolks into the cream sauce, whisking constantly.

◄ Over low heat, cook the sauce until thickened— when the whisk leaves a "path" in the pan. Stir in seafood, tomato, and chives.

◄ Divide the seafood filling among the four shells. Top with crumbs and bake until hot.

STUFFED LOBSTER TAILS

MAKES 4 TAILS
TOTAL TIME: 30 MINUTES

PREPARE:

2	steamed lobster tails (8 oz. each), split, meat removed

FOR THE SPICE PASTE, COMBINE:

1	T. fresh lemon juice
1	t. dry mustard
1/2	t. cayenne
1/2	t. kosher salt

FOR THE TOPPING, MIX:

1/2	c. panko crumbs
2	T. unsalted butter, melted
2	T. Parmesan cheese, grated
1/2	t. paprika

REDUCE:

2	T. dry sherry

ADD:

	Spice paste
1/2	c. heavy cream
4	T. unsalted butter, cubed

TEMPER AND ADD:

2	egg yolks
	Cooked lobster meat
6	oz. pasteurized crabmeat
3	T. fresh tomato, diced
2	T. chopped fresh chives

Preheat oven to 450° with rack in the top half.

Prepare lobster tails, steaming as on Page 7; remove meat and chop.
Combine the lemon juice, spices, and salt for the spice paste.
Mix panko, butter, Parmesan, and paprika for the topping.
Reduce sherry by half in a saucepan over medium-high heat.
Add spice paste, cream, and butter; stir until butter is melted. Turn off the burner.
Temper egg yolks with cream mixture. Return to sauce; cook over low heat for 1 minute. Add lobster, crab, tomato, and chives. Stuff shells with filling, sprinkle with crumbs, and bake 8–10 min.

spicy citrus Shrimp

A gift for you—

three elegantly simple

entrees that dress up the table

without requiring all your time.

Holidays are demanding—they require time, concentration, and patience. So I've come up with a few recipes that won't chain you to your stove, leaving you with more time to spend with friends and family. That's the *real* gift.

These recipes use simple preparation and cooking methods that produce results that virtually garnish themselves. For instance, take this Spicy Citrus Shrimp. It has all the "wow" of a restaurant quality meal and is on the table in half the time it would take to drive to a downtown eatery.

Chipotle chiles mellowed by a sweet orange flavor make this sensational sauce rich and spicy. The quick preparation and short cooking time is just a bonus that makes it a handy recipe for any last minute get-togethers.

menu

Spicy Citrus Shrimp

Parsley Rice

Buttered Green Beans

Spicy Citrus Shrimp

Dried, smoked jalapeños (chipotles) are packed in cans with a vinegary chile puree (adobo). Together they make up the base of this sauce.

Makes 6 Servings
Total Time: 30 Minutes

For the Sauce—
Combine:
- 1/4 cup unsalted butter, melted
- 3 chipotle chiles in adobo, minced
- 3 T. adobo sauce from chipotles
- 3 T. fresh lime juice
- 2 T. frozen orange juice concentrate, thawed
- 1 t. kosher salt

For the Shrimp—
Dust with 2 T. All-Purpose Flour:
- 1 1/2 lb. extra-large shrimp (16–20 count), peeled, deveined

Garnish with:
- 1/2 cup mango, peeled and diced
- 3 T. scallions, chopped

Preheat oven to 450°.
Combine all ingredients for the sauce in a large mixing bowl.
Dust shrimp with flour; combine with sauce. Transfer to baking dish.
Bake at 450° for 7 minutes; stir and bake an additional 7 minutes.
Garnish with mango and scallions before serving.

---

to make it a menu

Parsley Rice

Bring 3 cups water, 2 T. unsalted butter, and 1 t. kosher salt to a boil. Add 1 1/2 cups long grain rice; cover, reduce heat, and simmer about 20 min., or until water is absorbed. Stir in 1/4 cup chopped fresh parsley before serving.

Making shrimp sizzle

Layering the flavors of citrus, smoke, and spice is what makes this a fun and exciting dish. The combination of lime and orange does two things. First, it accents the spice of the chipotle, and second it cuts the heat of the adobo sauce with sweetness. Make sure the orange juice concentrate is at room temperature so the melted butter doesn't clump.

Extra-large shrimp provide a presence that is undeniable, and leaving the tail segment on them when cleaning adds a natural flair. But if you want to get every last bite of this shrimp, it's okay to remove the tail end. (See *Basics*, Page 25.) And to guarantee that each bite has plenty of zing, dust the shrimp with flour. It will thicken the sauce, coating the shrimp during baking.

Fresh mango completes the Latin influences of the recipe. Its cool creaminess echoes the smooth citrus sauce. If you can't find fresh mango, look for it in jars in the produce section of your grocery store.

Measure out adobo sauce from the canned chipotles and whisk it into the citrus mixture.▼

▲*Dust shrimp with flour and gently toss to coat. Don't worry if it's a little sticky—it loosens up when the sauce is added.*

▲*Add the sauce to the shrimp, then spoon the mixture into a shallow baking dish.*

▲*Stirring halfway through cooking allows the shrimp to cook faster and more evenly.*

Greek Salsa Chicken

With vivid flavors and colors, this chicken dinner brings the tastes of summer to the dead of winter.

I admit it, I play with food. I have fun with it, and that's how this recipe was invented. It's a regular party on a platter.

Traditional Greek ingredients are combined like a feta cheese salad, but used in a decidedly New World style—as a salsa. This Greek "salsa" can be tossed together in a flash, but what's great is it can be made hours ahead. It'll just get better as the ingredients meld over time.

Finish the pan-roasted chicken by topping it with the salsa. The heat from the chicken melts the cheese a bit and releases aromas from the herbs.

Making salsa dance

To keep things simple, I took the guesswork out of measuring the salsa ingredients. Instead, I'm calling for pretty standard package sizes. This way you can come home from shopping and literally toss the salsa together in a matter of minutes. And then, believe it or not, the main part of the recipe is done!

Big flavors like feta cheese, olives, and lemon are some of the signatures of Greek food. The Greeks tint and shade these flavors with herbs, and this salsa is no exception. *Fresh* oregano and parsley give the salsa a vitality that their dried counterparts could never do.

For golden brown, deliciously moist chicken breasts, quickly sear them on the stove top, then pop into a hot oven. "Pan-roasting" like this is an ideal method to cook bone-in chicken. This way the chicken slowly roasts in its own juices and isn't as apt to dry out so quickly.

to make it a menu

ROASTED POTATOES

Quarter 2½ pounds of small red potatoes, toss with 3 T. olive oil, and season with salt and pepper. Arrange on a baking sheet in a single layer, then roast at 450° for 50 minutes. Lightly toss with 2 T. white wine vinegar before serving.

Roasting these potatoes along with the chicken is a cinch. Place the potatoes on the lower rack in the preheated oven just before you sear the chicken. Place the pan of chicken on the rack above them. This way they get roasted by both the heat from below and by reflected heat from the pan above.

GREEK SALSA CHICKEN

For an even quicker dinner (without the roasted potatoes and lemon wedges), saute boneless, skinless chicken breasts for about 12 minutes, turning once. Serve with the Greek salsa.

MAKES 6 SERVINGS
TOTAL TIME: 1½ HOURS

FOR THE SALSA—
COMBINE:
3   packages (4 oz. each) crumbled feta cheese
1   pint grape or cherry tomatoes, halved
1   jar (4.75 oz.) pitted kalamata olives
½   cup minced fresh parsley
½   cup fresh lemon juice
½   cup extra-virgin olive oil
2   T. chopped fresh oregano
FOR THE CHICKEN—
SAUTE IN ¼ CUP OLIVE OIL:
6   skinless, bone-in chicken breast halves (8 oz. each), seasoned
SQUEEZE OVER CHICKEN:
2   lemons, cut into wedges

Preheat oven to 450°.
Combine all salsa ingredients in large bowl; cover and chill.
Saute chicken in oil, breast side down, in a large roasting pan over medium-high heat until browned. Turn chicken over.
Squeeze chicken with lemon juice, then nestle the squeezed lemon wedges around the breasts. Roast chicken about 50 minutes, or until it reaches 165° on an instant read thermometer. Transfer chicken and lemons to a large platter and top with salsa.

▲*Fresh oregano and parsley embellish the bold flavors of the salsa.*

▲ *If you don't have a roasting pan, browning the chicken in a large ovenproof skillet will work.*

Squeezing lemon juice over the top of the chicken enhances the seasonings and browning in the oven. ▼

◄*To serve, place the potatoes on the platter first so they can absorb the juices from the chicken and salsa.*

simple&elegant

hot chile Turkey

Rock your holidays with this spiced up version of roast turkey! A blend of Asian flavors and easy techniques puts plenty of flavor and color on the table.

Timid taste buds need not apply for this meal—this sweet and sour turkey packs a punch by using ingredients like Thai chile sauce reduced with balsamic vinegar. Tell Grandma to buckle her seat belt and hold on because she's never tasted a turkey quite like this!

The marinade for this recipe is its heart and soul. It not only gives the bird a deep mahogany color, but it flavors the turkey before and after cooking. Combining common Asian and European ingredients is what makes this rich brown "sweet and sour" marinade. Taking it one step further, the marinade is then boiled down to make a dense, highly flavored spicy sauce. But be careful—because it's so flavorful, it really should be used like a condiment. A little goes along way.

menu

Hot Chile Turkey

Brussels sprouts with Thyme

Gingered Sweet Potatoes, *Page 26*

Gobbler gastronomy

If you have to feed more than a few but less then a crowd, a bone-in turkey breast half is ideal. The rib-cage of the bone-in breast protects the meat from scorching on the hot pan as it roasts. Look for a breast half with other turkey products at the grocery store, or have the butcher split a whole breast for you.

The recipe still works with a boneless breast half—just reduce the roasting time by about 10 minutes. But *don't* buy a fabricated turkey breast roll. Its flavor isn't as good.

You can also save time by marinating the turkey overnight. The longer it goes, the deeper brown it becomes. The turkey looks good after only two hours of marinating, but looks better if it sits overnight.

Reserve the marinade and reduce it to make the sauce. Don't worry—boiling it down makes it safe for eating. Incidentally, this basic sweet and sour sauce has its roots in a classic French sauce: When sweet and sour sauce is boiled down with fruit, it's known as a "gastrique." But when a gastrique is made with hot sauce, *we* call it a "buckle your seat belts and hold on" sauce!

◄ *A Thai hot sauce called "sriracha" is a key part of the marinade. Find it in ethnic sections of your grocery store or at Asian markets. But if you don't like spicy food, it's all right to omit it.*

Browning the bird caramelizes the proteins and added sugars from the marinade. ▶

HOT CHILE TURKEY

Using an inexpensive balsamic vinegar is fine for this recipe. The delicacy of a fine balsamic would be lost.
MAKES ONE 3–4 LB. TURKEY BREAST HALF
TOTAL TIME: ABOUT 1¹⁄₂ HOURS + MARINATING

COMBINE WITH ¹⁄₂ CUP WATER:
1	cup yellow onion, chopped
¹⁄₂	cup low-sodium soy sauce
¹⁄₂	cup balsamic vinegar
¹⁄₄	cup honey
2–3	T. sriracha or Thai hot chile sauce
2	T. chopped fresh cilantro
2	T. fresh ginger, grated
2	T. toasted sesame oil
6	garlic cloves, minced

ADD AND MARINATE:
1	3–4 lb. turkey breast half

HEAT; SAUTE TURKEY IN:
¹⁄₄	cup olive oil

REDUCE MARINADE; STIR IN:
¹⁄₂	cup dried sweet cherries
2	T. chopped fresh cilantro

▲ *Remove turkey from the marinade; strain marinade into a bowl. Reduce the marinating liquid to make 1 cup of sauce.*

Combine marinade ingredients and water in a bowl, stirring with a whisk. Pour into a heavy-duty 1-gallon resealable plastic bag.
Add turkey. Marinate, chilled, at least 2 hours or overnight.

Preheat oven to 450°. Remove turkey from bag. Strain marinade through a colander into a large bowl; discard solids.
Heat oil in a heavy roasting pan over medium-high heat. Saute turkey, breast side down, 5 minutes, or until browned. Turn turkey breast side up, transfer pan to the oven, and roast 30 minutes.

Reduce heat to 400° and roast an additional 30 minutes, or until the internal temperature of the turkey reaches 165°. Remove turkey from the oven, tent with foil, and let rest 15–20 minutes while you prepare the sauce.
Reduce marinade in a medium saucepan, boiling until concentrated to 1 cup, about 15 minutes. Stir in dried cherries and cilantro; let sauce stand 5 min. off heat to soften the cherries before serving.

to make it a menu

BRUSSELS SPROUTS WITH THYME

Clean and trim 2 pounds fresh Brussels sprouts, *Page 24.* Cut each in half and thinly slice crosswise to shred. Heat 1 T. olive oil in a large skillet over medium-high heat. Add sprouts and saute 3 minutes. Stir in 1 t. chopped fresh thyme and season with salt and pepper.

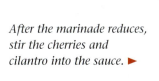

After the marinade reduces, stir the cherries and cilantro into the sauce. ▶

beef wellington

Ideal for hectic holiday times, a dinner of beef Wellington just makes it *look* like you were a slave to your stove. If your guests only knew.

Dinner parties during the '60s and '70s revolved around beef Wellington—it was beautiful, extravagant, and insanely popular. It's sort of taken a back seat to other dishes in recent years, but now is a good time to revisit this culinary stalwart. Today's cooks will no doubt appreciate the things that made beef Wellington a hit years ago.

First of all, there's just no arguing with Wellington's great flavors of beef tenderloin, pâté, mushrooms, and puff pastry. The combination has never failed to bring people to their knees, and they're all used here—generously.

Second, there aren't many dishes that rival Wellington's elegance. People will really feel special when they're served their very own "present."

But the biggest selling point of this dish has to be its make-ahead feature. The Wellingtons can be assembled up to a day ahead, then baked a short 30 minutes before serving. An elegant holiday meal has never been easier!

At the store

For all its fanciness, beef Wellington is made up of pretty common ingredients. Here's what to shop for.

Beef: If possible, buy center-cut beef tenderloin filets (filet mignon). Center cuts are evenly shaped, but if you can't find them, the next best option is to cut filets from a whole tenderloin, *see Issue 39*. Tenderloin steaks from the grocery store will work, but won't be as nicely shaped.

Pâté: This is the most exotic ingredient you'll need. Pâté [pah-TAY] is a ground meat spread often containing liver (pork, goose, and duck are typical). It comes smooth or coarsely ground, but here, use a smooth variety. This type of pâté makes a nicely textured filling.

Puff Pastry: In the '60s and '70s, home cooks had to make puff pastry—too much work! Today, look to the frozen food aisle. Pepperidge Farm makes a very good product.

CLASSIC BEEF WELLINGTON

MAKES 4 SERVINGS
TOTAL TIME: 2 HOURS + CHILLING

FOR THE BEEF—
SEAR IN 1 T. OLIVE OIL; CHILL:
4   filet mignon steaks, 2" thick (about 6 oz. each), seasoned
FOR THE PÂTÉ FILLING—
MASH:
8   T. (4 oz.) goose liver pâté (with truffles, if possible)
FOR THE DUXELLES FILLING—
SAUTE IN 2 T. UNSALTED BUTTER:
2   shallots, minced
4   oz. button mushrooms, diced
ADD AND SIMMER:
2   T. heavy cream
2   T. dry sherry or port
OFF HEAT, ADD:
1   T. chopped fresh thyme
      Salt and pepper to taste
FOR THE PASTRY—
THAW:
1   pkg. (1.1 lb.) puff pastry sheets

FOR THE BEEF—
Sear filets in oil in a hot skillet over high heat until well browned on one side, about 3 minutes. Turn; sear another minute then transfer to a plate (reserve pan for the duxelles). Chill beef at least 30 minutes. ▶

FOR THE PÂTÉ FILLING—
Mash the pâté in a small bowl until smooth. Chill until ready to use. ▼

French lesson
This pâté, bought at a national super-store chain, is smooth (mousse) and contains duck (canard) and pork (porc) liver (foie). It is flavored with truffles (truffe) and port wine (porto).

FOR THE DUXELLES FILLING—
Saute the shallots and mushrooms (chop the stems too!) for the *duxelles* [dook-SEHL] filling in butter over medium-high heat (use the same pan that was used to sear the beef). Cook 5 min., stirring occasionally.

Add cream and sherry; simmer until liquids are nearly evaporated. Off heat, add thyme, salt, and pepper; cool completely. ▶

◀ FOR THE PASTRY—
Thaw frozen puff pastry sheets at room temperature for 30 minutes, but don't let them get too warm or they'll be hard to work with. They may also be thawed overnight in the refrigerator.

cuisine technique

Assembling Wellingtons

TO ASSEMBLE—

ROLL OUT; CUT INTO SQUARES:
1   sheet thawed puff pastry

PLACE ON EACH SQUARE:
1   seared filet mignon, blotted dry

SPREAD EACH FILET WITH:
1   T. mashed pâté
1   T. duxelles

BRUSH PASTRY WITH; CHILL:
1   egg beaten with 1 T. water

BAKE WELLINGTONS. SERVE WITH:
    Port Wine Sauce, *Page 21*

Roll out thawed pastry on a lightly floured surface until about 13" square. Using a knife or pastry wheel, cut the dough into four squares. Place a cooled filet in the center of each square. Spread each filet with some pâté, then top the pâté with duxelles. ►

pastry cutouts

Decorating Wellingtons with cutouts of puff pastry may seem fussy, but it looks like a million bucks! Leaves and berries are easy to make, even if you're "decorating challenged" like me!

Using a paring knife, trim shapes out of pastry that is thawed but cold—it's hard to cut clean, even lines from warm dough.

Make vein imprints with the knife tip, then artfully "glue" the leaves and berries onto the Wellingtons with some of the egg wash. Chill completely, then brush the Wellingtons again with egg wash just before baking. The pastry puffs higher if it's cold when it hits the oven.

◄ Brush corners of pastry with egg and water mixture, then fold a corner up to the center. Fold the opposite corner up to the center, meeting the first corner. Press lightly to adhere.

Fold the other corners to the center in the same way, but this time, tuck in the sides as if wrapping a gift. Press corners to adhere. Gently stretch pastry over any open areas to enclose the meat. Place Wellingtons on an ungreased, parchment-lined baking sheet. ►

◄ Decorate Wellingtons with puff pastry cut-outs. Cover with plastic; chill at least 1 hour or up to 24.

Preheat oven to 425° with rack in the lower third. Brush Wellingtons with additional egg wash (to help in browning) and bake 20–25 minutes, or until pastry is puffed and golden. Do not bake longer than that or beef will be overdone. Serve Wellingtons with port sauce.

port wine *sauce*

Making sauces can elicit fear in even the most experienced cook. But with a dinner as special as beef Wellington, there's no getting around it—sauce is a must.

But this sauce is trouble-free. Used canned broth for easy preparation, but "doctor" its flavor with aromatic vegetables. Both port and red wine give the sauce deep, rich flavor and color, but you can use all of one or the other if you prefer. And forget about long simmering for body. A little cornstarch is all you need.

Do try to find truffle butter to finish the sauce (buy it at specialty markets). Aside from the flavor it gives the Wellingtons, it's terrific in scrambled eggs!

Truffle butter is butter that's been infused with black truffles—truffle flavor without the high price tag! No, it's not cheap ($9 for 3.5 oz.), but a little dab will do. It doesn't last long so freeze what you don't use. ▼

PORT WINE SAUCE

MAKES ABOUT 1 CUP
TOTAL TIME: 30–40 MINUTES

SAUTE IN 1 T. UNSALTED BUTTER:
- 1/2 cup yellow onion, chopped
- 1/4 cup carrot, chopped
- 1/4 cup celery, chopped
- 1 T. tomato paste
- 2 bay leaves

DEGLAZE WITH:
- 1/4 cup tawny port
- 1/4 cup dry red wine

ADD AND SIMMER; STRAIN:
- 3 cups low-sodium beef broth

COMBINE; WHISK IN:
- 2 T. cold water
- 2 t. cornstarch

FINISH SAUCE WITH:
- 1 T. red currant jelly
- 1 T. truffle butter, *optional* (if unavailable, substitute with 1 T. unsalted butter)
  Salt and pepper to taste

Saute vegetables, tomato paste, and bay leaves in butter until soft, 5 min.

Deglaze with port and wine, scraping bits from the bottom of the pan. Simmer until reduced, 5 minutes.

Add beef broth; simmer 8–10 minutes, then strain. (Sauce may be made ahead to this point and chilled.) Return broth to a clean pan and bring to a boil over high heat.

Combine cornstarch and water in a small bowl, smashing out lumps with your fingers. Whisk cornstarch into the boiling broth, stirring constantly until slightly thickened.

Finish with jelly and truffle butter. Season with salt and pepper, then serve with beef Wellington.

Saute vegetables and tomato paste. Deglaze with port and wine, add broth, then simmer. ▶

▲ *Whisk cornstarch mixture into strained, boiling broth; simmer to thicken.*

Finish with jelly and truffle butter. Add butter just before serving, or its "truffle-ness" will be lost. ▼

pork wellington

Does the holiday menu leave you with feelings of *déjà vu*?

Pork Wellington can breathe new life into your meal.

Traditions die hard and tinkering with the holiday dinner is a risky venture. But if you're daring to buck tradition a bit this year, here is the recipe to turn to. It's classic enough to appeal to those family members reluctant to change, yet different enough to satisfy cooks looking to spice up this year's holiday meals.

Pork tenderloin is an economical (and delicious) substitute for beef. And it only improves after it's been stuffed and wrapped in prosciutto! Like the beef Wellington, this can be made ahead and chilled, freeing up valuable time. One bite of it with Apple-Sage Sauce, and you just may invite it back next year!

Assembling the Wellingtons

Like beef Wellington, this pork version requires ahead-of-time work. Trim the tenderloins of fat and silverskin (the connective tissue on the surface). Then "butterfly" and stuff them with Boursin [boor-SAHN], a soft cheese flavored with herbs and garlic, or cracked pepper. (Herbed goat or cream cheese may be used in place of Boursin.)

Next, roll the tenderloin in thinly sliced prosciutto, then sear. After that, wrap each tenderloin in ⅔ of a sheet of puff pastry. The sheets are usually folded into thirds—simply unfold a sheet, and trim off and chill ⅓. Roll out the larger portion and wrap a tenderloin; do the same with the other one. Then cut decorations from the chilled sections.

Prepare tenderloins, trimming off silverskin and the thin tail at the end (reserve tail end for another use). Butterfly them for stuffing, making a 1"-deep incision down the length of each—do not cut all the way through. Stuff each tenderloin with half the Boursin.

Roll tenderloins in prosciutto. To do this, lay half the prosciutto slices in a single layer, overlapping them slightly. Place stuffed tenderloin at the base of the prosciutto and roll to cover. Do the same thing with the second tenderloin. Sear in oil in a large skillet over medium-high heat until prosciutto is brown and crisp on all sides, 5–8 min. Chill thoroughly.

PORK WELLINGTONS

MAKES 4–6 SERVINGS
TOTAL TIME: ABOUT 1 HOUR + CHILLING

PREPARE AND STUFF:
- 2   pork tenderloins (6–8 oz. each)
- 4   oz. Boursin cheese

ROLL TENDERLOINS IN; SEAR IN 1 T. OLIVE OIL:
- 6   oz. prosciutto (3 oz. per tenderloin)

TRIM; WRAP EACH TENDERLOIN IN:
- 1   sheet thawed puff pastry, rolled to a 16 x 12" rectangle

BRUSH PASTRY WITH; CHILL:
- 1   egg beaten with 1 T. water

BAKE WELLINGTONS. SERVE WITH:
     Apple-Sage Sauce, *below*

Trim pastry as described above, wrap pork, and transfer to a parchment-lined baking sheet.

Brush Wellingtons with egg-water mixture, then decorate with pastry vines and cutouts, *Page 20*. Cover with plastic; chill 1 hour or up to 24.

Preheat oven to 400° with rack in lower third. Brush with more egg wash for good browning.

APPLE-SAGE SAUCE FOR PORK WELLINGTON

To make Apple-Sage Sauce, follow the sauce recipe on Page 21, substituting **¼ cup apple juice or cider** for the **tawny port**. Use **¼ cup dry white wine** for the **dry red wine**. Finally, finish the sauce with **1 T. apple jelly** for the **currant jelly**, **1 T. truffle butter** (or unsalted butter), and **2 t. minced fresh sage**.

Bake tenderloins 30–35 minutes, or until golden (they cook longer and at a lower temperature than beef Wellington). Let rest 5 minutes before slicing. To serve, trim off the ends (they're doughy), then slice into 2"-thick pieces, allowing 2–3 per person. Serve with sage sauce, *left*.

basic**cuisine**

straightening **lobster tails**

Lobster tails curl naturally when cooked, and that's okay. However, for some recipes it's nice to keep the tail straight for looks.

To do that, split the tails in half lengthwise, Page 7. Holding the cut side up, run a skewer through the meat, as close to the upper shell as possible. Cook the tail as directed, then simply remove

the skewer when done. (This also works with shrimp.)

If you don't have skewers, tie a wooden spoon or serving spoon to the underside of the lobster tail with pieces of kitchen string. Then cook the tail as directed.

Tie a spoon to the lobster tail using cotton kitchen string in lieu of skewers. ▶

trimming **Brussels sprouts**

Trimming away the tough leaves and woody stems of Brussels sprouts helps them cook faster and makes them easier to eat. To trim, rinse the sprouts in cold water, then cut off about ¼" of the stems—just enough to remove the woody part. Discard any leathery, blotchy, or yellowing leaves.

If boiling or steaming the

▲ *Trim off the tough stems but don't trim too much—otherwise the sprouts will fall apart during cooking.*

sprouts whole, score an "x" on the stem with a paring knife to help speed up the cooking time, *see large photo above.* There's no need to score the stems if they're small, or if you're halving or shredding the sprouts before cooking.

filling **a pastry bag**

Filling a pastry bag is simple once you know a few tips. Get started by dropping the desired tip into the bag, pushing it into the opening so that it fits snugly.

To fill the bag, fold down the top to form a cuff. Hold the bag in one hand under the cuff, then add filling with a spatula. For easy handling, only fill the bag halfway.

Unfold the cuff and twist the top to close. Holding the twist in place with your thumb and forefinger, gently squeeze the filling to the tip, pressing out any air pockets.

▲ *To release the filling, apply pressure from the top of the bag, not the sides. Guide the bag with your other hand.*

cleaning **shrimp**

Cleaning shrimp is a two step process involving peeling and deveining. There are two good reasons to do it. First, peeling makes the shrimp easier to eat. And second, the "vein" (the shrimp's digestive track) is unattractive and may be gritty.

To peel, hold a shrimp firmly in one hand. Grasp the legs, then peel away the shell using your thumb to get between the shell and meat. Gently tug at the tail to remove.

Now, to devein, hold a peeled shrimp with its back facing you. With a paring knife, make a shallow incision along the back, running the length of the shrimp. The vein is usually dark, but can be opaque or coral. Remove the vein with the tip of the knife, or gently rinse the incision under cold running water until the vein is removed.

▲ *Grasp the legs to begin peeling away the shell.*

faster **with** fewer

mashed
potatoes

GINGERED SWEET POTATOES

Tip 2: Cooking sweet potatoes in coconut milk infuses them with flavor. Mash them in the pan along with the reduced coconut milk. These are great with the turkey on Page 16!
MAKES 5–6 CUPS; TOTAL TIME: ABOUT 30 MINUTES

BLT MASHED POTATOES

Tip 1: The "L" here is for leeks, not lettuce. Use equal-sized potato chunks to cook evenly. Be sure to salt the water for flavor.
MAKES 5–6 CUPS; TOTAL TIME: ABOUT 30 MINUTES

2¹/₂ lb. russet potatoes, peeled, diced into 2" cubes	2 T. sun-dried tomatoes packed in oil, minced
¹/₄ lb. bacon, diced	1 t. kosher salt
2 cups leeks (white part only), sliced	¹/₈ t. cayenne
4 T. unsalted butter, melted	2 T. chopped fresh chives
¹/₂ cup half and half, warmed	
4 oz. cream cheese	

Cook potatoes in salted water 15–20 minutes, or until tender.
Saute bacon until crisp; remove. Pour off all but 2 T. drippings. Saute leeks in drippings, then stir in bacon.
Drain potatoes, then return them to the pan. Dry briefly over medium heat, stirring constantly. Mash potatoes and fold in all ingredients.

▲ *Cook leeks in bacon drippings, then add cooked bacon.*

2¹/₂ lb. sweet potatoes, peeled, diced into 2" cubes
1 can (14.5 oz.) coconut milk
1 cup water
¹/₄ cup brown sugar
4 T. unsalted butter, melted
¹/₄ cup chopped fresh cilantro
3 T. fresh ginger, minced
1 T. jalapeño, seeded, diced
1 T. fresh lime juice
1 t. kosher salt

Cook sweet potatoes in coconut milk, water, and brown sugar for 15–20 min., or until tender. Mash by hand (for a chunky texture), then stir in butter.
Blend cilantro, ginger, jalapeño, and lime juice in a food processor until minced; scrape bowl periodically.
Stir cilantro mixture into potatoes along with salt.

Coconut milk mixture will reduce as the potatoes cook. ▼

▲ *Blend cilantro, ginger, jalapeño, and lime juice. Stir into mashed sweet potatoes.*

ROSEMARY AND CHEVRE MASHED POTATOES

Tip 3: *To test potatoes for doneness, insert a knife into the center—if the potato slides off the knife, it's done. Overcooking causes the potatoes to become waterlogged.*

MAKES 5–6 CUPS; TOTAL TIME: ABOUT 30 MINUTES

2¹/₂ lb. Yukon gold potatoes, peeled, diced into 2" cubes
3   sprigs rosemary, tied together
4   T. unsalted butter, melted
4   oz. chevre (goat cheese)
¹/₃ cup buttermilk
1   T. minced fresh rosemary
1   T. lemon zest, minced
1   t. kosher salt
¹/₄ t. black pepper

Cook potatoes and rosemary sprigs in salted water 15–20 minutes, or until tender. Remove sprigs and drain potatoes. Return potatoes to the pan and dry briefly over medium heat, stirring often to prevent scorching. Remove pan from heat.

Mash potatoes and stir in butter to coat. Add goat cheese; stir until melted. Fold in buttermilk, minced rosemary, zest, and seasonings.

◄ *Tie the rosemary sprigs together for easy removal.*

PESTO MASHED POTATOES

Tip 4: *To mash potatoes, use an old fashioned hand masher, electric mixer, food mill, or my favorite—a ricer. Never mash in a food processor or the potatoes will become gluey.*

MAKES 5–6 CUPS; TOTAL TIME: ABOUT 30 MINUTES

2¹/₂ lb. russet potatoes, peeled, diced into 2" chunks
6   cloves garlic, peeled
2   cups fresh basil leaves
¹/₂ cup Parmesan cheese, grated
1   t. kosher salt
¹/₂ t. crushed red pepper flakes
¹/₂ cup olive oil
4   T. unsalted butter, melted
³/₄ cup half and half, warmed

A ricer is the best tool for making fluffy, lump-free mashed potatoes. ►

Cook potatoes and garlic in salted water 15–20 min., or until tender. Drain; return them to the pot and dry over med. heat.
Blend basil, Parmesan, salt, and pepper flakes in food processor until minced. Drizzle in olive oil.
Mash potatoes; stir in butter, half and half, and basil mixture.

◄ *Stir in pesto, blending just until mixed.*

allabout

REAL butter

Once you know about this kitchen staple, bread will always play the supporting role to its lead act. So spread the word!

One of the things I remember from kindergarten is sitting in a circle, shaking a Mason jar of cream until it turned into butter. To my kindergarten palate, that butter didn't leave much of an impression. But after sampling 20 of finest butters in the world, it's pretty clear that there's a lot more to the stuff than a five-year-old can appreciate.

What is it?: Butter is nothing more than firm fat—think of it as semisolid heavy cream. Cream is what rises to the top of the pail after a cow's been milked. Just skim off this cream, churn it, and you'll have butter.

Butter consists of butterfat, water, milk solids, and sometimes salt. Butterfat is directly responsible for the taste and texture of butter—it's what makes it rich and creamy. The higher the butterfat, the lower the butter's moisture content. This lack of moisture is what helps cakes rise and pastries flake.

How is it made?: If you've ever beaten heavy cream too long, then you know the basics of butter making. By agitating (churning) cream, the fat globules link onto the air bubbles that are created. Constant churning warms and softens the globules to the point that they join together and solidify into butter. To prevent the joined fat globules from melting and becoming liquefied, churning occurs at rather cool temperatures.

Color: The color of butter is a reflection of the cow's diet and changes with the seasons. In warmer months, pastured cows feed on summer grass that contains a lot of carotene. This gives their milk, and thus butter, a yellow hue. To maintain uniform color throughout the year (winter butter is paler), annatto, a plant extract, is sometimes added.

Storing: Butter's high fat content makes proper storage important. Prolonged exposure to light and air causes the fat to break down and turn rancid. To prevent this, store butter in the coldest section of the refrigerator (*not* in the "butter shelf" on the door!), wrapped in packaging or covered in a dish. It'll start to taste stale after about 3 months.

Freezing is an accepted method for storing butter for longer spans of time. Well wrapped, it should keep for up to a year. But some butter experts argue that freezing changes the properties of the butterfat and water, causing it to "weep" more moisture.

Varieties of butter

Salted vs. Unsalted

Salt acts as a preservative and gives butter a longer shelf life. But the amount of salt added varies from one manufacturer to another. As a result, many cooks prefer to use unsalted butter, salting the dish as needed to better control the flavor. If substituting salted butter for unsalted, omit $1/4$ teaspoon salt per $1/2$ cup (1 stick) of salted butter.

European Style

Made both in Europe and the United States, European Style butter is churned longer and slower than other butters, thereby retaining more of the butterfat. European style has a minimum of 82% butterfat compared to regular butter's required 80%. The difference may not seem like much, but taste proves otherwise! It's great for baking and cooking, but its higher cost may limit this.

Which wrapper is better?

A foil wrapper is preferred over paper since it acts as a better barrier against unwanted odors and light exposure.

Light

This butter, with around 40% butterfat, was developed as a dairy-based alternative to margarine. Made from real butter, additional ingredients such as skim milk and water are added to reduce cholesterol, calories, and fat. Light butter can be substituted tablespoon for tablespoon for real butter, but its high moisture content changes the way it performs—avoid it in butter-rich recipes like shortbread.

Whipped

By increasing its volume with either air or nitrogen gas, whipped butter was created as an easy-to-spread butter for the table. It has a different texture than stick butter and is, therefore, not recommended for baking. In a pinch, substitute whipped butter by measuring its *weight*, not volume: 4 ounces of whipped butter is equivalent to $1/2$ cup of stick butter.

Clarified

Clarified, or drawn, butter is melted butter with the milk solids removed—this makes it great for sauteing since the milk solids are prone to burning. Ghee [GEE] is simply the Indian version of clarified butter. Its slightly nutty flavor is due to the fact that the milk solids are left in the melted butter until they've browned. Find ghee at ethnic markets and health food stores.

Cultured

Common grocery store butter is typically labeled "sweet cream," meaning it's uncultured. To make *cultured* butter, controlled, natural bacteria (like that used to make sour cream) are added to the cream, which is then left to ferment before churning. The result is a tangy, nutty-flavored butter. Its slightly higher acidity makes cultured butter softer and easier to work into dough.

For an online listing of purchasing sources for gourmet butter, visit **CuisineAtHome**.com

butter pecan tartlets

This is every baker's dream dessert—absolutely delicious, knock-out gorgeous, and rewardingly easy. You must've been good this year because Santa has come early!

This tartlet has the holidays in mind—it tastes awesome, looks cool, and individual portions make serving a snap. But what's better is that they're quick to prepare and freeze well. So when guests drop in, you're ready!

The crust for these tartlets is just like a buttery shortbread cookie. But it's made differently than most shortbread because *melted* butter is used rather than cold. This makes the dough easy to work with because there's no need

to worry about overworking it. It is, however, important to chill the dough before baking to solidify the fat so it doesn't melt out. Do not skip this step because it makes a huge difference in texture and flavor of the crust.

The chewy pecan filling in these tartlets doesn't need dressing up, but a simple garnish of unsweetened whipped cream does wonders. For a more decadent treat, serve them with warmed Chocolate Ganache, *Page 39.*

Making tartlets

Add sugar, vanilla, and salt to melted butter. Pour butter mixture into flour; blend to combine. ▼

▲Press 3 T. dough in each pan. Start in the center, press outward, and up the sides. Freeze until firm, then bake until pale golden brown.

BUTTER PECAN TARTLETS
MAKES EIGHT 3³/₄" TARTLETS OR ONE 10" TART; TOTAL TIME: 45 MINUTES

FOR THE CRUST—
MELT:
12 T. unsalted butter (1 ½ sticks)
OFF HEAT, STIR IN:
½ cup sugar
1 t. vanilla extract
½ t. kosher salt
BLEND INTO:
2 cups all-purpose flour

FOR THE FILLING—
SAUTE IN 1 T. UNSALTED BUTTER:
2 cups pecan pieces
BRING TO A BOIL:
½ cup sugar
½ cup corn syrup
¼ cup heavy cream
⅛ t. kosher salt
OFF HEAT, ADD:
2 T. bourbon, *optional*
1 t. vanilla extract
   Sauteed pecans
SERVE WITH:
   Unsweetened whipped cream
   Fresh mint sprigs

Preheat oven to 325° with rack in the middle.

Melt butter for the crust in a saucepan over medium-high heat.

Off heat, stir in sugar, vanilla, and salt until dissolved.

Blend butter mixture into flour. Press dough into 8 ungreased tartlet pans with removable bottoms. Freeze crusts for 15 min., then bake 25–30 minutes.

Saute pecans for filling in butter over medium-high heat. Stir constantly to prevent scorching.

Bring sugar, corn syrup, cream, and salt to a boil. Cook, stirring constantly, for 1 minute.

Off heat, add bourbon, vanilla, and sauteed pecans. Spoon filling into crusts; bake 10–15 minutes at 325°. When filling is set and tartlets are cool enough to handle, remove them from the pans.

Serve with whipped cream and sprigs of mint.

Saute pecans in butter until they're aromatic and butter browns, 3–5 min. This adds great flavor to the filling. ▶

◀ Boil sugar, syrup, cream, and salt for 1 minute—this helps thicken the filling. Add flavorings and pecans.

▲ Fill each crust (still in its pan) with ¼ cup filling. Mound it high for an impressive presentation. Bake until filling is bubbly.

▲If the bottom plate sticks to the crust, use the tip of a knife to carefully pry it off.

wares
gifts for cooks

For the cook who has everything, here are some suggestions—from clever stocking stuffers to upscale kitchen classics.

For an online listing of purchasing sources, go to **CuisineAtHome**.com

UNDER $10

Pour Tops ▶

These versatile spouts allow easy pouring of olive oil, vinegar, or almost *any* liquid in a controlled stream. The graduated plastic rings adjust to fit most bottle openings.

$5.00
(set of two)

▼ Pig Tail Food Flipper

Looking like a pig tail, the stainless steel tip of this kitchen and grill tool is pin-sharp to lift everything from pancakes to steak to hefty racks of ribs. It's easy on the wrist, handles up to 14 pounds, and pricks instead of jabs, so meat doesn't lose juices.

$9.95

$5.95

▲ Drop, Smidge, Pinch, Hint Spoons

Ever wonder just how much a drop, smidge, pinch, or hint really is? While there's no precise answer, these novel stainless steel measuring spoons provide a good guideline.

UNDER $20

▼ 3-in-1 Egg Slicer

This slicer cuts through hard-cooked eggs like butter! Use the first tier of wires to make wedges; the second tier for even slices, length- or width-wise. Mushrooms and strawberries slice perfectly too.

$14.99

$19.95

▲ Joyce Chen Scissors

These little scissors (just 6½" tip to tip) are indispensable. The unusual design provides powerful leverage for cutting most anything—from chicken bones to lobster shells to flowers. Fits both right and left hands of all sizes.

$13.99

▲ Round Cutters

Plain round stainless steel cutters cleanly cut out biscuits, cookies, cake— just about anything in any size! The 11 circles range from ³/₄"–3⁵/₈" wide, are 1¹/₄" tall, and nest neatly in a tin for storage.

$39.95

▲ Mortar and Pestle

Individual craftsmanship means each mortar (hand-carved in Thailand) is *slightly* different. But all are about 5" tall, 7" in diameter, hold 3 cups, and weigh 12–15 pounds! Of course, a substantial pestle is included for serious herb and spice grinding.

▼ Pizza Stone and Peel

A quality baking stone paired with a wooden peel will please any pizza maker or inspire the novice on your list. Porous pizza stones create crispy crusts that no pan can imitate. And this 14 x 16" stone carries an unrivaled lifetime warranty. The peel is the ideal tool for transferring pizza to and from the hot stone.

$39.95

▼ Magnum Plus Peppermill

This sleek 9" model is the favorite grinder in our test kitchen. Boasting large storage capacity and easy-to-clean acrylic casing, it quickly dispenses pepper (with a wide grinding range) from a durable nickel-plated steel mechanism. Be sure to give some Tellicherry peppercorns with the mill!

$45.00

▼ Cutting Board

So sturdy it will probably be handed down to future generations, this 16-pound board is made from end-grain hard maple that does more than provide a pretty pattern. It produces an extra-hard surface allowing the board to stand up to heavy use. Made in Vermont, it's 16" square, 2½" thick, and reversible.

$99.99

▼ Chateau Laguiole Wine Opener

$129.00

Pamper your favorite wine connoisseur with this luxurious French-made opener. Smooth olive-wood inlay surrounds solid stainless steel construction in a shape curved to fit the hand. It features a serrated foil cutter, a five-turn spiral "worm" that penetrates the length of the cork, and a leather case.

▼ Stainless Steel Bowls

Every kitchen needs a stainless steel bowl—and a set of three is better still! These graduated bowls have handy pouring lips, and measuring lines that mark cups, quarts, and liters. Purchase these bowls separately or splurge and give the set—they are sure to last a lifetime.

$81.85

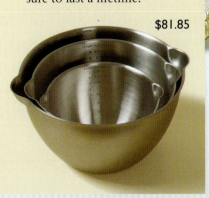

asian
chicken lollipops

In the appetizer arena, good chicken wings can't be beat. But these gussied-up ones are sure to make the party swing!

Let's cut to the chase here—these chicken lollipops are really just wings that've undergone minor cosmetic surgery. Happily, no flavor has been sacrificed in the makeover. Coated in Japanese panko crumbs and sesame seeds, they bake up golden and crisp, with a built-in handle that makes these wings perfect finger food!

The term "drummette" can be confusing. Contrary to what you might think, they are *not* mini drumsticks, but from a portion of the wing, *see sidebar, Page 35*. Drummettes are so popular now that bags of them are often stocked in the frozen meat section of the grocery store. Buy them (unbreaded, of course). They are a great time saver.

"Lollipopping" is a bit fussy, but simple to do. Just be sure to scrape the bone clean for the nicest presentation. This also gives you plenty of handle to hold on to when dipping into the two flavorful Asian sauces!

CHINESE CHICKEN "LOLLIPOPS"

MAKES 3 LB.; TOTAL TIME: ABOUT 1½ HOURS

PREPARE:
3   lb. frozen chicken
      drummettes, thawed

COMBINE:
2   cups panko crumbs
2   T. sesame seeds
2   T. unsalted butter, melted
1   t. kosher salt
¼   t. toasted sesame oil
¼   t. cayenne

WHISK TOGETHER:
2   eggs
2   T. mayonnaise
1   T. chili garlic sauce

SERVE WITH:
     Asian Flavored Remoulade
     Sweet Chili Dipping Sauce

What is a drummette?

Chicken wings have three sections—the wing tip and two meaty portions. The drummette is made from the part that connects the wing to the bird's body.

Preheat oven to 425° with racks in the lower third. Coat two baking sheets with nonstick cooking spray.

Prepare chicken as shown below, scraping the bones well.

Combine panko, sesame seeds, butter, salt, sesame oil, and cayenne in a bowl.

Whisk eggs, mayonnaise, and chili garlic sauce together in a second bowl. Dip chicken in egg mixture, then dredge in crumbs, coating all sides. Place on prepared baking sheets and bake 40 minutes, turning chicken over after 20 minutes. When done, the drummettes should be golden and crisp all the way around.

Serve with one or both dipping sauces, *right*. (Dipping sauces may be made 1–2 days ahead of time and chilled.)

Use kitchen shears to snip the tendons around the top of the drummette. ▲

Push the meat to the base of the drum-mette with the back of a paring knife. ▶

Dip the drum-mette in the egg mixture, then dredge in the crumb mixture. ▶

easy sauces

ASIAN FLAVORED REMOULADE

MAKES ABOUT 1 CUP
TOTAL TIME: 15 MINUTES

COMBINE:
½   cup mayonnaise
¼   cup scallions, minced
¼   cup red bell pepper, diced
¼   cup chopped fresh cilantro
1   T. garlic, minced
1   T. fresh ginger, minced
1   T. fresh lime juice
1   T. brown sugar
1   t. dry mustard

Combine all ingredients in a mixing bowl. Transfer remoulade to a dish and chill until ready to serve.

SWEET CHILI DIPPING SAUCE

MAKES ABOUT ¾ CUP
TOTAL TIME: ABOUT 30 MINUTES

SIMMER:
¾   cup water
½   cup rice vinegar
½   cup brown sugar
3   T. low-sodium soy sauce
3   T. garlic, minced
¼   t. crushed red pepper flakes

Simmer all ingredients in a saucepan over medium heat. Cook until reduced by half, about 20 minutes. Serve at room temperature.

chimichurri
meatballs

Cocktail meatballs and parties go hand in hand—people love them! Try this Latin-inspired appetizer at your next holiday gathering.

I'm a big fan of cocktail meatballs, speared out of BBQ sauce with frilly toothpicks. But the holidays tend to demand something more refined, and these parsley-sauced meatballs dress up a buffet table with ease.

In Argentina, people thrive on beef and chimichurri, a pungent parsley and garlic sauce. Not a meal goes by that doesn't involve the sauce in one way or another. Taste it and you will understand why—it's addictive.

But authentic chimichurri is a little strong for a cocktail party, so this recipe backs off on the garlic and red pepper flakes a bit. Whatever you do, resist the urge to whip it up in a food processor—it doesn't look as nice. Chop everything by hand, and be sure to serve the sauce within an hour or two of making it. The flavor will be freshest then.

Feta cheese definitely *isn't* Argentinian, but its salty bite helps balance the rich meatballs.

▲ *Hand chop parsley leaves and stems for the chimichurri sauce, then blend with remaining ingredients.*

A small ice cream scoop (#100) is great for portioning meatballs. Roll lightly between your hands to shape evenly. ▼

CHIMICHURRI MEATBALLS

MAKES 4 DOZEN MEATBALLS; TOTAL TIME: ABOUT 1 HOUR

FOR THE CHIMICHURRI—
COMBINE:
1	bunch minced curly leaf parsley, leaves and stems
1	cup extra-virgin olive oil
1/2	cup red wine vinegar
2	T. minced fresh oregano leaves (or 1 t. dried)
2	t. sugar
1	t. crushed red pepper flakes
	Minced zest and juice of 1 lemon
	Salt to taste

FOR THE MEATBALLS—
BLEND; SHAPE AND FRY IN 2 T. OLIVE OIL:
1	lb. ground chuck
1/2	lb. ground pork
1/4	cup panko crumbs or dry bread crumbs
3	T. scallions, minced
2	t. garlic, minced
2	t. kosher salt
1	t. black pepper
1	egg

GARNISH WITH:
1/2	cup feta cheese, crumbled

Combine all ingredients for chimichurri in a large bowl. Let stand at room temperature up to two hours to blend flavors.

Blend all meatball ingredients in a bowl; do not overwork. Test for seasoning, *see sidebar.*

Form 1" balls. Heat 1 T. oil in a nonstick skillet over medium-high heat. Fry half the meatballs until cooked through and browned all around, about 5 minutes. Transfer to a platter that has some of the chimichurri spooned onto the bottom; top the meatballs with some of the sauce and tent with foil to keep warm. Fry remaining meatballs in additional tablespoon of oil, add them to the platter, and top with more chimichurri. **Garnish** with crumbled feta.

Seasoning tip

Before forming the meatballs, fry a little of the meat mixture until cooked through. This allows you to taste the meat for seasoning and adjust it as needed.

▼ *Fry meatballs, shaking the pan to turn them rather than using tongs. This will help preserve their shape.*

▲ *Top meatballs with sauce and feta; serve immediately. Meatballs may also be kept in a heated chafing dish, but serve the sauce on the side or else the bright green color will fade.*

CHOCOLATE MOCHA
baked alaska

Baked Alaska was the glamorous scientific wonder of the dinner party era. Now it tastes better, is mostly made ahead, and individual servings are showier than ever!

Perfect plating
- *chill serving plates ahead*
- *swirl a small pool of melted ganache in the center of each chilled plate*
- *top with baked Alaska*
- *dust with powdered sugar*
- *drizzle more ganache over entire plate*

There's a whole generation that doesn't know what baked Alaska is all about. It's mainly cake and ice cream that's covered with meringue. So what's the big deal? It's actually *baked* in the oven—and the ice cream stays intact!

The secret to this wonder is in its construction. It's really quite logical. Cake and ice cream are frozen together, then covered with meringue. The meringue acts as insulation, protecting the ice cream from the heat. In the process, the brief time in a hot oven is enough to brown the meringue and form a crunchy exterior. The cake acts as a buffer from below—it warms through but shields the ice cream.

This baked Alaska improves on its impressive reputation by increasing the flavor and making individual desserts. But the biggest bonus is that these Alaskas are conveniently formed in a muffin tin, using mostly purchased ingredients. A creamy layer of chocolate ganache is sandwiched between really good ice cream and soaked pound cake. And all of this (except the final step of meringue) is assembled ahead—who could ask for anything more?

MOCHA BAKED ALASKA

MAKES 6 SERVINGS

FOR THE GANACHE—
HEAT AND WHISK TOGETHER:
- 8 oz. semisweet chocolate, broken into pieces
- 1 cup heavy cream

TO ASSEMBLE—
PREPARE:
- 1 purchased pound cake (10.75 oz.), sliced, cut into rounds
- 6 t. coffee liqueur (or 4 T. strong coffee)
- 1 recipe Ganache, *above*
- 1 qt. coffee ice cream

BEFORE BAKING, PREPARE:
- 1 recipe Meringue, *Page 40*

Smart assembly

Making baked Alaska is more about assembly know-how than cooking. Here's the scoop.

Assembling Alaskas ahead (as little as a day or up to a week) insures that the ice cream is frozen solid so it can withstand baking—this is important! It also limits last-minute preparation.

A jumbo muffin pan is great for forming individual portions. Line it with jumbo muffin liners or large pieces of plastic wrap. Custard cups, ramekins, or a regular muffin pan also work.

When using store-bought ingredients, quality is key. I don't usually specify brands, but here I'll make an exception. Starbucks Java Chip ice cream tastes fantastic—if available, use it! Sara Lee pound cake (located in the freezer aisle) makes a perfect Alaska base and doesn't crumble.

Ganache, a rich chocolate sauce, is the only ingredient not purchased. But it couldn't be easier to make—just melt chocolate and heavy cream together.

FOR THE GANACHE—
◄ **Heat** chocolate and cream in a bowl over simmering water or in the microwave. Whisk to combine. Chill 30–60 minutes until spreadable. Reserve the extra ganache for plating.

TO ASSEMBLE—
Prepare pound cake, slicing it horizontally into three layers. Cut two rounds from each layer, matching the size of your jumbo muffin tin openings. ►

◄ **Pour** 1 t. liqueur (or 2 t. coffee) onto each round, then spread with 2 T. ganache. If ganache is too thick, warm it slightly until spreadable.

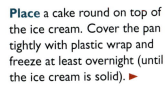

◄ **Press** 1/2 cup ice cream into a lined muffin tin. If necessary, use your fingers to smooth the ice cream. Leave 1/2" space on top for the cake round.

Place a cake round on top of the ice cream. Cover the pan tightly with plastic wrap and freeze at least overnight (until the ice cream is solid). ►

Meringue rules

Follow these rules and you're pretty much guaranteed to be successful. There's one thing though—don't attempt to make meringue in humid weather. It can't stiffen properly.

Equipment: Clean tools that are free of any fat are very important for volume. Meringue whips best in stainless steel; a glass bowl is second best. A hand mixer handles the job fine, but if you have a stand mixer, use it—the whipping action is better yet.

Eggs: When separating eggs, make sure absolutely no yolk gets into the whites. Just a trace of egg yolk (fat) will deflate the foam.

Beating: Incorporating sugar into the whites is a building process—be patient. Beat it in a tablespoon at a time so it can dissolve before adding more. After all the sugar is added, continue beating until stiff peaks form. Meringue needs to be sturdy to form "insulation" and keep the ice cream from melting.

Meringue instructions always say "don't overbeat." How can you tell when to stop? Gauge by time, feel, and look. Beating takes about 10 minutes total. Finished meringue is smooth, creamy, *very* stiff and shiny, and stark white. Overbeaten, it's dry and lumpy. Underbeaten is not yet extra-stiff.

Finishing: First, chill a baking sheet in the freezer to help the ice cream stay frozen. For easy removal, line the frozen pan with parchment and coat with non-stick spray. Place the Alaskas on the parchment, cake side down, then spread the meringue—work quickly to avoid ice cream melt!

MERINGUE

MAKES 8 CUPS
TOTAL TIME: ABOUT 10 MINUTES

BEAT, THEN ADD:
6   egg whites, room temperature
1/2 t. cream of tartar
1/8 t. table salt
SPRINKLE BY TABLESPOONS:
1   cup sugar
MIX IN:
1   t. vanilla extract

Sprinkle in sugar 1 T. at a time, beating 20 seconds between additions. Meringue slowly increases in volume and stiffness, becoming shiny. When *very stiff*, mix in vanilla. ▶

▲ Generously cover each Alaska with 1 cup meringue, spreading to form cloud-like swirls. Be sure meringue reaches the parchment, creating a barrier so ice cream doesn't leak.

Beat whites at med. speed until frothy; add cream of tartar and salt. The cream of tartar speeds up the beating process and helps stabilize the finished meringue. ▼

◀ Continue beating (use high speed for a hand mixer, medium-high for a stand mixer) until the whites hold a soft peak. Now you can begin adding the sugar.

Baking

Bake 4–5 minutes in 500° oven with rack in the top third. Bake just until tips are nicely darkened. If a little ice cream leaks, don't worry about it. Immediately transfer Alaskas to chilled plates.

LEMON MERINGUE
baked alaska

LEMON MERINGUE BAKED ALASKA

MAKES 6 SERVINGS

FOR THE LEMON SYRUP—
WHISK TOGETHER; HEAT:
- 1/3 cup fresh lemon juice
- 3 T. sugar

TO ASSEMBLE—
PREPARE:
- 1 purchased pound cake (10.75 oz.), sliced, cut into 6 rounds
- 1 recipe Lemon Syrup, *above*
- 1 jar (10 oz.) lemon curd
- 1 qt. vanilla ice cream

BEFORE BAKING, PREPARE:
- 1 recipe Meringue, *Page 40*

Whisk together lemon juice and sugar for the syrup; warm over medium heat until sugar dissolves. **Assemble, prepare, and bake** Alaskas according to instructions on Pages 39–40.

Meringue paired with lemon makes this baked Alaska version a flashier cousin of lemon meringue pie! Pound cake is transformed into lemon cake as the lemon syrup soaks in. Then a tangy layer of lemon curd punches up the citrus flavor. Curd is a smooth, tart-sweet spread made with egg yolks, sugar, butter, and juice. Buy a jar of lemon curd for this—it's available at grocery and gourmet stores, and is a shortcut that won't count against you.

This lemon baked Alaska goes together just like the mocha recipe, but uses vanilla ice cream, and replaces the liqueur and ganache with lemon syrup and curd. Follow the very same assembly, freezing, meringue, and baking instructions as with the Mocha Baked Alaska on Pages 39–40. Serve these right out of the oven on chilled plates and sprinkle with powdered sugar.

◄Dip top half of each cake round briefly in the lemon syrup.

◄Spread 2 T. lemon curd over each dipped round.

42 *online* **extra**

For more baked Alaska flavor combinations, go to www.CuisineAtHome.com

from **our** readers

Q&A
questions & answers

PAN READY?

When a recipe reads "heat oil over medium-high heat," just how long should it be heated before using?

Pat Watts
Tacoma, WA

Oil temperature is important since it helps the food brown properly and keeps it from soaking up too much oil.

The easiest way to tell when oil is hot enough is by adding something to it, like a scallion, and seeing how the oil reacts. It's ready when bubbles immediately form around the edges.

Visually, the oil is ready when it "shimmers" on the surface. If the oil smokes, it's too hot and is starting to break down.

Never test oil by adding water droplets. They cause the oil to splatter and pop violently.

CLOVE QUESTION

What are cloves?

McKenna Lewis
Birmingham, AL

Cloves are the unopened flower buds of a small evergreen tree native to the Spice Islands in Eastern Indonesia. Their name comes from the Latin *clavus*, meaning "nail," which perfectly describes their appearance. Historically, visitors to the Chinese emperor were encouraged to nibble on cloves as breath mints.

Besides studding oranges during the holidays, cloves flavor a wide spectrum of dishes. Used either whole or ground, they're in everything from American gingerbread to Indian curries.

Stored in an airtight container in a cool, dry place, whole cloves will stay fresh for about a year; ground cloves 3 months. After that, they start losing their pungency. They're still usable, but you may need to add more.

EGG ROLL VS. SPRING ROLL

How are egg rolls and spring rolls different from one another?

Austin Potter
Richfield, MN

Nearly every Asian cuisine has its own version of egg rolls and spring rolls, making them hard to define. The fried appetizer we know (egg rolls) were originally called spring rolls! Small and delicate, they were a festive food served in spring to celebrate the Chinese New Year.

These rolls were a hit and were soon made year-round. That's when they evolved into larger rolls wrapped in a thick egg dough that blistered when fried. The name changed to egg roll, and today is the broad definition of filled wrappers that are fried.

Other countries adopted spring rolls as well. Depending on where you are, today's spring rolls may be either fried or "fresh" (that is, not fried). And they can be wrapped in anything from rice paper (as Vietnamese spring rolls are) to lumpia, a thin flour dough used widely in the Philippines.

STORING BREAD

How can I store bread so that it stays fresher longer?

Norman Craig
Jacksonville, FL

The best way to store bread depends on the *type* of bread it is. If it has a soft crust, keep it in a plastic bag; a paper bag is better if it has a crisp crust. Store both types at room temperature.

Artisan-style, preservative-free breads are really only good for about a day. A paper bag will keep crusts crisp, but it also makes the bread stale quicker because there's more exposure to air. Plastic bags will keep soft bread soft (and will soften crisp crusts) but heat and humidity cause it to mold. To combat this, many use the refrigerator for storage. This does slow mold growth, but temperatures just below freezing cause sugars in bread to crystallize, drying it out.

The only real win situation is to eat freshly baked bread as soon as possible. And if that's not an option, wrap in plastic and freeze.

PEPPER MILL CLEAN-UP

The grinders of my pepper mill are sticky. How can I clean them?

Barbara Burnett
Albuquerque, NM

Peppercorn residue can build up over time, making the grinders sticky and difficult to turn. That's why it's a good idea to clean your mill every six months or so.

▲ *To remove the sticky peppercorn residue, grind raw rice.*

▲ *Dust the bottom of the mill with a dry, soft-bristled brush.*

To do this, grind enough raw rice (start with 1 tablespoon) through the mill to push through any clogged peppercorns. Then brush off the pepper dust that has collected around the bottom.

Depending on the exterior surface of the mill, it can simply be wiped clean with a common household furniture polish, glass cleaner, or damp cloth.

Avoid exposing the mill to water and steam. Moisture rusts the metal grinders and turns the peppercorns in the mill rancid.

tell**me** *more*

Fennel

A Mediterranean native popular in Italian cuisine, fennel is both a vegetable and an herb. The herb variety, which is bulbless, is grown mainly for its seeds. The variety found in stores, *right*, is the vegetable, called Florence fennel or *finocchio*. The entire plant is edible—the stalks can be used to flavor soups and sauces; the bulb can be added to salads or sauteed; and the fronds make a delicate garnish.

Fennel and seafood is a classic pairing, but it tastes great nearly any way you want to cook it—I like it roasted. Raw, it's crisp and tastes a little bit like licorice (that's why it's often mislabeled "sweet anise"). Cooked, the texture becomes tender and the flavor mellows.

Fennel is available year-round but is in season from late fall through early spring. Look for bulbs with no sign of browning and bright, healthy fronds. Wrapped in plastic and stored in the refrigerator, fennel will stay fresh up to one week. Any longer and it begins to toughen and lose its flavor.

STATEMENT OF OWNERSHIP, MANAGEMENT, AND CIRCULATION (REQUIRED BY 39 USC 3685)

Publication title: Cuisine at home. 2) Publication number: 1537-8225. 3) Filing date: September 12, 2003. 4) Issue frequency: bimonthly. 5) Number of issues published annually: six. 6) Annual subscription price: $24.00. 7) Complete mailing address of known office of publication: 2200 Grand Avenue, Des Moines, Polk County, Iowa 50312-5306. 8) Complete mailing address of headquarters or general business office of publisher: 2200 Grand Avenue, Des Moines, Iowa 50312. 9) Full names and complete mailing address of publisher, editor, and managing editor: Donald B. Peschke, 2200 Grand Avenue, Des Moines, Iowa 50312; Editor: John Meyer, 2200 Grand Avenue, Des Moines, Iowa 50312. 10) Owner: August Home Publishing Company, 2200 Grand Avenue, Des Moines, Iowa 50312; Donald B. Peschke, 2200 Grand Avenue, Des Moines, Iowa 50312. 11) Known bondholders, mortgagees, and other security holders owning or holding 1 percent or more of total amount of bonds, mortgages, or other securities: none. 12) Does not apply. 13) Publication title: Cuisine at home. 14) Issue date for circulation data below: July/August 2003. 15) Extent and nature of circulation:

	Average no. copies each issue during preceding 12 months	Actual no. copies of single issue published nearest to filing date
A. Total number copies (net press run)	223,610	271,823
B. Paid and/or requested circulation		
1. Paid/requested outside-county mail subscriptions stated on Form 3541	169,458	218,978
2. Paid in-county subscriptions	0	0
3. Sales through dealers and carriers, street vendors, counter sales, and other non-USPS paid distribution	14,224	14,008
4. Other classes mailed through the USPS	0	0
C. Total paid and/or requested circulation	183,682	232,986
D. Free distribution by mail		
1. Outside-county as stated on Form 3541	179	169
2. In-county as stated on Form 3541	0	0
3. Other classes mailed through the USPS	0	0
E. Free distribution outside the mail	0	0
F. Total free distribution	179	169
G. Total distribution	183,861	233,155
H. Copies not distributed	39,749	38,668
I. Total	223,610	271,823
J. Percentage paid and/or requested circulation	99.90%	99.93%

16. This statement of ownership will be printed in the Nov/Dec 2003 issue of this publication.
17. I certify that the statements made by me above are correct and complete. (signed) John Meyer, Editor

grand**finale**

piggyback lobster tails

Have you ever wondered how restaurants get that lobster tail meat to sit up on its shell? It's easy as long as you know the technique called "piggybacking."

First, using kitchen shears, cut down the center of the tail's shell up to the fan—do not penetrate the meat as you do this. Now, pull the shell apart until it cracks (about 2") so you can lift out the meat without tearing it.

Gently lift the meat through the cut, pulling up and out towards the fan. Leave the tail end of the meat connected and close the shell. Now, lay the meat back on top of the shell. Clean any remaining vein or bits of shell by rinsing under cold water.

Cut the back of the shell (not the meat) up to the fan. Kitchen shears work best. ▶

Pull top of shell apart and lift meat out, leaving it still connected at fan. ▼

Broiling is a good method for cooking piggyback tails. Lightly brush the lobster tails with butter and set them 6–8" under the broiler. Broil just until meat is firm and starts to split slightly. This takes about 5 minutes for a 4-oz. tail.

Cuisine at home.